Daniel Boardman Purinton

Christian Theism, its Claims and Sanctions

Daniel Boardman Purinton

Christian Theism, its Claims and Sanctions

ISBN/EAN: 9783337028183

Printed in Europe, USA, Canada, Australia, Japan

Cover: Foto ©Lupo / pixelio.de

More available books at **www.hansebooks.com**

CHRISTIAN THEISM

ITS CLAIMS AND SANCTIONS

BY

D. B. PURINTON, LL.D.

VICE-PRESIDENT AND PROFESSOR OF METAPHYSICS IN WEST VIRGINIA UNIVERSITY

NEW YORK & LONDON

G. P. PUTNAM'S SONS

The Knickerbocker Press

1889

The Knickerbocker Press

Electrotyped and Printed by

G. P. Putnam's Sons

PREFACE.

ANALYSIS is the best key to clear and easy thought. Systems of truth, like machines, are often so complicated as to baffle thought, until they are taken to pieces. Theism is such a system. This fact has been observed in the following treatise. Arguments have been correlated and each assigned to its proper place. Elements in each argument have been carefully distinguished and separately set out. The character of every part, and its relation to the whole, have been invariably indicated. And the entire discussion has been simplified, as far as possible.

The author has three objects in view :

1. To construct a progressive argument which shall be, not only logical in its methods and correct in its general conclusions, but likewise defensible in each individual part and item of it.

2. To free the subject, as far as may be, from those obscurities and difficulties of which students in Theism are wont to complain.

3. To present the subject—without dodging any of its profound problems—in such clear and simple manner as to commend it to the general reader who is willing to think as he reads.

The theist ought not to be satisfied with few readers, especially when the atheist is writing for the many.

No apology is needed for presenting theistic thought in

a new form. While truth is changeless, its aspects may vary. Much of the material here employed is the common property of mankind. Any book claiming entire originality, on a subject like Theism, must foredoom itself to just ridicule. In order to avoid tedious and distracting citations in the text, references are made, at the close of each chapter, to some of the works to which the author is indebted, and in which the subject of the chapter is more fully discussed.

And yet this volume is neither a reprint nor a compend. Old thoughts have been put to a new use, and new thoughts added. It is hoped that the plan of treatment here first presented, in which each attribute of the Deity is to be established by a separate and independent argument, will commend the work to thoughtful men, and particularly to those who may have honestly doubted the validity of theistic methods hitherto employed.

This form of the theistic argument has grown up out of the daily demands of the lecture-room, and the author is not without hope that it may be found useful and convenient as a text-book in natural theology.

The current opinion may be true, that authors usually write because of their profound conviction that the world needs their thought, and is waiting for it. The author of this Essay has written, because of his conviction that he needed to utter his thought. Having uttered it, he is content. If thereby he may be the means of contributing, even in the slightest degree, to that interest which men ought to feel in the greatest of all truths, his labor will not have been in vain.

West Virginia University, July, 1889.

CONTENTS.

INTRODUCTION.

GENERAL OUTLINE OF THE SUBJECT.

CHAPTER I.

INTELLIGENCE IN NATURE ; OR, THE EUTAXIOLOGICAL ARGUMENT.

CHAPTER II.

VOLITION IN NATURE ; OR, THE TELEOLOGICAL ARGUMENT.

CHAPTER III.

THE PERSONALITY OF GOD ; OR, THE INTUITIVE ARGUMENT.

CHAPTER IV.

THE GOODNESS OF GOD ; OR, THE HISTORICAL ARGUMENT.

CHAPTER V.

THE UNITY OF GOD ; OR, THE MONISTIC ARGUMENT.

CHAPTER VI.

INFINITY OF GOD ; OR, THE CAUSAL ARGUMENT.

CHAPTER VII.

ANTI-THEISTIC ERRORS.

CHAPTER VIII.

EVOLUTION AND CHRISTIAN THEISM.

CHAPTER IX.

IMMORTALITY.

CHRISTIAN THEISM.

INTRODUCTION.

GENERAL OUTLINE OF THE SUBJECT.

SECTION I.

CHRISTIAN THEISM AS A FACT.

CHRISTIANITY is not the effete product of a Hebrew myth. It is a momentous fact in the world,
positive, persistent, and fruitful. It has a history.
Twenty centuries attest its permanence. Like any other
fact, it challenges investigation. In its origin, character,
and continuance, it asks to be accounted for. This demand
is both wise and reasonable. It must be met honestly and
fairly, both by its friends and by its foes. All questions
concerning it, whether clear and palpable, or obscure and
difficult, must be treated with patience, modesty, sincerity,
love of truth, and intellectual honesty.

That such treatment should be accorded to it, is evident
from the nature of Christianity as a mere fact in the world.
It is widespread, profound, and far-reaching. It dominates the creeds, touches the hearts, and colors the lives
of the leading races of men now upon the earth. Nor
is this all. It cannot be denied that Christianity is historically connected with the development and progress of

the race, with the fairest types of civilization hitherto attained. If intelligent, thoughtful men are expected to deal carefully and patiently with the simplest facts of science, of history, or of practical life, how much greater the necessity of dealing thus with the questions of Christianity, a fact of most transcendent importance, past, present, and future.

But Christianity is not a mere fact. It is likewise a system of doctrine and belief. True, it is a fact, historical and actual, and so can never be resolved into a mystical chain of mere speculative ideas. And yet it embraces ideas, it generates thought. It includes doctrines concerning God, man, and redemption ; concerning the origin and destiny of creation, and the true purport of history ; concerning human duty, the nature of evil, and its relation to God, man, and the universe ; concerning virtue, holiness, and immortality. These are undeniably among the most profound and important questions with which human philosophy has to deal ; and yet concerning every one of them, Christianity sets forth, with no uncertain sound, its own system of positive truth. As such it invites comparison with any and all other systems, and will fearlessly abide the result thereof, if only it be made in the spirit of candor and absolute honesty. Christianity bears its own burdens, and asks no favors.

Such in brief is the nature of the Christian religion as a fact and a system of doctrine among men. The more minute statement and justification of its individual doctrines belong to treatises on Ethics and Systematic Theology, and are therefore foreign to the present purpose. Christian Theism includes but two subjects—(1) The being and nature of God and (2) His revelation of truth in the Old and New Testament Scriptures.

SECTION II.

CLAIMS OF CHRISTIAN THEISM.

Christian Theism advances immense claims upon the intelligence and devotion of men. What these claims are in themselves, and what they necessarily involve, must be plainly recognized in any worthy discussion of theistic questions. It will be well to consider them at the very outset.

I. THEIR NATURE.

These claims are characterized by certain distinguishing traits, the chief of which may be readily pointed out.

(1) *They are Positive.*

Christian Theism makes no uncertain, indefinite, meaningless claims. They are clear, strong, sure. They are enduring, unchangeable. Indeed they could not be otherwise, since they refer to the unchanging principles of eternal truth. The requirements of a government, a social compact, a political party, or a family may be one thing to-day and quite another to-morrow; but the fluctuating, uncertain aspects of human progress affect not the claims of God. Based upon his own immutable nature, they change not. They may be unknown, misunderstood, distorted, abused; man's recognition of them may be strangely vacillating, their hold upon the human conscience may vary in extent and in power, but the claims themselves vary not. Theology is properly a progressive science, but nothing can ever be added to the truths of Theism. While God is God and man is man, they must remain essentially the same.

(2) *They are Bold.*

They assert themselves in open day. They assume no apologetic tone. They ask nobody's pardon for existing or speaking. They cry aloud, and spare not. They marshal themselves in the open plain, and challenge the whole world to battle. They never lower their flag, nor reverse their arms. The character of the "Church militant" has become proverbial. Viewed in a purely historical light, the circumstances under which these claims were first instituted and proclaimed to the world mark them with a boldness which is truly phenomenal. A runaway slave, an obscure and poverty-stricken carpenter's son, a handful of ignorant fishermen in an insignificant provincial country—these were the agents through whom the claims of Christian Theism were first presented to the world. Compare these outward human conditions with the Ten Commandments of Moses, the Sermon on the Mount, and the many calm, intrepid, masterful words of Jesus and the Apostles, and the boldness of their utterances is seen in no uncertain light. It must be remembered, moreover, that this boldness is entirely independent of all circumstances. When Christianity was weak and obscure, and hardly beset by malignant and powerful foes, its claims were just as bold and regal as they now are when it stands at the centre of civilization and numbers its followers by millions. It is easy enough to be brave when out of danger, but the old fable of the wolf and the lamb cannot be applied to the claims of Christianity.

(3) *They are Radical.*

They go to the bottom of things. They are not satisfied with surface work. They lay hold upon the very roots of knowledge, thought, and life. Their profundity is equalled only by their importance. Christianity has, in these days, been constantly termed the great conservative force of civilization, and that not without reason, for such, in some measure, it certainly is. Praise and censure alike have been heaped upon it in its conservative capacity. And yet it is just as certainly radical in character and tendency. It may be doubted whether any other system ever propounded among men has uprooted so many philosophies, antagonized so many beliefs, revolutionized so many customs, renovated so many hearts, recast so many lives. In its own expressive language, Christianity lays the axe unto the root of the trees.

It proposes the absolute and final settlement of questions involving the coolest judgment, the clearest reason, the profoundest research, the greatest knowledge, the wisest forecast. Some of its questions, indeed, lie on the surface, and appeal successfully to the child or the savage, but these by no means exhaust the list. There are others that furnish never failing food for thought to the wisest sage, the most radical philosopher, the most patient thinker.

(4) *These Claims are Uncompromising.*

Christianity strikes hands with no one. It pools no issues, compounds no results. As it asks no favors of other systems, so it grants none to them. It admits no partners, acknowledges no equals, suffers no superiors. Other religions are not so exacting.

In the old hymns of the Rig-Veda, for example, a curious fact may be observed concerning the many gods therein revealed. It seems that there is no jealousy whatever in the hearts of these celestial beings; for the worshipper is at full liberty to take his choice among them, and then to ascribe absolute supremacy to any one of them whom his fancy may lead him to adore, or his necessities constrain him to propitiate. Agni, Indra, Yama, and Varuna will receive these empty honors by turn, with

the utmost relish and the sweetest amiability. Not so
with Jehovah. He is a jealous God. He will have all or
none. He makes no compromise, admits no partnership,
brooks no rivalry. His claims are absolute and uncondi-
tional. He never yields one of them. He seeks the con-
quest of the world, and never capitulates on any terms
short of complete surrender.

2. THE EXTENT OF CHRISTIAN CLAIMS.

Adequate knowledge concerning any thing must include
not only its nature, but likewise the extent of its being.
Very much may depend upon tracing its form, measuring
its magnitude, exhausting its content. Whether a thing
be large or small is often the most suggestive question
concerning it. Its character may be good, while its size
is fatally infinitesimal. The value of a coal mine depends
upon its depth quite as much as upon the analysis of its
coal. So is it with Christianity. A proper estimate of
its claims must take into account their extent as well as
their nature. It needs but a hasty survey of them to
show how extensive they are.

(1) *They Extend to Every Human Being.*

The Bible claims to be the word of God as God to man
as man. It is Heaven's message to the entire race, and
nothing less. Whatever may be true of its first utterances,
its last word knows no Jew, no Gentile, no Greek, no Bar-
barian, no bond, no free. It comes to all men alike, places
them on a common footing, deals with them impartially,
prefers its claims on common grounds, announces a common purpose, pursues it by common methods, inspires
common hopes, leads to a common end.

As the Vedic gods are so amiably indifferent in regard
to matters of personal supremacy among their followers,

so are they likewise as to the number of followers they shall have. Their demands in this line are not at all exorbitant. They seem perfectly satisfied with the adoration of a single race or nation. This is true also of all the gods alike. Neither Ahura, nor Dyaus Pitar, nor Zeus, nor Jupiter ever dreamed of asking the fealty of the whole race of man. But precisely this Jehovah does demand. He will be satisfied with nothing less than the willing homage of all men of every nation, clime, and tongue, so long as men shall dwell upon the earth. The claims of the Christian religion are absolutely world-wide.

(2) *They Extend to Every Thought and Action.*

The Christian religion is not a garment to be put on and off at pleasure. It is not a masque to be worn on Sunday and discarded during the week. Undoubtedly such use has often been made of it. Not a few of its advocates to-day are using it merely as a convenience or an ornament. But, however much such souls may need adorning, and however beautiful Christianity may be, it is not designed for beauty and outward ornament alone. It is a matter of fact to be believed, a matter of precept to be obeyed, a matter of life to be practised. It lays claim to the whole man, takes cognizance of every act of his life. It rises with him in the morning, sits with him at the table, goes with him about his daily business or pleasure, gathers with him around the family fireside, retires with him to his bedchamber, and even wanders with him through the misty vales of dreamland. Plato's ideal ethics may require little more than a nominal belief, but Christian ethics extend to the minutest details of every-day life.

Nor are they content even then. They probe the inmost recesses of the heart and pitilessly drag to the light the very thoughts and intents thereof. They weigh the motives, analyze the choice, characterize the purpose. They ask a man, not only what he does, but why he does it ; not only how he appears, but what he is. There is no particular department of being or life which he can set apart for Christian duties to the exclusion of the rest. Every duty is a Christian duty. So must every purpose, thought, and act be. Whatever other gods may require, it is certain that the God of the Bible proposes to reign not only over all men, but in all men. He would set up his throne in the human heart, and rule without a rival there.

(3) *They Extend to Man's Religious Nature Only.*

The Bible addresses itself to man as a religious being. Were he not such a being, it would have no message to him whatever. The universality of its claims, as just set forth, depends upon the universality of the religious principle in man. Man has been justly styled a religious animal. He can no more outgrow or escape his religious nature than he can his appetite or his digestion. He may change his religion, as he does his food, with Protean rapidity, but religion of some kind he must have. Men have been found without art, science, poetry, history, institutions, governments; but nowhere upon the earth has any race of men ever yet been found utterly devoid of religion. Proof of this statement will be given hereafter. (Chap. V.)

The Bible is exclusively a religious book. It is not a treatise on philosophy, metaphysics, science, or politics. It gives no instruction in these things. While its moral precepts in their guiding force are universally applicable, still it is not a text-book of human wisdom. While it exalts truth, it does not exhaust it. Let it always be remembered that the Bible leaves men entirely free to seek after truth in fields of human thought, wherever by honest seeking it may be found. Revelation is intended as an aid to man's natural powers, and not a substitute for them. It is in no sense a premium upon idleness and mental inanity. It·is confined strictly to the domain of religious truth, wherein such aid is imperatively necessary. But suppose man had no religious nature. Conceive him just as he is physically and mentally, with the religious element left out. In that case, there could be no place for the Bible or any system of Christian Theism. The only field in which revelation is necessary would be utterly beyond his comprehension. This principle is in no wise contradictory to that of the preceding topic ; for it is man's religious nature that lays hold of his entire being, and enforces the universal claims of Christian Theism.

3. THINGS INVOLVED IN THESE CLAIMS.

It is not enough to consider the claims of Christian Theism in their nature and their extent. What they involve must be noticed. They are not themselves fundamental. Indeed, no claim of any kind can be fundamental. It must be built on something, must have something beneath it, on which it rests.

Beneath such huge claims as appear in the Christian system there ought to be a base of adamant. The strength of the foundation must correspond to the weight of the column it has to support. This basal support may not always be visible. It may be hidden beneath the surface, but honest digging will bring it to light. Thus it is with the claims of Christianity. The foundation facts are not always displayed. They are not argued, perhaps not even stated, but they are there, nevertheless, and are assumed as though beyond question or dispute.

(1) *Christianity Involves the Existence and Character of God.*

It is true, the Scriptures nowhere elaborate an argument to prove that God exists. They do make a very uncomplimentary remark concerning him who hath said in his heart "There is no God." But they do not argue the point with him. They manifestly assume the existence of Deity as a first truth to be universally admitted, or as a conviction to be gained without the aid of Revelation. They begin with God and end with God. He is the Alpha and the Omega. Neither do they give the rationale of his nature. They do attribute to him illimitable and incomprehensible perfections. They affirm his infinity in wisdom, power, truth, justice, holiness, and love. They dwell largely upon those attributes of Deity which are of special interest to helpless, imperfect, and dependent creatures. But they offer no sort of argument as to the intrinsic nature of the Infinite, or as to the compatibility of his attributes. These things are also manifestly taken for granted. The Scriptures come to us as the utterances of a self-existent Deity whose being and all-sufficiency are everywhere assumed.

(2) *The Knowableness of God.*

Knowledge of his mere existence is of no avail to man. Proofs of his being may be infallibly conclusive, and may yet leave untouched the essential doctrines of the Bible. A man may freely admit that there is a God, and at the same time utterly repudiate the entire Christian system. The number of men who, as a matter of fact, do this thing, is historically great, and is probably not diminishing. Matthew Arnold may have believed in "A Power not ourselves that makes for righteousness"; but he believed not in the Bible. Herbert Spencer may talk of an "Infinite and Eternal Energy, from which all things procceed," but Herbert Spencer has no use for the Bible. The god of his philosophy is the Unknown and the Unknowable. However he may be able to reconcile these terms, he certainly means by them that there is an impassable barrier between us and God, that we can never know him, and that therefore the sum of all Theology possible to man may be written in two words, God exists.

Now this barrier to the knowledge of God may reside in God himself, or in man, or in both. On the one hand, the absolute and infinite may be essentially unutterable, incommunicable. If so, an absolute and infinite God can never be known. He dwells forever in the solemn solitudes of his own fathomless being. Man is shut out by an impregnable wall. Every avenue is barred against him by all the power of infinitude itself. The mightiest intellect cannot approach unto God, and the fault is in God himself. But, on the other hand, ignorance of God may be chargeable to man. It may result from the nature and limitations of human knowledge. If man's knowledge depends entirely upon laws of the human understanding, and has no necessary correspondence to the world of objective reality, then he can never be sure of any thing, excepting only the aforesaid laws of the human understanding. Whatever necessary beliefs may be drawn from the Practical Reason, it is certain that according to the philosophy of Kant, Hegel, and Fichte, no man can ever know God. In either case, it is manifest that no revelation of God to man could ever take

place.   But the Bible proceeds upon the assumption that
God can be known, and that man can know him.

(3) *A Veritable Revelation.*

Christian Theism involves the assertion that God has
actually made a revelation to man.   This is a vital point.
God's existence and capacity to be known, man's existence and capacity to know God, are all meaningless
terms until they are realized and united in an act of
revelation.   Certain Egyptian hieroglyphics may be de-
cipherable, and my capacity to decipher them may be
unquestioned, and yet I may remain forever in ignorance,
not only of their meaning, but even of their very existence.   If God has not actually revealed himself to man,
then Herbert Spencer is right, and religious agnosticism
is the soundest philosophy.   But Christian Theism insists
that such a revelation has actually been made, that it is a
matter of fact, a plain historical truth susceptible of historical proof.   On any other supposition, the repeated
utterances of Christ and the Apostles are either impious
blasphemy or ridiculous nonsense.

But more than this.   It is claimed that this revelation
is contained entirely in the canonical books of the Old
and New Testament Scriptures.   A terrible curse is pronounced upon him who adds thereto or takes therefrom.
The canon is closed.   The Bible professes to hold an un-
compromising and indefeasible monopoly on revealed
truth.   Every purchaser, to the end of time, must come
to the inexhaustible treasure-house of the Word, and
buy for himself and not for another.   Verily God has
spoken to man, or the whole Christian system is a stupendous and blasphemous imposture.

SECTION III.

These sanctions are authoritative and convincing. They must furnish justification and enforcement to the claims themselves. If they are adequate, the claims stand; if inadequate, the claims fall, and both go down together.

A commander must be able to show his commission. Christian Theism proposes to command the whole world, and these sanctions are its commission. Let them be carefully examined.

I. THEY ARE ADDRESSED TO THE REASON.

Any other appeal would certainly be unworthy and insufficient. Man's reason is at once his highest power, his distinguishing trait, and his ultimate guide. It is his only test of truth. He must constantly employ it in the discovery of truth and the detection of error. Moreover, he must carefully guard against misusing it. The abuse of reason is the most prolific source of error in the world. He who would find the truth must seek it without prejudice, must approach it in a spirit of absolute impartiality, and must be ready to follow whithersoever it leads. This is always difficult to do. Peculiarly so is it, when such vast personal interests are at stake, as in the case of Christian Theism. But the very vastness of these interests makes it all the more important to follow the dictates of right reason, in settling the momentous questions of religion. What! Shall a man employ his reason in deciding the trivial and momentary affairs of ordinary life, and refuse to use it concerning questions of character, duty, and destiny? Shall he exhaust his highest powers in considering the physical aspects of nature, in studying the moons of Jupiter, the tail of a comet, or the interstellar ether, and doggedly close the eyes of his understanding against those things which make for his own enduring felicity when moons and stars and comets shall have faded from the sky? Surely nothing can be more unreasonable than such an employment of human reason.

And yet it has been repeatedly and boldly asserted that the Christian religion discourages the use of reason, that her sanctions forbid it. This would be a grave charge, indeed, if it were true; but it is not true. It is a baseless slander upon Christianity. " Come, let us reason together," is one of her first words. And the sanctions of the whole system are manifestly addressed to the reason.

(1) *They do not Stand on Blind Authority.*

It is not denied that Bible truth stands on authority. It does so stand. But that authority is not blind. It submits itself to reason. And here the functions of reason in relation to truth must be carefully distinguished. They are twofold: first, the discovery of truth; and second, the test of truth. Some truths can be discovered by the reason alone, some cannot; but all alike must be brought to the test of reason. It must be more reasonable to believe a thing than to reject it, or else its appeal as truth is nugatory.

Christianity claims to reveal truth upon the authority of Deity himself. Now this procedure is reasonable enough, provided the claim to Divine authority be established. But even then, it is not at all complimentary to the powers of human reason; for it plainly implies that the truth so revealed could not be discovered by reason.

It is therefore quite natural that the pride of human reason should be touched thereby, and deeply offended. If the philosopher, by the unaided use of his own powers of speculation and research, might find out God to perfection and gain a knowledge of his will, he would be justly proud of such an achievement. A comfortable sense of proprietorship in the truth so discovered would doubtless give him an ardent attachment to it.

But such is not the plan of the Gospel. The man of most imperial intellect must sit, side by side, with the ignorant and the lowly at the feet of Jesus. Humble and dependent as a little child, he must there receive the truth of God from the King of truth himself. His reason is called upon to discover nothing whatever. It is merely expected to appropriate and test that truth which is already discovered and proclaimed unto it. This pleases not the pride of human reason, and the man of speculative mind turns away from Gospel truth with proud disdain. Let him remember, however, that in doing so he rejects reason no less than Revelation. For the sanctions of Revelation make their appeal at the bar of his reason, and without prejudice or pride, should be tried only before that high tribunal.

(2) *They do not Rest upon mere Ecstatic Fancy.*

One extreme in religion begets another. The cold and rigid demands of reason have floated us into the ice-bound regions of rationalism. Reaction takes place. The counter-current sets in. The fervid breath of ecstatic feeling wafts us back into the torrid kingdom of fancy. We are all aglow and wellnigh stifled with the heat. Yesterday we were in danger of death by freezing. To-day we are about to ignite. The apostles of this subtle and sultry faith declare to us that they are gazing on truth direct, that like seers of old they have beatific visions, that they are caught up into the third heaven, that they behold things divine which no man can utter, and that one moment of such rapt revelation out-weighs a lifetime of icy logic and barren speculation.

Now these enthusiasts are doubtless sincere in their beliefs, and there may be in them a grain of truth, and to some minds a modicum of religious assurance. It may be, and doubtless is, true that moments of spiritual exaltation come to every earnest worshipper, wherein he feels the potent charm of sovereign truth and love as he never felt before. And yet, the sanctions of Christian Theism are in no sense dependent upon such moments of religious ecstasy. When based upon Christian principle, these experiences are true and good; but they figure poorly when brought as witnesses to the bar of reason. Christianity needs not their testimony.

(3) *These Sanctions are not Matters of Habit Simply.*

The formation of proper habits is undeniably a good thing. It is not to be discouraged, nor its power despised. It should be freely admitted and widely utilized in religion as elsewhere. And this is equally true whether it refers to the individual or to the race.

It is manifest, however, that mere habit cannot change the moral character of an act. If the act be right in itself, no repetition of it can make it wrong. And, on the other hand, if the act be wrong, the uninterrupted practice of ages and generations of men can never make it right. The same is true of a belief, and preëminently so of any form of religious faith. It may be right for me to believe to-day as I did yesterday, but it cannot be right *because* I believed it yesterday. It may be right for me to worship the God of my fathers, but it cannot be simply because my fathers worshipped him. I may have two excellent reasons for venerating my ancestors: first, because they were my ancestors; and second, because of the good qualities they may have personally possessed. But my veneration for them can never justify me in imbibing an error or practising a delusion; even they may have done both. Nay, more. It cannot excuse me from investigating for myself any truth which they may have believed or practised.

The Christian religion, recognizing this just principle, calls upon no man to accept its truth because his father did, or because it may have been the habit of his ancestors. He who joins a church because his father belonged to it, professes a creed because it is popular, or pins his religious faith to a priestly robe, is to be pitied or despised. Certainly he is not the most intelligent exponent of the Christian faith.

2. CHRISTIAN SANCTIONS ARE COMMENSURATE WITH CHRISTIAN CLAIMS.

They are justly expected to cover the same ground. Any thing less than this would vitiate the entire system. A man must not claim to be a major-general and show the commission of a lieutenant. Christianity must not lay claim to the entire field of religious thought and action, under the authority of sanctions that cover only a part of that field. The building must not be broader than its foundation. As the Christian structure is worldwide, so is the measure of its foundation.

(1) *Its Extent.*

Christianity presses home its claims upon every member of the human race; but its accompanying sanctions are likewise universal.   The proofs of Christian truth are indeed varied and diversified.   In its quiver there is some arrow that can reach every man's heart.   There is judicial and metaphysical evidence for the philosopher, inductive and deductive evidence for the logician, historical evidence for the antiquarian, linguistic evidence for the philologist, personal testimony for the man of affairs ; and there are intuitive and experimental proofs for all men alike, high or low, rich or poor, learned or ignorant, busy or idle.

Christianity is cosmopolitan.   Other religions flourish in certain latitudes and among certain races.   This one alone flourishes equally among men of every race or tongue or clime.   Now this universal adaptation is found not only in the claims of Christianity, but also in the provisions by which their authority is maintained.   It has sanctions that bring conviction to the mind of every rational human being, no matter what language he may speak, or beneath what sky he may dwell.

(2) *The Scope of Christian Authority.*

By scope of authority is meant the subjects to which it applies, concerning which it speaks.   Manifestly there are many important fields in the domain of possible truth in which Christian Theism utters no voice.   Concerning such truth, of course, she needs show no credentials.   She confines her utterances to two subjects alone. *God* and *the Bible*, are the burden of Christian Theism. For the proofs concerning them, both internal and external, both physical and moral, both historical and inferential, she is responsible.   And, furthermore, she asks not to be relieved of this responsibility.   She is willing to be judged by her ability to establish the being of God and the inspiration of the Bible. Those "mawkish and invertebrate systems" of misty sentimentality, which tender-footed theologians in these days are attempting to construct, under the modest title of "Advanced Christianity," and which utterly ignore the inspiration of the Divine Word, are abhorrent to every principle of Christian Theism. The possibility of the supernatural is a vital hypothesis in the Christian system. Without it, the system is contradictory and self-destructive. Christianity, like the ancient temple of Dagon, rests on two pillars. These pillars are God and the Bible. If either of them shall ever be torn down by the Samsons of infidelity, the whole temple will lie in ruins. If we would measure its strength, we must examine these massive columns. This is the scope of Christian Theism. It has just two themes : first, *Theism*, or evidences concerning the being and nature of God ; second, *Revelation*, or evidences concerning the inspiration of the Bible.

(3) *The Matter of Certainty.*

The sanctions of Christianity are commensurate with its claims, in clearness and certainty. As there is no uncertain sound about the one, so there must be none about the other. As men are left in no manner of doubt concerning the imperative character of Scriptural precepts, so must they be cleared of all reasonable doubt concerning Scriptural authority. The language of the Bible is not simply advisory, it is uniformly authoritative. Thus saith the Lord. That the Scriptures do speak by the authority of the Almighty God, it shall be the purpose of the second volume of this work to prove. In this divine authority lies the chief value of the Bible. Many of its doctrines and precepts might possibly be discoverable by laborious and patient processes of human reason, but when thus discovered they would be of little avail. They would fail to command the homage of men. The very method of their approach would be against them. They would come to us with the tottering step of infancy, rather than the firm, elastic tread of mature age. They would speak the hesitating language of doubt and disagreement, rather than the commanding words of unquestionable certainty. They might engage attention, but could never command obedience. They might reinforce the intellect, but not the heart. The will, the conscience, and the moral powers, which are in greatest need of reinforcement, would be left untouched. Man always knows better than he does. He needs more knowledge, to be sure, but by far his greatest need is a constant, clear, and commanding monitor to awaken the conscience, arouse the affections, and dispose the will toward that which is true and good. Such a monitor the Holy Scriptures furnish to every man who accepts their authority. If they did nothing else than this, they would even then be of priceless value.

3. THE SANCTIONS OF CHRISTIAN THEISM ARE SUI GENERIS.

A brilliant German writer once said of his mother-tongue : " It is separate, unmixed, and only like itself." So may it be said in a higher sense of Christianity ; it is only like itself. But these words must not be pressed too far, in either case. It is certainly not meant that the German language has absolutely nothing in common with other tongues, for that would be contrary to fact, and in defiance of the universal laws of philology and linguistic growth. Neither is it meant that Christianity has nothing whatever of fact, truth, or purpose in common with other systems of religion. Many of its doctrines may indeed be found elsewhere. It is meant, however, that the sanctions of Christianity are unlike all others, both in importance and in method.

(1) *In Importance.*

If Christianity be true at all, it is eternally and transcendently true. It is incomparably the most momentous system of truth ever addressed to men. It takes hold on two worlds. It unites origin, duty, and destiny. It declares all other religious systems essentially and eternally false. It declares God to be true, though all men be found to be liars. It assumes, upon principles of its own, to fix all men in a state of immortal felicity or of endless woe. Now the sanctions of such a system as this must be of supreme and universal importance.

If I am a Brahmin, it matters little to me whether Christianity or Islamism shall prove true, for my religion will admit either. I can witness with equal composure the ascendency of the crescent or of the cross. If I am a Pagan, I can receive with entire unconcern the most convincing proofs of any religion whatsoever; for I already believe in lords many and gods many. But if I am a Christian I can do no such thing. The establishment of any other system is the ruin of my own. Jehovah-God is either the All-Father, or else the most stupendous myth in the universe. This is the question of all questions. Its proofs are of unparalleled importance.

(2) *In Method.*

The sanctions of Christian truth are necessarily unlike all others in their method of approach to the human understanding. This is peculiarly the case with the underlying doctrines of Theism. The question of the being of God is unlike all others. Its proofs ought to be unlike all other proofs. No man need ever expect to demonstrate God, for it cannot be done. Men have often tried it, and as often failed. Even Bishop Butler, in his early days, came near ruining himself in the vain attempt. Atheists have often taunted theists with these chronic failures. They say: "If your God actually exists, why do you not demonstrate it?" At this challenge thoughtless theists have grown pale with alarm, and equally thoughtless atheists have exulted with delight. Both are wrong. These failures are by no means alarming; they are positively encouraging. On the other hand, a rigorous deductive demonstration of God's being would be fatal to Theism. The error consists in admitting the rationality of the atheist's demand to demonstrate God.

Let us look into this matter a little more deeply and see just what it is that the atheist asks of us. What is a strict deductive demonstration, anyhow? It is simply the employment of two related propositions in such a way as to bring to view the truth they contain. It simply unfolds what they already enfold. What then is its effect? It simply classifies the object or objects denoted by a certain term (as Cæsar) among the objects denoted by a certain other and general term (as mortal). Now we begin to see what the atheist wants. He modestly asks us to classify God! And because we very properly decline to do so, he looks extremely wise, and declares it as his candid opinion that we have no God. He seems not to realize that the God of Christian Theism cannot be classified; and this for the obvious reason that he is the one only God, and there is no other being like him in existence. If we were polytheists, we might submit our gods to the rules of logical deduction. But we cannot demonstrate Jehovah without degrading him.

Let there be no misunderstanding of this statement. In avoiding one palpable error, let us not fall into another. It must not be inferred that no proofs of God's existence are to be required. Such a demand is reasonable and will be promptly met. Theism has many lines of cumulative argument, which it shall be the chief purpose of the following pages to present. What we insist upon at the outset is, that no single direct argument in syllogistic form shall be either demanded or admitted. The very nature of the truth to be established forbids it.

CHAPTER I.

INTELLIGENCE IN NATURE; OR, THE EU-TAXIOLOGICAL ARGUMENT.

SECTION I.

DIFFICULTIES IN THE PROOF.

IN constructing a cumulative argument for the establishment of Christian Theism, the two subjects which
it includes must be separately and successively treated.
These, as already stated, are Theism and Revelation.
The subjects themselves will determine the proper order
of their treatment. They are closely and logically related. It is manifest that if there be no God, there can
be no Revelation. If the being or nature of God be
doubtful or unknown, to the same extent will the genu-
ineness of Revelation be doubtful or unknown. The
first truth must therefore be proved before attempting
the second. Theism must be established on a firm footing before revealed Theism can be touched

Herein a serious difficulty presents itself. In these
days of Inductive Philosophy, men are accustomed to
proceed from the particular to the general, to reason
from facts to laws. Naturally easy to the mind, this process has the added facility of habit and the commanding
prestige of success. In the case of Theism, however,
this process must be reversed, and the proof of the gen-

eral truth must be given first. But, by the very nature of the case, a general truth is more difficult of proof than a particular fact. Facts stand on simple testimony, general truths do not. Facts are palpable, obtrusive; general truths are not. Facts appeal to consciousness and the senses; general truths appeal to the understanding, the reason, the judgment, the intuitive powers. To all men the first appeal is intelligible and powerful. To most men the second is surrounded with a degree of difficulty or obscurity, and requires no little effort. Now Revelation is a matter of fact; the being of God is an eternal truth, but not a fact. If I could assume the great fact of Revelation, and proceed therefrom to argue the being and character of God, my way would be easy, my task light. Such a course, however, would be illogical in the extreme—a most flagrant *petitio principii.* In purely theistic studies the Bible must be resolutely closed, and no aid therefrom be either asked or admitted. This principle is so plain that it need not be mentioned, were it not for the undeniable fact that Natural Theists have repeatedly overlooked it.

Another and more serious difficulty confronts us. It arises from the nature of the truth to be established. The more general a truth is, the more difficult is its proof. The wider a law is, the longer men are in finding it out. The history of every branch of human knowledge bears out this statement. Numerous illustrations of its truth in the growth of chemistry, geology, astronomy, and biology, will readily occur to any one acquainted with the history of these sciences. But the being of God is the most general truth possible or conceivable. If it is true at all, it is the truth of truths, the law of laws, the all-embracing, all-penetrating, omnipotent truth of the universe. It is deeper than the lowest depths, higher than the loftiest heights, broader than the widest breadths, impassable, immeasurable, eternal. The very statement of such a truth exhausts the widest reach of mind, baffles the firmest hold of thought, transcends the utmost bound of language.

Surely its proof is in no sense a light undertaking. It can never be accomplished by purely categorical methods. The atheist must not circumscribe us in our arguments. When he calls for proof, as theists we agree. When he proposes to limit us to a single argument, we protest. Truth limited to a particular field may, and doubtless does, have its own appropriate method of proof, to the exclusion of all others. But the truth of Theism is absolutely unlimited, and must not be restricted to any particular kind of proof. Any kind of argumentation which addresses itself with convincing force to a normally constituted human being must be freely admitted. There will be occasion in this work to employ arguments, inductive, deductive, intuitional, historical, and causal. The liberty to do so is claimed not as a privilege, but as a *right*, based upon the nature of the task to be accomplished. If any man should deny the reasonableness of this claim, such denial must argue, either intellectual dishonesty on his part, or else such an abnormal view of reason as renders all reasoning with him impossible. In either case, theistic proofs can have no access to his understanding, and there is nothing in these pages for him.

I am persuaded, however, that no thoughtful man will question the propriety of employing different methods of proof in Theism. The necessity for it is by no means alarming. The absence of such necessity would, on the contrary, give just cause for alarm. The man who thinks he has proved God by a single syllogism, would better look well to his syllogism. The circumstance is unpleasantly suspicious, to say the least of it. To make light work of a difficult task, is usually to slight it.

More than two centuries ago, Henry More, a learned English divine, claimed to have "demonstrated that there is a God," and declared that he had abstained from reading any treatises on this subject, that he might the more undisturbedly write the easy emanations of his own mind. But, as might have been expected, both the demonstration and the "easy emanations" have long since ceased to be quoted by the intelligent theist, unless it be as matters of history, or subjects of just derision. The fact is, Natural Theology has suffered immensely from just such men. William Derham is by no means the only writer on this difficult subject who seems to have considered "the observations so obvious" as to need little thought or research. Neither is he the only writer who, as a necessary consequence, has vainly deceived himself into the belief that he was demonstrating God's existence, while, as a matter of fact, he was merely amusing himself and nauseating his readers by the repetition of stale platitudes and meaningless commonplaces concerning the greatness of God's wisdom and power, and the benignity of his providence. Against all such friends of Theism, we may justly adopt the French proverb and exclaim " Good Lord, deliver us."

Natural theologists are specially liable to this error, and should be specially on their guard against it. We cannot reach God at a single leap, nor rend his veil at a single stroke. We must be content to take a step at a time and look well to our footing. We must empty our minds of the all-pervasive conviction of God's existence, and set out on our theistic pathway as *terra incognita.*

The first step will lead to an Intelligence in the universe. To take this step will be the sole attempt of the present chapter. If the existence of such Intelligence shall be established, even that will not prove the existence of a God ; but it will give us one element of God, and that by no means an inconsiderable one.

This, then, is the present task—to prove Intelligence in nature. For this purpose I employ the principle of Eutaxiology. This term, derived from the Greek words εὖ, τάξις, and λόγος, and meaning well arranged, is used to name that branch of Theism which treats of order and harmony in nature.

It has often been falsely identified with Teleology, which treats of purpose or end in nature. The two subjects, while closely allied, are nevertheless logically distinct, and will be discussed separately. It is manifest that order may be seen where no purpose whatever is discoverable. Such order furnishes a legitimate argument in Eutaxiology, but none whatever in Teleology. Unmindful of this distinction, the old Teleologists made ludicrous blunders in attempting to show the purpose of every orderly result in nature. The purpose of the starry heavens, for example, may be extremely uncertain, but their order and beauty are clear enough. We see order everywhere in nature. Order implies a pre-conceived plan to which the numberless phenomena in question have been made to conform. But plan implies intelligence. Order and harmony are, therefore, marks of intelligence. This is the fundamental principle in Eutaxiology.

Let us turn to the animal kingdom for an illustration. It is readily found in the doctrine of morphology, **or** typical forms. Among vertebrate animals, for instance, the prevailing type of a limb is, that there be first a single bone, then two bones placed side by side, then small connecting bones, then five bones side by side, and, lastly, five digits. Many animals differing from one another immensely in other respects persist in retaining this identical type of limb. In fact, it is admitted to be a persistent idea which is capable of moulding the hand of a man, the wing of a bat, the paw of a lion—a veritable plan in nature, requiring intelligence for its conception and execution. Eutaxiology contains these two elements therefore: (1) The fact of order in nature ; (2) a previous plan necessary to the production of that order.

SECTION II.

THE EUTAXIOLOGICAL SYLLOGISM.

The importance of syllogistic forms is vastly overestimated. They are not necessary either to the discovery of truth, or even to the process of reasoning. Reason is a universal gift of man. Its proper use does not depend upon strict logical forms. In the study of nature logical and correct conclusions often flash upon the mind with a spontaneous and convincing force which is quite independent of formal logic. One needs but look to the starry heavens for an illustration of this truth. The harmony and beauty written there are read in no syllogistic light. They appeal to every man. "Their line is gone out through all the earth, and their words to the end of the world." In the silent majesty of their nightly course they tell the story of a Creative Intelligence. The lesson they impress is simple and universal. The conclusion they enforce is irresistible. And yet it depends not on the refinements of logical form. Logic is useful, however, as a protection against error. It corrects us when wrong and assures us when right. To satisfy the most exacting critic, therefore, the Eutaxiological argument will be put into strict syllogistic form. Here it is:

Major Premise.
Order and harmony are marks of intelligence.
Minor Premise.
Nature displays order and harmony.
Conclusion.
Nature displays marks of intelligence.

There is no logical fault in this argument. If the premises are true the conclusion must follow inevitably. Let these premises be carefully examined.

I. THE MAJOR PREMISE.

By this proposition it is meant that order and harmony are invariably conjoined with intelligence. If this be true, and order and harmony are found in nature, then the existence of intelligence in nature is proved beyond all peradventure. In discussing this premise its meaning must first be determined.

(1) *Its Truth Discriminated.*

It is not necessary to say that by intelligence in nature I make no reference whatever to the voluntary actions of men and of animals. Of course they are a part of nature, and order in their action is a mark of intelligence; but this intelligence is undisputed, and so need not be dwelt upon in the present discussion.

Neither does this proposition mean that intelligence never produces disorderly results. In other words, it does not claim that intelligence is invariably conjoined with order, but that order is invariably conjoined with intelligence. Just as organism is not always conjoined with life, but life is always conjoined with organism. In the case of order and intelligence, both these propositions may be true, but the latter only is vital to the argument. It may be true that intelligence is always orderly, but concerning that truth Eutaxiology is supremely indifferent.

Neither is it asserted that order and intelligence are joined together as cause and effect. This may, indeed, be the law that binds them ; intelligence may be the cause and order the effect. But this is not the particular truth on which the mind dwells in the present argument. In fact, it is not in the least necessary to it. What the particular nature of the relation between order and intelligence may be, is a matter of indifference so long as I know that the relation itself is invariable. To recur to the former illustration, I need not enquire whether or not animal life is a mere product of organism. I know that it never exists without organism, and that is sufficient. In like manner, if order is always and everywhere a mark of intelligence I need not trouble myself about the nature of this fact. If the two are inseparabley bound together, I need not demand a chemical analysis of the material from which have been forged the links of the binding chain.

(2) Its Truth Established.

Having freed this major premise from some possible misunderstandings, I now proceed to the direct establishment of its truth. Is order an invariable mark of intelligence ? To some the truth of this statement may seem self-evident. A careful analysis will, I think, show that it is not. I arrive at this truth by a process of induction,.

the steps of which are somewhat as follows : I am continually conscious of orderly results as the products of the
action of my own intelligence. This is the habit of my life
from earliest infancy. Moreover, I have likewise observed
similar results flowing from the action of other intelligences. My fellow-men are constantly furnishing examples of order as a mark of intelligence. Orderly results,
to some degree, are likewise produced by the lower animals. Here I have three classes of facts, the first produced
by myself, the second by my fellow-men, the third by
animals.

Now these facts are alike in that they are all orderly.
They all exhibit this same distinguishing feature. But the
first I know to be necessarily connected with my own
intelligence. The second are performed by beings like
myself, to whom I find it logically impossible to deny
intelligence, and are just such results as, if done by myself, would show intelligence. I therefore infer by a mental necessity that they are marks of intelligence in my
fellow-men. And this inference is not at all contingent.
I am as certain of it as of my own existence. The third
are performed by beings not like myself, it is true, but
still possessed of a degree of intelligence, of whose existence there are manifold and independent proofs. The
orderly results themselves are in perfect accordance with
this degree of animal intelligence. The two are inseparably bound together, and the one is the mark of the other.
And so it turns out that these three classes of orderly
results are all infallible marks of intelligence.

Let it now be remembered that these three classes
comprehend all the orderly results with whose origin I am
acquainted. But the fact of order is by no means so
circumscribed. It pervades all nature. It is seen alike

in leaf, and flower, and shell, in forest, and mountain, and ocean, in earth, and air, and sky. Now this widespread order in nature is the thing to be accounted for. What is its origin? I reply at once and without hesitation, that it is the action of a pervasive and marvellous intelligence. I reach this result by the legitimate and well-known process of induction. What has been found invariably true of all known cases of order-making I carry over to the unknown and logically infer to be likewise true of all cases whatsoever. This is but a simple act of sound induction, as every logician will attest.

And there is no manner of doubt about it. I know that order is an invariable mark of intelligence, just as certainly as I know that every man is a vertebrate, and that the law of gravitation is universal. So sure am I of this truth that it is perfectly satisfying in every possible case of order, actual or conceivable.

Suppose some Galileo of the nineteenth century should construct a telescope so marvellously superior in both magnifying and illuminating power as to render visible the minutest objects on the surface of the moon. Suppose that, by the use of this instrument, a system of accurate pentagonal figures should be discovered, whose sides were formed of successive triangles, equal, equiangular, and equi-distant. Would any sane man doubt for a moment that some intelligence had at some time been at work on the surface of the moon? If the same figures had been found on the surface of the earth, whether upon mountain summit, or upon ocean beach, he would doubtless attribute them to man. This is perfectly natural. It obviously results from the fact that man is the only being of mundane existence, whose intelligence is adequate to account for the facts. But he could never

think of attributing the telescopic fact of order just supposed to human intelligence, from the equally obvious
consideration that man's lunar existence is impossible.
So that the induction in question is manifestly far wider
than the human race.   It out-measures the earth, scales
the heavens, reaches the utmost limits of the known universe, and proclaims the existence of superhuman intelligence wherever order and harmony are found.   The
truth that order is a sure mark of intelligence is certainly
as clear an induction as man is capable of making in any
field of thought whatever.

2.   THE MINOR PREMISE.

" Nature displays order and harmony."   This will be
remembered as the second proposition in the eutaxiological syllogism.   It only remains to make good this
statement, in order to establish the argument beyond
question.

The careful reader need not be reminded that this
argument takes no account of those types of intelligence
to be found in the voluntary actions of animals and of
man.   The thing to be established is the existence in
nature of an intelligence utterly beyond these special
types, and independent of them.   In proving, therefore,
the display of order and harmony in nature, all reference
to such cases thereof as may imply the intelligence of
man or of animals, must be avoided.

It is obvious that, setting these aside, the proof of a
single case of order in nature is sufficient to establish the
proposition in question.   As I desire, however, not only
to prove the existence of intelligence in nature, but also
to show something of its all-pervasive, all-abounding
character, I shall not stop with a single example.   It will

be wise to enlarge somewhat on this point, for another reason. If there be intelligence anywhere in nature, it is quite reasonable, though not necessary, to expect it everywhere. If nature is, in any sense, the great workshop of intelligence, then surely some tokens of the workman will be scattered throughout the main building, and not confined to some obscure corner of an insignificant annex. The eutaxiologist may, indeed, not be able to recognize them all, but the longer he searches, the more will he find. The researches of modern science have already furnished an interesting and instructive list of these tokens. Every department of nature is full of them. It would be tedious, as well as useless, to burden these pages with a detailed statement of them all. Only a few representative types need be examined.

(1) *In Inorganic Matter.*

The science of chemistry abounds in examples of order. They are both numerical and formal. Every molecule of matter of every possible variety is a definite mass of atoms built together with the most exact arithmetical and geometrical relations. The most accurate structures built by the hand of man cannot compare with these products of nature in the numerical and formal exactness with which their elements are combined. There is vastly more order in the construction of a molecule than of a mansion.

Chemical symbols are nothing more than the expressions of the kind, number, and connection of atomic elements in these molecular structures. Moreover, these atomic blocks in the molecule do not combine invariably and indifferently, as so many bricks in a wall. Atoms of different elements possess a different number of combining sides. Hydrogen, for instance, has but one, and is said to be univalent, oxygen has two, and is bivalent ; carbon four, and is quadrivalent. Indeed, these atoms seem like stones designed by the architect for an exterior or interior place in the building, and having their faces cut accordingly.

Again, in their gaseous form all elements show a remarkable numerical order in their relative determinate weights and volumes in all compounds, involving numbers which are multiples of the atomic weights of the respective elements. These relations are not merely proximate, but are strictly exact.

The well known nitrogen series has been cited as a notable example of these structures. Witness the multiples of fourteen and sixteen running through the series :

	Nitrogen by weight.	Oxygen by weight.
Nitrous oxide	28	16
Nitric oxide	14	16
Nitrous trioxide	28	48
Nitric peroxide	14	32
Nitric pentoxide	28	80

Could any more exact numerical order be well conceived? It must be remembered, moreover, that this order is not an exceptional thing. It runs through the entire foundation on which the physical structure of things is built. The whole physical universe is but an aggregation of such orderly chemical structures. To the chemist there are tokens of order all through the workshop.

Crystallography furnishes striking examples of order and mathematical relations. They are to be observed in the edges, angles, surfaces and solids of crystalline forms. Snowflakes crystallize in a variety of radial forms, based in every case upon a constructive angle of 60°. The filaments of sal-ammoniac in solution, preserve an angle of 45° or 90°. The physicist finds no less than six different systems of crystals, characterized by the number, direction, and relative length of their axes. There is an exact symmetry of surfaces and angles in them all. We are told, moreover, that the position of the planes is mathematically related to the relative lengths of the axes.

Geometry, as well as arithmetic, is at work in the realm of inorganic matter, producing orderly results, both numerous and marvellous.

(2) *Order in the Vegetable Kingdom.*

The prevalence of order among plants is evident from their very classification into families, genera, and species. Nearly all these classes of plants are based upon elements of order and symmetry in the individual plants themselves. The very possibility of scientific classification is a convincing evidence of widespread order in the vegetable world. Surely there is no inherent physical necessity whereby great families of plants should be forced into one invariable type. Hap-hazard forms and violations of order would accord quite as well with the necessary demands of vegetable life. But not so. Nature is everywhere full of plan, order. An examination of vegetable life discloses this truth on every side.

The first thing that strikes us is number. Whole families of plants seem to be carefully constructed on a numerical relation of parts. The Liliacæ, for instance, are based on the number three. And so of other orders. But this relation is manifestly not at all necessary. It is an evidence of plan, but not of necessity.

Phyllotaxy abounds in curious and interesting cases of

numerical order. Leaves on a stem, flowers about a disc, are usually attached in the form of spirals. These spirals vary in the relative movements of generatrix and pole, for the different orders of plants. They are named and distinguished by the number of circuits around the stem as compared with the number of leaves contained in those circuits. These give a series of ratios; one half representing one circuit and two leaves; one third, one circuit and three leaves; two fifths, two circuits and five leaves; three eights, three circuits and eight leaves.

Scientists have called attention to two curious circumstances concerning this series of fractions. The first is, that each succeeding fraction is formed by the addition of the numerators and denominators of the two preceding ones; and the second, that they represent the ratios of the times of revolution of the planets about the sun, when expressed in days. "The period of Uranus is half that of Neptune, the period of Saturn is one third that of Uranus, the period of Jupiter two fifths that of Saturn." As an explanation of this law of phyllotaxy, it has been claimed that these particular arrangements of leaves about the stem are simply for the purpose of securing the best possible exposure to the sunlight. The explanation fails for two reasons. In the first place, the best possible exposure to sunlight cannot be shown to be a fact thus secured. The very nature of the law forbids it. If three eighths, for instance, represents the most economical arrangement about one perpendicular, cylindrical stem, then it is manifestly impossible that one half or two fifths should represent precisely the same thing in the case of another stem equally perpendicular and cylindrical. In the second place, it is not purpose that is to be explained, but *order, plan of structure.* If, therefore, it be shown that order in a given case may be utilized for any purpose whatever, that demonstration can neither remove the fact of order, nor account for it without intelligence.

Another remarkable field of orderly results in the vegetable kingdom is found in its exquisite symmetry and beauty of form, arrangement, and color. All this beauty, of which nature is so full, results from symmetry of form and proportion, and delicate combinations of color. And this is true both of a landscape as a whole, and of the separate objects of which it is composed. It is likewise true in general of all objects alike in the vegetable kingdom, whether large or small. The stately symmetry of the oak, the poplar, and the pine may not be discoverable in any mere details of form, but it is none the less surely and strikingly visible to every lover of nature. Then there is the more delicate symmetry of leaf and stem, and flower and disc. There is scarcely a leaf in the forest, whose exquisite symmetry of outline and delicate shadings of color do not surpass the skill of human art. Mark the most admirable symmetry displayed in the petals, stamens, and anthers of flowers. Observe also their orderly and delicate use of colors. Flowers never display irregular and unsightly patches of white and red and blue and gold, in promiscuous mixture—a hideous daub. They are always mingled in delicate outline and systematic order.

No man can make a careful study of plants and flowers without being imbued with the spirit of order, symmetry, and beauty that pervades them everywhere.

(3) *Order in the Animal Kingdom.*

Forms of order and symmetry among animals are found to be much more complex and complicated than those heretofore discussed. This is not at all surprising. As we rise to higher types of being we must expect to meet combinations more complex in every respect. Take an illustration. Biologists tell us that albumen in some form is the physical basis of all animal life. Now a molecule of water consists of three atoms, while that of albumen contains 2,316 atoms. Who can wonder that, if cases of order should occur in albuminous forms, they should become somewhat complicated? As a matter of fact, order and symmetry do exist in most pervasive and comprehensive forms, in nearly every species of animals. These symmetries are very various and very noticeable. They extend to both the exterior and the interior structure. Indeed, they are so universal as to be termed typical forms, which are supposed by many to dominate the structures of the various species. The very names of the sub-kingdoms refer directly to these typical forms. Mollusca and radiata, for instance, have a circular symmetry, while that of vertebrata is clearly bilateral. There is again the greatest conceivable variety in these sub-kingdoms. But one thing seems to remain constant, and that is the simple idea of order and appropriate symmetry. Animate nature has been aptly likened to the work of an architect who is building every imaginable variety of houses, but all under the guiding principles of a given style of general architecture.

Again, the element of color in animate nature is so employed as to display striking forms of order and symmetry. The markings of insects, fishes, beasts, and birds are not disorderly, but are fashioned for the most part into forms of regularity and beauty.

Now these forms and colors of the several types are all undoubted cases of order in nature. It will not do to say that they are simple physical necessities. Variations from symmetrical forms are sufficiently numerous and sufficiently pronounced to dispel any reasonable suspicion of necessity, in symmetrical structures, wherever they may be found. Neither do this symmetry and beauty arise from mere considerations of utility in service. There are many instances of both wherein no useful function can possibly be discovered. Take the exterior symmetry and beauty of the human form, for example. There is no particular physiological necessity or advantage in that. On the contrary, the most vital physiological functions are performed by organs that are by no means symmetrically disposed in the body. The heart, lungs, liver, and stomach are all such. The fact is, that the internal symmetry of the human structure is not at all complete. Wherein, then, lies the necessity that the exterior should be so assiduously rounded out into forms symmetrical and beautiful? But so it is; and the fact, whether it proves any thing else or not, does certainly show a clear case of plan and order in the structure of the human frame.

The human hand has often been cited as an instrument of design and utility. But it is also one of exquisite symmetry and beauty. Observe its wonderful delicacy of outline, flexibility of parts, dexterity of motion, expressiveness of posture. Who can say that nature exhibits no plan or order in its unique structure?

The human face is also a thing of marvellous symmetry and beauty. In its structure, nature seems to have reached the very summit of her skill as an order-worker. Who can behold an innocent, intelligent human face without emotions of the deepest admiration?

I cannot better close this topic than in the eloquent

words of another, to whom I am already indebted for much of this part of the argument herein condensed.

He says: "The human face—furnished with its vigorous senses reaching to the stars, in turn looking out of the depths of space and the silence of eternity; its features, the seat of versatile thought, the medium through which the soul is flashing all the changeable lights of emotion; the voice, meanwhile, uttering, like a chorus in articulate sound, the burden of this passion—[the human face] is that hand-breadth of surface in which two worlds touch each other and blend at the zenith of beauty."

(4) *Order in the Cosmos.*

The term "Cosmos" has been shamefully abused. It has been unceremoneously dragged into any use which the necessity, convenience, or fancy of philosophers might dictate. Sometimes it stands for the world, sometimes for the earth; sometimes it includes the whole universe, sometimes the physical creation or only a portion thereof. In these pages it will be used in its broadest sense to include the whole created universe. In this sense, strictly considered, the present topic, "Order in the Cosmos" would evidently include all possible order. It is designed, however, to mention only a very few instances which are of such a nature that they could not properly be ranked among the chemical, botanical, or biological examples just given.

And here I am confronted at once with the law of gravitation—the most general conception hitherto attained in the physical universe. It would seem like a hazardous undertaking, indeed, to attempt the extraction of individual instances of order from a principle so widespread and absolutely universal. A little examination, however, shows it to be just the contrary.

The very fundamental law of its action is an admirable embodiment of order. Every particle of matter in the universe attracts every other particle, directly as its mass, and inversely as the square of its distance. Now let us see just what is involved in this well-known law, so often and so carelessly quoted. A forcible writer has set forth its meaning somewhat as follows :

It means that every molecule of matter is tugging away at every other without interruption and without weariness. It means that every little fellow knows just how to tug, in what direction, and how hard. It means that each is an accurate mathematician, for he must work according to inverse ratios, and that of the second power. If one little atom on the surface of Sirius should, by mistake, conduct the attraction business of his office on the ratio of cubes instead of squares, it would eventually disrupt the universe. It means that every worker must be an accurate observer with both microscopic and telescopic powers of vision, and likewise a brilliant clairvoyant of marvellous range. For he must know the exact distance and direction of every atom in creation ; else how can he determine with what strength and at what angle to pull at him ? It means that he carries a "ready reckoner" of most incredible capacity ; else how can he figure out with unerring accuracy, the proper ratios of countless millions of atoms, each of whose distances is constantly varying at every conceivable instant of time, and always arrive at the desired results with such simultaneous celerity as to enable him to conduct his attraction business absolutely without interruption and without mistake ? If, through carelessness, incapacity, or stupidity, one single atom should miss his reckoning for a single instant, the disastrous consequences of his indiscretion would permeate the entire creation. As a matter of fact, no such mistake or delay is ever made.

And is there no order here? Verily there is, and that, too, of the most intricate character. This one law of gravitation—so simple and yet so intricate—makes of the whole physical universe one vast system of orderly existence and harmonious activity—a far-reaching plan, which implies constructive intelligence of immense capacity and boundless sweep.

But this is not all. The special applications of this law are likewise along the line of harmony and order. It is, indeed, a very wonder-worker of celestial harmonies. It stands like a mighty giant in the sky. With its two arms of power, centripetal and centrifugal, it hurls innumerable and massive worlds through the mazy depths of unmeasured space, and at the same time binds them to the invariable symmetry of their orbital movements. The order and precision with which planets and stars and suns hold on their mysterious way through the sky, are due to special applications of this law. This statement cannot be better illustrated than by reference to Kepler's famous laws of planetary motion: (1) Planets describe elliptical orbits. (2) The radius vector of any planet describes equal areas in equal times. (3) The ratio between the squares of the periods of revolution of any two planets is always equal to the ratio between the cubes of their mean distances from the sun. These three laws disclose the most exact mathematical order, both discrete and continuous. But upon these three laws hang almost the entire science of astronomy. And they themselves are based in turn upon the wider law of gravitation. Even gravitation itself may yet be found to be only the application of a wider, deeper law, which the mind of man has not yet compassed.

And these are but a few of the stately symmetries of the starry heavens. What a world of beauty and harmony and order they present in their nightly sweep to him who has eyes to see it! And is there no pre-conceived plan, no constructive intelligence in all this? Well might Napoleon, in answer to the speculations of the French atheists, point to the star-set sky and exclaim: " But who made all these?" It was a sound argument in Eutaxiology.

3. THE CONCLUSION.

If the preceding considerations have established the truth of the premises in the eutaxiological syllogism, then the conclusion must follow as a logical necessity. If order and harmony are marks of intelligence, and nature displays order and harmony, then it is certainly true that nature displays marks of intelligence. There is no illicit process here of any conceivable kind whatever. But if nature shows marks of intelligence, then either there is now intelligence at work in nature, or there has been at some previous time, or both. In either case, the existence of intelligence, other than that of man and the lower animals, is infallibly proved. And just this is all that Eutaxiology proposes to do. Her task is accomplished.

SECTION III.

OBJECTIONS.

It would certainly seem that no additional word need be uttered in defence of this straightforward argument in Eutaxiology which has just been set forth. But, as ever, the objector is abroad in the land. He has formulated sundry and diverse objections against the doctrine taught herein, which it is proper to notice as briefly as the nature and the number of these strictures will admit.

1. CONCERNING LAW.

The philosophers who make this objection have a most exalted idea of law, particularly of natural law. They consider it wellnigh omnipotent—capable of doing and accounting for every thing. In short, they deify law. They evidently forget that natural law, so-called, is nothing but an expression for the uniform activities of nature, and can account for nothing whatever. When we speak of "the reign of law," we use words figuratively, for a law of nature is a thing of method, and not at all of origin or cause. The very existence of law implies a law-maker; and so, instead of explaining events occurring under it, must needs be explained itself.

But the objection of these champions of natural law runs thus : "What you call order in nature is nothing in the world but the operation of law. There is no order in it, no pre-conceived plan, no constructive intelligence back of it. It is all the result of mere laws of matter."

Now this is evidently an attempt to explain the orderly results in the universe on purely physical principles. Its purpose is to explain away all intelligence from nature. These theorists, having denied to mind its proper work in orderly results, assign that work to purely physical and organic activities. This forlorn undertaking may be honest enough, but it cannot be credited with much penetration. Mark the inconsistency and essential weakness of the thing. In explaining the course of these organic processes on which these theorists stake so much, there is not a man in the list who does not constitute them, directly or indirectly, into seats of "unconscious or supra-conscious intelligence" of some kind or other. Now intelligence is manifestly intelligence, whether conscious or otherwise. But let these gentlemen tell us what sort of thing this " unconscious intelligence " of theirs may be. We are justly anxious to know, for it certainly plays a leading part in their philosophy. It is not matter. It can, therefore, do nothing by virtue of physical properties. It is not mind, for that word is utterly repudiated. The very existence of a species of absolutely and eternally unconscious intelligence, is an impossible conception. But let its existence be magnanimously granted. What could it do in bringing to pass the orderly results of nature? I have shown that these results involve number and form. What does unconscious intelligence know about form? They likewise involve complicated mathematical relations. What can unconscious intelligence do in mathematics? They likewise involve the independent and co-etaneous action of vast numbers of material objects at immense distances asunder. What can unconscious intelligence do toward marshalling into orderly and effective movement the confused and scattered battalions of such a heterogeneous host? The battle-field is far too vast, the soldiery too numerous, for this unconscious, comatose commander. And yet these gentlemen naively assure us that he is adequate to the task; for, say they, there is no other in the field, and the cosmical army is actually moving in orderly and triumphant array.

The fact is that this unconscious intelligence is a wonderful affair. It accomplishes most wonderful results. Indeed, it must be infinitely superior to conscious intelligence. Human mind is conscious intelligence in its typical form. Surely no one will deny this, if he believes in intelligence at all. But human mind could never do an infinitesimal part of the work so confidently assigned to this unconscious intelligence in nature. Consciousness must then be a bad element in mind—a regular burden to the intellect, a clog to its operations! Let us be rid of the burden at any cost. Let the scales of consciousness drop at once from our mental vision. Let us adopt the prayer of Buddha, and ask to deposit our worn-out consciousness in some humble corner of the opalescent realms of Nirvana!

Seriously, that kind of unconscious intelligence which these philosophers are constrained to postulate is quite good enough for the eutaxiologist. It is fully equal to any thing in that line which his argument establishes. True, he regrets their unfortunate and improper use of the term "unconscious," and would earnestly suggest that they leave it off altogether. But he is not disposed to quarrel about a word.

2. CONCERNING CAUSATION.

The attempt has been made to involve Eutaxiology in the disputes concerning cause and effect. It is put thus: "Order is considered a mark of intelligence by an inference from the law ' Every event has a cause.' But this law itself is in dispute as to its origin. One philosopher says it is an intuition, another deems it an induction, while a third views it as a simple matter of association. The whole thing is adrift in uncertainty. Eutaxiology is therefore a mere matter of unsettled opinion."

Now concerning this objection, it must be admitted that the causal principle is in some sense involved in all reasoning whatsoever. This is no new idea. Leibnitz considered it one of the primary laws of logical thought, and stated it thus: "Nothing happens without a reason why it should be so rather than otherwise." By others it has been styled the Law of Sufficient Reason.

Eutaxiology is certainly a sample of the reasoning

process, and must, therefore, have the principle of causation lying somewhere beneath it. But it must be remembered that this causal principle (be its origin what it may) is practically so universally recognized as never to be brought into question. No logistic syllogism is ever questioned as to its validity, by virtue of its relation to the proposition: Every event has a cause. All we ask is: "Are the premises true? Is the logic sound?" This practical truth has been forcibly illustrated by reference to a criminal trial at court. Suppose that a prisoner is at the bar on trial for murder. The prosecution proves incontestably that the victim died by a mortal wound, that he and the prisoner were closeted together at the time of the murder, that they were alone, that the prisoner had every motive for killing, that immediately after the sad event, a concealed weapon, covered with blood, was found upon the person of the prisoner, that the victim had no weapon whatever, that upon careful examination the blood-spots were found to contain minute discs of that form and size which invariably betoken human blood. The defence admits all these facts, but he insists that there is some difference among philosophers about the law of sufficient causation. The death of the victim did occur, but, then, it may possibly have had no cause whatever. These spots are undoubtedly on the prisoner's weapon, but they might have come there by mere chance. Opinions differ. Will you take an innocent man's life, on a simple matter of opinion?

How long would such a defence hang a jury of intelligent men?

But suppose he argues further about the blood-discs; says it is uncertain whether these peculiar forms are a result of the constitution of human blood, or the constitution of human blood is a result of these peculiar forms. It is a matter of entire indifference with the jury as to which is cause and which effect, or indeed as to whether there be any cause and effect in the case. That is not the question. The only pertinent question is, "Do these peculiar discs invariably betoken human blood?" With that answered in the affirmative, the case is perfectly clear and certain.

Just so with the eutaxiologist. He cares nothing at all about causation in orderly results. He only asks "Does order always betoken intelligence?" And the proof that it does puts the case of intelligence in nature beyond all possible question.

3. CONCERNING NECESSITY.

This objection states that the order of nature flows necessarily from the properties of matter; and as matter itself is eternal, and therefore all its properties are eternal, the order of nature is adequately accounted for without intelligence.

Both of the statements involved in this objection are decidedly questionable. Chalmers, for instance, denies the first, and insists that the wonderful order-making in nature results, not from necessary properties of matter, but from what he styles *arbitrary collocations* thereof. He takes the solar system as an illustration. Gravitation is conceded to be an out-flow of the necessary properties of matter. But gravitation can destroy systems and worlds as well as preserve them. The question as to which result shall take place in a given system, depends quite as much upon certain peculiar conditions thereof as upon the general law of gravitation. The integrity of the solar system, for example, depends upon five con-

·ditions of planetary movement: (1) smallness of the orbital inclinations, (2) slightness of orbital eccentricities, (3) motions all in the same direction, (4) the incommensurable character of the periods of revolution, and (5) the relative vastness of the central sun. Now all these conditions are apparently arbitrary. There is no known property of matter which could possibly have prevented any one of them from being otherwise than it is. But the slightest change in any one of them would be sufficient to destroy the stability of the entire solar system. Hence it has been justly argued that the evidence of intelligence in nature is to be found in these arbitrary collocations, even though matter should be proved to be eternal.

But the eternity of matter is not proved. It may be that what Chalmers deems arbitrary collocations of matter may yet turn up as the results of necessary properties of matter—the action of physical laws as yet undiscerned. What then? Would these orderly results become any the less evident marks of intelligence? Have we not already seen that this very law of gravitation is full of such marks? It makes no sort of difference when these principles were implanted in physical nature, nor how long they shall remain there; if so be they are only there, they are certain marks of intelligence. If they were there from the beginning, it only goes to show that intelligence was there from the beginning. And such a conclusion would work no damage whatever to the present argument. Kant has truly said, that if matter has such properties that it must produce a beautiful and orderly world, then an intelligent being must have created matter and endowed it with these properties.

Eutaxiology agrees, and insists that if order is a neces-

sary out-flow of matter, it is thereby none the less certain
that " this goodly frame of things " must have proceeded
from an intelligent author.

4. CONCERNING UNIVERSALITY.

It is objected further that the very abundance of order
in nature is fatal to Eutaxiology. Those who bring this
objection take a view of the subject quite the opposite of
the preceding. They are eager to admit that order exists
everywhere. They even insist upon it. They assert that
order pervades every corner and cranny of creation ; that
from molecule to mountain, from atom to star, its sway is
absolutely universal. " Now it is evident," they argue,
" that a universal thing cannot be the mark of any thing
whatever, for a mark of any thing is simply a sign by
which we recognize it and distinguish it from all other
things. But a universal sign cannot distinguish one thing
from another, for the good and sufficient reason that it
pertains to all things alike. If order is unlimited, it can
be a mark of nothing, unless it be of mere existence."

Now this argument is specious, indeed. At first sight
it looks sound and strong. But the trouble seems to be
that it is too strong. It proves entirely too much. It
destroys all distinction between mind and matter. It
denies human intelligence. If it means any thing, it
means that there can be no evidence of the existence of
mind anywhere. It puts out God and man at one breath.
There is no God, and man is but a form of matter. Orderly results from human intelligence are a myth, for
there is no evidence that there is any human intelligence.
Consciousness is a lie, memory a fraud, experience a delusion, reason a cheat. For by all these am I certified that
certain orderly results are the outflow and token of my
own intelligence.

Any theory which necessarily leads to such wholesale philosophical iconoclasm must be wrong somewhere. Let it be granted that the first statements in the argument are true. Let us suppose that order is universal; that only proves the universality of intelligence. The sign is co-extensive with the thing signified. But what of that? A universal thing ought to have universal tokens. If intelligence does pervade matter everywhere, it is on that account none the less intelligence. The mere multiplication of a thing cannot change its nature. Neither is matter any the less matter. The co-existence of the two in nature presents no new philosophical difficulty, for they are admitted to co-exist in man.

The eutaxiologist starts out to prove the existence of intelligence in nature. If in so doing he arrives at the universality of that intelligence, he is not at all alarmed thereby. On the contrary, he is decidedly pleased with such a conclusion. Moreover, he is not arguing for human intelligence. Its existence is universally conceded. And so this ponderous objection falls harmless at his feet.

5. CONCERNING PURPOSE OR END.

The preceding objections all smack of atheism. This one comes from the theist. He complains that Eutaxiology utterly ignores the principle of adaptation and design ; that it antagonizes the methods of Teleology— the world-renowned and historic champion of Theism— and insolently usurps its proper ground. If true, this would certainly be a serious charge. And it really is a serious matter, because it is the criticism of a friend. One may expect to be misunderstood and misrepresented by enemies, but not by a friend or brother. Now the eutaxiologist and the teleologist are natural brothers in philosophy. They are fellow-soldiers fighting on the same side of a great issue. They cannot afford to disagree. And they need not. The simple fact is that the teleologist is mistaken as to the purpose of his theistic brother. And so, without meaning to be unjust, he has made charges that are totally false.

(1) *As to Ignoring Adaptation.*

Eutaxiology does not ignore this broad principle in nature. It freely admits it. True, it is not used, simply because it is not needed. Plan may imply adaptation to an end, but that adaptation need not be shown in order to prove intelligence in plan. The fact of order is enough for that. And so adaptation is left in the domain of Teleology, where it rightfully belongs. Because two soldiers fight in the same cause is no reason why they must use exactly the same weapons.

(2) *As to the Matter of Antagonism.*

There is none whatever. There can be no possible war between plan and purpose. And this tells the exact relation between Eutaxiology and Teleology. Indeed, these branches of Theism may be briefly and fittingly described as *Plans and Purposes in Nature.* They are in perfect harmony. Their methods may be different, but they are certainly not belligerent. In fact, they dwell together in unity. Every plan pre-supposes a purpose, and every purpose executes a plan.

(3) *As to the Charge of Usurpation.*

It likewise is false. Teleology has hitherto assumed the burden of proving the existence of God. That is an herculean task. Eutaxiology does not attempt it at all. It does propose to demonstrate the existence of intelligence in nature. With this simple task it is satisfied; with this single step it stops. And yet this is no light task, no insignificant step toward the proof of God. It will be of great service to Teleology in the larger work yet to be accomplished. With this intent the truth established by Eutaxiology is cordially proffered. Let it be cordially received, and let these two stand together as co-workers in the greatest and best of all causes.

REFERENCES.

Hick's " Critique of Design-Arguments."
Bascom's " Natural Theology."
Bowne's " Studies in Theism."
Cooke's " Religion and Chemistry."

CHAPTER II.

VOLITION IN NATURE; OR, THE TELEOLOGI-
CAL ARGUMENT.

SECTION I.

SCOPE OF THE ARGUMENT.

A CONSTRUCTIVE work presupposes a plan. The architect matures his plans and specifications before a hammer is lifted or a stone moved. And so of every builder. The plan must be definite and consistent or the structure will fail of perfection. This principle is universal. It is just as binding in the mental world as in the physical.

Now an argument is a mental structure. It has parts, relations, and purposes. It must, therefore, have a plan —a type of construction. And this plan must be strictly in accordance with the scope of the argument.

Teleology, as the term implies, treats of purpose, design, or end in nature. It is pre-eminently argumentative; it seeks to prove something. Following this law of mental structures, it has a definite plan—a scope of being. Unfortunately the true scope of the teleological argument has been so persistently obscured, misunderstood, or overlooked that it must be set forth somewhat in detail before attempting the construction of the argument itself.

1. WHAT IT ATTEMPTS.

This topic will be discussed most clearly by subdividing and considering it historically, negatively, and positively.

(1) *What has been Heretofore Attempted.*

Teleology is an old science. Its field and purpose have long been well known. As was intimated in the last chapter, it proposes to prove the existence and goodness of God. This has been its burden for centuries. Volume after volume has been written in support of this purpose. Arguments have been constructed, inferences drawn, and exclamations made in view of the greatness of the under-taking, and the more or less comfortable assurance of its successful accomplishment. Teleologists are for the most part accustomed to hunt through nature and collect there-from a formidable array of facts wherein there is more or less evidence of purpose or design. They expatiate on these facts, bring out vividly their elements of special and wonderful adaptation to the purposes for which they are designed, and finally close the argument with a glowing panegyric on the wisdom and goodness of God.

Concerning this teleological history, three observations may be made. *First*, this practice is not universal. There are here and there exceptions to it. *Second*, it is mani-festly proper and useful to bring out these facts in nature, and to adore the Goodness and Wisdom to which they point. *Third*, it is not so manifestly proper and useful to attempt, in a single argument, to prove the existence, the wisdom, and the goodness of God.

It is very possible that teleologists have hitherto been attempting too much. Many of them have undeniably fallen into logical and philosophical indiscretions which their enemies have not been slow to utilize against them. In their eager and commendable desire to see God, they have taken too long steps, and have consequently made ugly slips here and there. They are beginning to see this mistake and to correct it. The teleological watchword of to-day is a word of caution and patience. Let us not, either in worship or in philosophy, rush into the presence of God *per saltem.*

(2) *What Should Not be Attempted.*

The line of thought under this head has already been indicated. If the principles heretofore stated are correct, it is clear that the teleologist should not attempt the direct demonstration of God. To satisfy the Christian Theist this demonstration must include intelligence, volition, personality, goodness, unity, and infinity. Other elements there are, indeed, which are associated with these in our idea of the Deity, but these at least are fundamental and essential. It would certainly seem that any attempt to prove them all by a single argument must be foredoomed to failure. In my use of the principle of Teleology I shall not attempt so much. The existence of all these elements in the Deity must, indeed, be established. Nothing less than that can satisfy Christian Theism, whose justification is here undertaken. But I prefer to divide the task, take a step at a time, make sure footing, and proceed cautiously in easy stages. One step has already been taken, and Teleology will take another. Eutaxiology has established one element of God; Teleology is relied upon to establish one more and that is all. Other proofs will readily be found for other elements, and this historic pack-horse of Theism will not henceforth be weighted with the whole burden.

(3) *What May Properly be Attempted.*

Teleology is expected to prove something. It is agreed on all hands that this expectation is just. The only difference of opinion is as to what and how much shall be attempted or required. The history of philosophy has no more curious page than that on which this question is brought to solution. Teleologists have been strangely at variance concerning it. Shall Teleology be used to prove the being of God? Or, assuming his existence, shall it proceed to demonstrate his wisdom and goodness? Or can it suffice to establish all the attributes of Deity? Theoretically these various methods have had their respective advocates, but practically these distinctions have been almost universally ignored, and the entire load of theistic proofs has been jumbled together and thrown onto the patient back of Teleology. This is a mistake, and has wrought great damage to Theism. But how much ought to be attempted in the teleological argument? The old teleologist said six things; I say one. *Volition* is the one single element of Deity which I shall attempt to prove by the use of this argument. And certainly this is the most natural and proper thing to attempt. To be convinced of this fact, the reader has only to notice two things: *First*, that the key-note of Teleology is purpose or design, and *secondly*, that volition is the formation of purpose. A volition is simply that mental act of which a purpose is the proper product. Now, if Teleology deals with purpose in nature, and if purpose and volition are inseparably connected as act and product, it is surely within the rightful province of Teleology to prove the existence of volition in nature. This one task will be committed to it.

2. WHAT TELEOLOGY EMPLOYS.

The principle employed in Teleology is that of design or purpose. It has frequently been termed the principle of final causes. This expression is unfortunate for two reasons. *First*, it falsely identifies design with the principle of efficient cause. The distinction between the two cannot be readily maintained. If by efficient cause we mean all those things without which certain subsequent and correspondent phenomena cannot take place, then it is evident that final causes must be included among them. But if we mean something else and less than this, and still hold on to final cause, there is absolutely no place to draw the line of limitation about efficient causation. Philosophers have recognized this difficulty. Even M. Janet, from whose masterly work entitled " Final Causes " I have drawn a considerable part of the present argument, fails to distinguish on this point. He says: " No one denies that the final cause may be reduced to the efficient cause . . . and it matters not whether this cause is called final or efficient." And yet if any one should ask this able writer to change the title of his book to " Efficient Causes," he would justly object to such a flagrant misnomer. If no distinction is to be made and strictly maintained, it were vastly better not to attempt any. *Secondly*, a more serious objection is that design, purpose, end is not cause at all. A cause is that which has power to produce inevitably the particular phenomenon which is its proper effect. Ends have no such power at all. They are simply motives presented to the will. If the will be free, it can choose these motives or set them aside. And this must be true of all free will, whether in God or man. God doubtless acts in view of motives. These motives have reference to ends to be accomplished. And yet these motives or ends are not the cause of God's action. He is under no anterior necessity to follow them. For, if so, he is not God at all. Volition, or the determination of the divine will, is undoubtedly the cause of all things. But without that, mere design, or purpose even, would have remained unproductive forever.

For these reasons, I shall avoid the term *final causes* altogether, and shall hope to escape some of the errors at least, into which its use has betrayed the wisest philosophers.

With this necessary caveat in mind, let us now inquire into the nature of the principle which we call design, purpose, or end. Is it a first principle, of à priori origin? Contrary to many philosophers, I am constrained to reply in the negative. It will be remembered that first principles of thought must possess three elements, *originality*, *universality*, and *necessity*. But design does not seem to possess all these elements. It evidently lacks universality. This fact is made evident by comparing the two principles of Causation and Design.

It is a necessary and universal law of the mind that whenever a phenomenon appears to us, we suppose for it some pre-existent condition or phenomenon which we term its cause. And this we are obliged to do in all cases whatsoever—it matters not what the nature of the phenomenon may be. But it is not so in the case of Design. Very many of the phenomena which present themselves to us seem to be without any end ; or at least do not either impress us with such an idea or impel us to seek it. There are others, again, in which this idea is produced with definite clearness and irresistible force. It is plain, then, that while causation is a universal principle, design is not. And yet we constantly apply the principle of design, and that with quite as much ease and certainty, as are attached to causation. Let us illustrate. Two carriages collide on a thronged thoroughfare. It was a mere coincidence and nothing more. Two ships are befogged and collide at sea. That, too, is a coincidence. But suppose the same ship strikes your vessel broadside at every port you enter for a dozen successive voyages, without interruption. That is no coincidence. It is intentional, and you know it.

You go out on a clear night in August and witness a brilliant display of shooting stars. Again in November the same phenomenon is observed. Next year the same pyrotechnics of the sky are repeated, at exactly the same periods of the year, and so on for a score of years. Now you are not satisfied that this uniform repetition is a mere coincidence. There must be some reason for it.

The very fact of coincidence itself is what needs explanation. There is doubtless a physical cause for each individual shower of stars. But this is not all. The peculiar and persistent order in the phenomena addresses the mind as a thing utterly distinct from the individual phenomena themselves, and demands explanation.

Wandering over a desert, you find half buried in the sand an antique statue, of beautiful form and exquisite proportions, and you justly conclude that the chisel of the sculptor has been there.

Beneath fallen leaves in a vast and trackless forest, you discover an accurately chiselled implement of stone, evidently shaped for cutting. Upon further search, you find many more of the same pattern and in the same vicinity. Their existence there in such numbers must be accounted for. They certainly never grew there. Somebody must have made them. This is your firm conviction, and no man can eradicate it. Nor is this all. They must have been made with a purpose; and this fact is just as sure as the other.

Now journey to a volcanic region, and see the terrible volleys of fire and smoke and molten matter as they pour forth over the burning mountain-side. You are very sure that this impressive phenomenon before you has an adequate cause, whether you know the nature of that cause or not. But it brings to your mind no idea whatever of necessary purpose or design. One phenomenon carries with it an unalterable conviction of design, while another vastly greater and more impressive in character, gives not even a hint of it. Whence arises this difference? If design be a universal principle, how could any such difference ever exist? And further, granting that it is not universal, by what necessity or by what warrant do we invariably recognize end or design in the one phenomenon, and not in the other? These questions demand a careful response.

A phenomenon may have two possible relations, and only two. It may be related to the past, or to the future, or to both. It is doubtless true that every phenomenon does, in some sense, carry both these relations; but, in many cases, the necessity thereof is not at all apparent. That volcanic action, for example, is necessarily connected with the past, and certain future events will likewise flow from it; but this latter fact is by no means apparent in the action itself, nor essential to it. The attempt of teleologists to show that volcanoes are designed to prevent earthquakes, is exceedingly weak and flimsy. On the other hand, the formation of those stone implements found in the forest, looks both ways; backward to its cause, and forward to its purpose. And the latter relation is just as essential to their existence as is the former.

Every event must have a cause, and must therefore look to the past. But it is not correspondently true that every event must have a purpose, and must therefore look to the future. A fiery horse becomes unmanageable and runs away on the street. At that very moment, an absent-minded philosopher, lost in deep reverie, crosses the street. A collision ensues which results in the sudden death of the philosopher. That is an important event. It certainly had an adequate cause, but who can see any purpose in it?

The fact seems to be that wherever we recognize purpose or end in action, it comes to us as an induction, and not as a first principle. If this be true, it will account for the clearness and force of this conviction in some cases, and its entire absence in others. That it is true will be shown in subsequent sections of this chapter. For the present it will suffice to determine and describe those cases in which this induction will always be applicable.

It may be said in general that whenever phenomena concur in orderly repetition or agreement, the human mind requires an explanation, not only of the individual phenomena, but likewise of their order or concurrence. This requirement calls for two principles, the first of which is *mechanical*, the second *teleological*.

Janet puts them thus:

"*First principle.*—When a certain coincidence of phenomena is remarked constantly, it does not suffice to attach each phenomenon in particular to its antecedent causes; it is necessary also to give a precise reason for the coincidence itself.

"*Second principle.*—When a certain coincidence of phenomena is determined, not only by its relation to the past, but also by its relation to the future, we will not have done justice to the principle of causality if, in supposing a cause for this coincidence, we neglect to explain, besides, its precise relation to the future phenomenon."

The author's use of "the principle of causality" may be objected to; but it is not at all vital in the statement here made, which is otherwise a clear and forcible expression of the principles involved in concurrent phe-

nomena. The meteoric showers illustrate the first principle; the marble statue and the stone hatchets illustrate
the second.

This principle of purpose or design in concurrent phenomena constitutes the subject matter out of which the
teleological argument is constructed. It determines the
scope of Teleology as to what is employed therein.

3. WHOM TELEOLOGY ADDRESSES.

Our examination of the scope of Teleology will not be
complete without enquiring into the range of its application. A system may be very broad in meaning, comprehensive in elements, far-reaching in method, universal in
relation, and at the same time very limited in its application. Just so with an argument. Its subject matter may
be extensive, its foundation broad, and yet may address
itself to very few persons. It may be of such a nature
as to transcend the comprehension of ordinary men.

Such is not the case with Teleology. It comes to every
man of every age and every race. It brings its argument
with commanding force to every human mind. It is not
the exclusive property of the astute philosopher, the
analytical thinker, the learned savant. All men recognize
a plain case of design with equal ease and certainty.
And nature, moreover, is full of such cases. Who does
not know that eyes were made to see with, ears to hear
with, tongues to talk with, hands to grasp with, feet to
walk with? No labored argument is necessary to convince the plainest man that there is design in these provisions of nature. The conviction comes to him with
spontaneous, irresistible force. He cannot doubt it if he
would, and would not if he could. He may not know
the technical language of the schools in which the argu-

ment is formally expressed, nor even the name of the process; but he realizes the result just the same, and that, too, with intense vividness and certainty.

Teleology has always been popular with the masses. In this respect it stands in decided contrast with Eutaxiology. This latter system, based upon order, symmetry, and harmony in nature, addresses itself with peculiar force to the scientist, the scholar.

It will be remembered that nearly all the striking examples of order heretofore advanced, are furnished by the researches of modern science. There are a few cases, it is true, that are independent of all scientific research, and are, therefore, applicable to all men alike. Such, for instance, is the nightly array of the starry heavens. These cases, however, are exceptional. The great bulk of the evidence in Eutaxiology depends upon the work of the learned scientist. But by that very fact such evidence must lose much of its force when presented to an untutored mind. Take, for example, the doctrine of typical forms. It is one of the strongholds of Eutaxiology. But the idea it depends upon is quite a complicated and metaphysical one. It is with great difficulty that the utterly unlettered man can grasp the general notion of a preconceived typical skeleton or crystal-bearing matrix which runs through some vast portion of nature, and dominates the growth of organisms or of structural forms therein.

Dr. McCosh is undoubtedly right when he states that the ancients attended to the principles of order as well as of adaptation. And yet the ancients had no science of Eutaxiology. This is not a matter of surprise, for they could not have developed such a science. With their limited and erroneous conceptions of nature it was impossible. The strongest points in the argument are of modern origin.   And many more will doubtless be discovered in the future.   Eutaxiology has much to hope from the exercise of that spirit of universal investigation which employs itself in tracing the action of general laws and uniformities in nature.

Teleology, on the other hand, is measurably independent of this spirit.   Its proofs are not recondite and critical.   It is based upon facts, rather than law.   Its message is to all.   It speaks the language of the common people.   And this is right.   In the rich storehouse of Theism there ought to be supplies for all.   Let each take his own, and all may be satisfied.

SECTION II.

THE TELEOLOGICAL SYLLOGISM.

The argument in Teleology is capable of being put into logical form.   It can be framed into a syllogism.   All that was said in the last chapter concerning syllogistic forms applies here with equal force.   A vast majority of the writers on this subject have hitherto massed their facts and hurled them in solid phalanx against the enemy, without the least regard for logical form.   It must be admitted, moreover, that many of those that have made use of the syllogism have fallen into serious logical fallacies.   For instance, "design implies a designer."   This favorite teleological premise is a mere truism—the second term is involved in the first, and nothing can be proved by it.

My purpose in this discussion is critical as well as argumentative.   I want to produce conviction, it is true, but am even more desirous to test the correctness of that conviction. I shall argue design in nature, and shall present convincing evidence of its existence therein ; but above all I shall attempt to test the validity of this time-honored argument and to show its exact bearing upon the question of Theism. For this purpose the syllogism is the most natural and valuable instrument. The teleological argument may be formulated thus :

Major Premise.

Rational and useful results produced by the concurrence of suitable causes, imply volition.

Minor Premise.

Rational and useful results so produced exist in nature.

Conclusion.

The existence of nature implies volition.

This argument is straightforward and logical. I shall endeavor to establish the truth of the premises and thereby prove the conclusion.

I. THE MAJOR PREMISE.

Like the major premise in Eutaxiology, this also is an induction. Let us carefully examine the circumstances under which it is made.

In the investigation of nature, we observe certain effects which are rational and useful in their character. We observe, moreover, that these effects are produced by a concurrence of causes in themselves distinct, separate, and independent of one another. Each cause can be traced to its proper effect, and the combination of these individual effects can be seen to constitute the rational result observed. But no one of these causes, acting alone, could ever have produced this result. Nay, more ; the combination of any number of them could not have accomplished it. The abstraction of a single one of the numerous causes whose con-joint action produced the given result, would have proved fatal to its character as rational and useful. Now the question arises : How came these particular efficient causes to conspire for the pro- duction of such a result ? Out of the myriads of possible combinations, who made such wise selection of these exact causes, and these only, that are suitable to this rational and useful end? The same strangely fortunate concurrence of causes is repeated in nature again and again, a hundred, a thousand, a million times. How comes this inveterate habit of nature? Out of what necessity does it spring? This is the problem. The perfect analysis of any or all the concurring causes does not solve it. There is something behind them, some constructive power which brings them together. A good illustration of this power is drawn by a recent writer from the constructive energy of man.

Yonder stands a beautiful mansion. Physical causes conspired to produce it. Every brick has a certain chemi- cal constitution and history. The mortar and plaster have been comminuted by adequate physical causes. Every beam has been formed in strict accordance with the laws of vegetable growth, and brought to its present shape by the attrition of physical implements. The exact position of every single element in the structure, from foundation stone to turret, can be accounted for by purely physical causes. And yet, when you have gone the rounds and exhausted the entire list of physical causes, you have scarcely begun to account for the building. Behind them all, and over them all, there was a great constructive en- ergy which selected, combined, and guided them all to the production of this rational and useful result. That energy resided in the mind of the architect. Just so it is in nature.   A rational result is produced by the concurrence of adequate and suitable causes.   This concurrence is the thing to be explained.   The individual causes themselves cannot account for it, for each of them is exhausted in the production of its own appropriate effect.   It will not do to suppose another physical cause like unto them, for its effect would be purely physical also.   That would be like an attempt to explain the building by supposing an additional bricklayer or carpenter or hodcarrier, instead of the plan and purpose of the architect.   There is one explanation and only one that can satisfy the mind.   It is taken for granted that these various causes were made to concur in order to produce a given result.   The combination had a purpose in it, and that purpose looked to the future event.   It was clearly a case of design.   No other assumption accounts for it ; this one does perfectly.   And this explanation is entirely natural and spontaneous on our part.   It costs us no effort whatever.   The conviction of design is brought home to us by the very presence of the objects themselves.   " We see a thought realized in nature, and so recognize in it a forethought."

And men have always done thus.   The design-argument has impressed the philosopher and the peasant alike.   Socrates, Aristotle, Cicero, Galen, Newton, and Paley have enforced it.   A statue, a watch, an engine, a building, have been successively drawn into this service. But, however it may be illustrated, there is no manner of doubt that the observation of adaptation in nature inspires all men of all ages with the conviction that a designing mind conceived and executed that adaptation. This is the fact ; but what is its origin, and what its meaning?   How comes this universal conviction ?

I answer by referring to my major premise :   Rational

and useful results produced by the concurrence of suitable causes, imply volition. If this be true, and if these cases of adaptation are such results so produced, then will this universal conviction of mankind be amply explained and justified. Let us see as to the truth of the premise.

As already stated, this proposition is an evident induction. Every sound induction must proceed originally from matters of personal experience. Observation, testimony, analogy, and the like, are surely admissible, but our own experience must furnish the original starting-point. Otherwise, while the induction itself may be logically correct, we can have no absolute assurance that the supposed facts upon which it is based may not be erroneous from top to bottom. A material fallacy will invalidate the conclusion, in spite of all logic.

But this teleological induction is based upon personal experience. Every man is daily conscious of forming purposes and executing them in both physical and mental acts. The purpose gives character, direction, and limitation to the acts performed. But the purpose itself implies an act of volition, in order to be executed. In other words volition is the mental act, and purpose is the psychical product of that act. Purposes never grow spontaneously. They must be formed by the mind ; and the act by which they are formed is termed volition. It is evident, then, that the existence of purpose or design presupposes volition.

Take a simple illustration. I have just written and posted a letter. But I had a purpose in view when I did it—yes, even before I began to prepare to write. I wanted some information from a friend at a distance, and I wrote for it. This purpose determined every act, physical or mental, by which the communication was produced and mailed. But for this purpose, the acts would not have been performed. It must be noticed, moreover, that all these acts were selected and correlated by a thing yet in the future. When each was performed it had, of course, its appropriate cause in the past. But we might search forever among these efficient causes and not find any explanation of the letter. The concurrence and correlation of such causes, and such only as were suitable to produce this particular rational and useful result, while as yet the result was itself in the unknown future—these are the things to be explained. The causes did not correlate themselves. The constructed result did not correlate them surely, for at that time it did not exist. There was just one thing that could do this constructive work, and that was the idea of the future result which existed in my mind before a single cause began to co-operate toward its production. That it actually did the work, is a matter of personal consciousness with me. I know that I wrote that letter, that I did it for a purpose, that I correlated certain causes suitable to carry out that purpose, and that I myself formed that purpose by a direct act of volition of my own. Here, then, is one rational and useful result produced by a concurrence of suitable causes, which does imply volition. And I am as sure of it as of any thing in existence. But this is not all. My experience is filled with just such products. I am conscious of producing them every day of my life. The great majority of my conscious acts are of this character. Furthermore, I see other men acting just as I do. You write a letter. You aver that you had a purpose in writing. The letter itself is admirably adapted to accomplish the very purpose had in view at the time of writing. It is just such as I would have written for that purpose. The whole affair has the unmistakable marks of design. I am compelled to believe that this letter is the outcome of purpose, just the same as my own. Here, then, is another rational and useful result, produced by the concurrence of suitable causes, which implies volition. This result is entirely beyond my own experience, and yet I recognize volition in it. It is the same truth as before.

Thus, in the acts of ourselves and of all men, we are furnished with constant and innumerable examples of the truth of the major premise under discussion. And there is not a solitary exception. Every such rational and useful product, accomplished by means of human activity, is found invariably to imply volition. There is no question about it.

But is this truth applicable to the activities of nature likewise? This is the central question on which the teleological induction turns. An affirmative answer carries' with it the establishment of this premise upon an impregnable foundation.

The industry of man is undeniably based upon purpose, design. It uniformly has an end in view. This much we know. The industry of nature is not known to us personally, as regards its origin or purpose. Now every case of human purpose is a case of adaptation. And, conversely, every case of adaptation in human activity, is a case of purpose. But when we see nature doing just such things as we do with a purpose, and cannot do at all without a purpose, we generalize the known law and say that nature acts with a purpose. This is an ordinary inductive inference, and nothing more. In every known case of adaptation we have found purpose, and hence volition. Here is a new case in which adaptation is evident. It must be like all the rest, and therefore implies volition.

Two difficulties have sometimes been put in the way of this induction.

First difficulty.—It is claimed that there is no reason to think that nature acts in the production of her works as man acts in the production of his. The fields of activity are so utterly unlike that we cannot compare them; and so we are not warranted in passing from the industry of man to that of nature.

If this objection means any thing, it means that man and nature are terms in complete opposition to each other, and absolutely without analogy; that there is no passing from the world of mind to the world of nature; that the two are mutually independent, and have nothing whatever in common, and that, therefore, we cannot attribute the mode of action found to exist in the one to the industry of the other.

But the statement thus developed is manifestly false. Man is not at all opposed to nature. Neither is he out of analogy or independent of nature. On the contrary, he himself, in his physical being, is a part of nature. His organism is fitted up in her laboratory, and daily supported from her alembics. He freely accepts her chemical and physical laws, and works under them. His body is certainly subject to her laws of animal and vegetable life. His soul, whatever be its origin and character, is certainly not independent of his body. His powers of perception, memory, imagination, and even reason itself, are necessarily connected with the realm of matter about him. Neither is his industry independent of nature. He works within nature, uses her materials, employs her forces, submits to her laws, modifies or enlarges her results. Moreover, it is only by knowing and obeying her laws that he can reap any benefit from his own industry. The two industries are therefore not in opposition, but in strict and close analogy with each other. They are two species under the same genus, and we have a perfect right to pass from the one to the other in a purely inductive inference. There is really nothing in the way of this process, but, on the contrary, a strong antecedent presumption in its favor.

Second difficulty.—Another obstruction has been placed farther back in the pathway of our induction. It is stated that even man's industry is not always dependent upon volition; that we do many things daily without any definite intention; and that acts produced automatically from habit or otherwise, without any reference to an end, are easily mistaken for intentional acts. As an illustration of this difficulty, M. Janet cites the case from an old curate who had become insane, and used to recite with the utmost eloquence the famous exordium of Father Bridaine. It was impossible for strangers who heard him to suspect that he was not speaking intelligently, and with the definite purpose of moving his auditors. And yet the poor old man was an utter imbecile, in the last stages of senile dementia, unable to utter two consecutive words with intelligent purpose.

The obstructionist, reinforced by a goodly array of such instances, proceeds to argue that what we so often mistake in man, we may mistake altogether in nature; and so it may turn out, after all, that there is no intentionality or volition in nature whatever. "Your induction," says he, "is a little premature."

In dealing with this difficulty, I frankly admit the facts upon which it is based. It is true, in the first place, that we do often perform acts without any intention whatever, and in the second place that we may be misled by our fellowmen as to the intentionality of their acts. But these facts have no bearing at all upon the present induction. They are true enough, indeed, but absolutely irrelevant.

I do not claim that all human acts are intentional. They are not. As a matter of fact, many of them are instinctive. I am talking about a *certain class* of human acts, namely: *such as produce rational and useful results by the concurrence of suitable causes.* Of these acts, and these only, the proposition in question affirms that they imply volition. Of any and all other possible acts, human or non-human, it has nothing to say. They concern it not in the least. So long as there are such human acts as I have described, the premise is safe. There can be no manner of doubt that there are such. I know, for instance, that no man can build a mansion by dropping bricks into a hole, or compose a poem by pulling letters out of a box, or construct a geometrical figure by throwing dice over a plane. There are some human achievements that are impossible without pre-existing intention, and everybody knows it. More than this. We can all recognize this element of intentionality in the things themselves. It matters not whether we see them done, or even know who did them.

Just so it is in nature. I find activities there which bear the same undeniable marks of intentionality. There may be other activities there which do not bear such marks; but that matters nothing. I need not prove that all nature is one unbroken complex of intentionality. That may be true, or may not; and if true, it may be beyond my powers of demonstration. There may even be doubtful cases which give some false show of intentionality, and deceive me thereby. But all these possibilities combined can raise no presumption whatever against the induction here made. If there are any unmistakable cases of design in nature, that is sufficient. So long as eyes are made to see with, for example, I need seek no farther in nature. The object of my search is found, the induction established.

Before leaving the major premise it will be well to notice the exact extent and value of the induction upon which it rests. The steps of the inference are simply these. I know that certain products of my own activity are intentional; I infer, by a mental necessity, that similar products arising from the activity of my fellow-men are likewise intentional; I characterize, identify, and generalize these products, and infer that all products whatsoever of the same class, wherever found or however produced, are also necessarily and invariably intentional. If, then, such products exist in nature, they give indisputable evidence of design or intention in nature. That there are such products, it is the special province of the second premise in Teleology to show.

2. THE MINOR PREMISE.

This proposition, stated in full, is as follows: Rational and useful results produced by the concurrence of suitable causes exist in nature. It will be seen that this statement includes five things:

(1) There must be results.

(2) These results must be rational and useful.

(3) They must be produced by the concurrence of causes.

(4) These causes must, of course, be suitable.

(5) The results must exist in nature.

In other words, I reject from this proof every result that is not rational and useful; every result, whether rational or otherwise, that is produced by a single cause;

and every result, whether rational and concurrent or otherwise, which is not produced by the direct operations of nature. When all these have been rejected, however, there are myriads left which naturally and properly fall under the teleological syllogism. I shall select from them a very few only which may serve as examples of this truth, and fix our thoughts upon it.

And here I find myself encumbered with an embarrassment of riches; insomuch that I scarcely know how to proceed in the employment of them. Whole volumes might well be written in the enforcement of the proposition under consideration. Indeed, whole volumes have been so written. Under the popular title of "Adaptations in Nature," the bulk of teleological literature for two hundred years has expended itself upon this very theme. It is certainly neither necessary nor desirable to re-array this immense host of facts which show adaptation in nature; they already stand out in bold relief in many able treatises heretofore written on this subject. I shall content myself with the selection and presentation of a very few which may be taken as types of all the others.

Before proceeding to the facts a single remark must be made concerning the use of the term *adaptation*. It will be employed to denote in brief that fitness which results from the co-ordination of suitable causes to produce a certain rational end, or accomplish a certain purpose. I shall speak freely of adaptations in nature, in the sense just explained, and for the sole purpose of avoiding a tedious circumlocution.

Another preliminary remark must be made. In animate nature there are striking adaptations of two kinds, *functions* and *instincts*. In the former the structure of the organ is most prominent; in the latter, the co-ordinate action of organs.

(1) *Functions.*

By adaptation of functions is meant the fitness of an organ to perform its appropriate function. The structure of the eye for purposes of vision furnishes a most striking example of functional adaptation. It is very old. Many men have already used it. Indeed it has with some justice been called the classical argument in this line. But I shall not avoid it on that account. It is not in the least enfeebled by age. Nor is it obsolete. Like the rising sun and the revolving seasons, it keeps itself in perennial freshness and vigor. So long as eyes are made to see with the argument will hold. When Adam first beheld with rapture the glory and beauty of this fair creation, fresh and pure from the hands of the Almighty, he illustrated the utility and rationality of vision. From that day to this the argument holds its grasp with undiminished force, and I am persuaded it will continue to do so till the last man shall stand upon the earth.

Vision is manifestly a useful end to be achieved. In its accomplishment nature has before her a complicated problem. Let us notice some of the conditions necessary to its solution.

First.—There must be light. There must be some adequate means of communication, rapid and facile, between the organ and the object of vision. The exact nature of this medium is still unknown to science; but its reflecting and refracting properties are known, and are found to be indispensable to the act of vision. In an atmosphere of inky blackness, ten thousand eyes would avail nothing.

Secondly.—There must be a nerve sensitive to this light. This neural sensitiveness is no slight or unmeaning affair. There are in the body many nerves of exquisite delicacy, but without this power. How long, for instance, would it take the rays of a tropical sun, shining in his meridian splendor upon the palm of a man's hand or the tip of his tongue, to produce a well-authenticated case of vision? And yet these members are not at all wanting in delicacy of nerve-power.   The fact is that the optic nerve must be specially fitted for its special business.

Thirdly.—There must be an optical apparatus. This is necessary in order that the contact between the light and the nerve may be properly regulated. Without it, light, indeed, could be distinguished from darkness, but no distinct vision of individual objects would be possible. This impossibility results from the diffusive property of light. Rays of light from a luminous body radiate in every possible direction, unless an opaque obstacle be in their way. So that a single luminous point will lighten an exposed surface of any extent.   Let this surface be the retina, and every single point thereon will receive light from every single point of the luminous object.   A dazzling flood of light might ensue, but distinct vision could not. In order for vision, it is necessary that rays of light from individual points of the visible object shall affect corresponding individual points, like placed on the retina.   For this purpose all other rays, whether direct or reflected, must be shut off.   This requirement presents a difficult mechanical problem.   Nature has solved it in two ways: first, by *isolation*, and second, by *convergence*.   The first method is seen in the *composite* eyes of insects and crustaceans.   It "consists in placing before the retina, and perpendicularly to it, an innumerable quantity of transparent cones, which allow to reach the nervous membrane only the light following the direction of their axes, and absorb by means of the pigment with which their walls are lined, all that strikes them obliquely."   The marvellous geometrical adjustment necessary to the success of this method is evident from the fact that some 15,000 or 20,000 cones are employed in a single eye. Nature must indeed be a skillful artist.

But the most exquisite perfection of skill is required in the second method, which is called convergence. This is employed in the well-known organ commonly called *the eye*, which is found in all vertebrate animals, as well as in some others. It is needless and would be tedious to go into all the minute details of its wonderful mechanism. It is, in general, a sort of enclosed box—a camera obscura, somewhat like the photographer's instrument bearing that name. Observe its remarkable character. It is not a Pandora's box, but it is equally wonderful. Its necessary elements are most curiously and skillfully combined.

(1) There is the sclerotic, a solid membrane which forms the globe of the eye.

(2) There is the cornea, a transparent point in the sclerotic, which admits the rays of light.

(3) There are converging media, the vitreous humor, the aqueous humor, and the crystalline lens, which serve to focalize the luminous rays.

(4) There is the retina, or extension of the optic nerve, to receive the image of the object to be seen.

(5) All these elements are accurately adjusted to each other in the axis of the eye.

(6) The pupil is adjustable to the dimensions required for admitting or shutting out the light.

(7) The optical focus is adjustable to a longer or shorter distance.

(8) The direction of this focus is readily changeable.

(9) The whole adjustment is absolutely achromatic, it corrects the aberration of light.

(10) The entire apparatus is protected and lubricated by means of external conformations—the eye-lids, eye-lashes, and overjutting brows.

Now here is an instrument of admirable delicacy, accuracy, and power. Its construction is both rational and useful in the extreme. It is made by the concurrence of a multitude of different causes, some within the organ and some without it, some apparently connected in origin, and some of origin separated by millions of miles ; but all suitable, and, so far as we can discover, necessary to the coördinated result of vision. Can any thing be plainer than that these causes have been made to concur in order to produce the given result? In other words, there is adaptation in it. Eyes are made to see with, and there can be no doubt about it. As a mere work of art, the eye is a marvel of beauty and perfection. As a useful instrument, it is none the less so.

Two objections have been raised against it as a useful structure. It is said, in the first place, to be imperfect, weak, and inaccurate. It is urged that an ordinary telescope is superior to the eye in these respects.

This objector would do well to remember two things.

First. That the range of the eye is far superior to that of the telescope—it can take in objects near and far, great and small, at every conceivable angle, and that, too, without any artificial variation or readjustment of eye-pieces.

Second. That its capacity is immeasurably superior to that of the telescope. It can see. Who ever yet put a little telescope into the head of a blind man, and caused him to see thereby? Man has sought out many ingenious and useful inventions, but nature is still ahead.

The second objection strikes, not so much at the function, as at the very structure, of the instrument itself. It is claimed that there are useless and unnecessary parts. At least the crystalline humor is said to be of this character. The proof of this statement is supposed to be found in the fact that those blind from cataract, can, after its removal, see without the crystalline medium. Now there is no doubt about this fact; but the inference drawn from it is a clear *non sequitur*. Men do not and cannot see as well without the crystalline lens as with it. I may be able to feed myself comfortably with one hand; but that is no manner of reason why I should be restricted to the use of one hand in the gustatory process.

And, besides, there may be other reasons for the combination of these three humors in the eye. There are, indeed. The crystalline humor, for instance, has recently been found to have two other functions. One pertains to the difference of density between the aqueous humor and the medium through which the light comes to the eye. It is evident that the less this difference is, the greater ought the convexity of the lens to be. A man sees in the air; a fish in the water; an amphibian in either. The fish must have the greater convexity of lens, and he has it. The amphibian must have a readjustment of lens, and he has it. Is there any principle of hydrostatics by which the pressure of the water could cause this displacement of lens? Nay, verily. It is the crystalline humor that admits the needful result.

But again, it has another distinctively useful function. The ability of the eye to change at will the focus of distinct vision, has long puzzled physicists. Place a minute but brilliant object at a distance of ten inches from the eye. It is in the focus of distinct vision. Now remove it to a distance of twenty, or even thirty inches, and it is still in that focus. This instantaneous change of focus has hitherto defied the principles of optics. It has recently been traced, however, to the crystalline humor, which is capable, it seems, in response to the will, of changing at once its degree of convexity. These changes of curvature have been accurately measured to the thousandth of an inch, and found to correspond exactly with the requirements of the changed focus. The laws of optics are justified, and the crystalline humor has abundantly established its right to exist. Meanwhile a new and most striking case of forethought in the eye has been disclosed This old classical argument, it seems, is not yet exhausted. The teleologist tenders his thanks to the objector for calling attention to these most interesting facts.

I have dwelt somewhat at length upon the organ of vision, because it was necessary in order to bring out the striking and unmistakable marks of adaptation to be found in it. It would be an easy and pleasing task to point out equally numerous and convincing proofs of design in the other organs of the human body. For the sake of brevity, however, I forbear ; and content myself with the mere mention of a very few.

(1) The organ of hearing, and its nice adjustment to the sound vibrations of different media, as air and water.

(2) The shape of the teeth, so well fitted for cutting, tearing, and grinding ; their order, strength of base, and method of insertion, so admirably conformed to their respective use ; and the peculiar enamel which so completely covers and protects them.

(3) The epiglottis—that draw-bridge of the trachea, which automatically shuts and opens to keep out the food and let in the air.

(4) Those curious valves of the veins, which led Harvey

to his famous discovery of the circulation of the blood. In the veins and chyle-ducts they open toward the heart, while in the arteries the reverse of this is true.

(5) The structure of the heart; its division into two large apartments and subdivision into two smaller ones; and its valves and concentric muscles, all adapted to the delicate and vital function of the organ as a whole.

(6) The respiratory apparatus, joining the blood-bearing vessels on the one hand, and the air-bearing vessels on the other, and making, in each pulmonary cell, the necessary exchange of oxygen and carbon.

(7) The organs of locomotion, varying greatly to meet the diverse necessities of walking, flying, creeping, or swimming, but all describing arcs of progressive motion by some parts of the body.

(8) The human voice, that marvel of beauty, variety, flexibility, compass, and strength ; that delicate exponent of thought, emotion, character, and purpose, so immeasurably superior to all other instruments of sound.

(9) The sexual organs developed in different animals, by a plain prevision of nature, and carefully adjusted to the necessities of reproduction and the preservation of the species.

(10) The wonderful and admirable harmony of the entire organism. The adaptation of each organ, not only to its own individual function, but to all the other parts, is such as to bind all into one definite and integral unity of organism and function. No part is wanting, none is superfluous. The whole system is both symmetrical and useful—a thing of incomparable beauty and utility.

The adaptations of functions are certainly both numerous and striking. There is in nature another distinct field of adaptations scarcely less fruitful, which must be hastily surveyed.

(2) *Instincts.*

Instinctive actions differ from those that are rational in two important respects; they are not learned by experience or by imitating others; they are always performed in the same way, without choice, change, or improvement, from an unthinking impulse rather than an intelligent prevision either of methods or of results. Eminent naturalists tell us that the effects of instinct " may sometimes be modified by experience, but they never depend on it."

" Hardly are all the parts of the young bee dried, hardly are its wings in a state to be moved, when it knows all it will have to do during the rest of its life." It immediately sets out in search of honey-bearing flowers, leaving the common habitation, loading itself, and returning alone without guidance or experience. It invariably finds its way back home again with the same unerring precision from the first trip as from the hundredth. A young child may stray away from home and be lost— a young bee, never. More than this. It begins its work, not from the impulse of its own necessities, but rather for the common good. Maraldi states that he has seen bees return to the hive loaded with two large balls of wax on the same day that they were born. He also says that young wasps go at once in search of food, which they bring back and divide among the grubs.

It is very evident that these acts are for the future good of the individual and the species, and that they are performed spontaneously from innate capacities, and not from imitation, calculation, or habit. These innate capacities are received from nature, and show a high degree of art, design, purpose. If a human inventor should succeed in making a machine capable of performing automatically the ordinary acts of the humblest insect, his name and fame would be immortalized. Edison would quit the field.

A careful analysis and description of the various instincts of animals would be appropriate and instructive at this point. For the sake of brevity, however, I content myself with inserting an abridgement of the summary given by Janet. It is somewhat as follows:

(1) *Instincts of Individual Preservation.*

(*a*) Inclination to take food of certain kinds and in certain amounts. This often changes instantaneously with the necessities of the animal. Certain insects, for instance, are carnivorous in their larvæ state, but in their after development become herbivorous.

(*b*) Means by which carnivorous animals obtain their prey. The ant-eater digs a funnel-shaped hole in the sand and hides his trap at the bottom. The spider makes a snare of his web. The fish throws water drops on the insects he intends to devour.

(*c*) The well-known instinct of accumulation for future need. The squirrel lays by stores of nuts for winter, and carefully deposits them in a place of safety. The ant is no less provident. The lagomys pica, of Siberia, cuts and cures hay, and stacks it away in mows for winter use.

(*d*) Instincts of construction. The rabbit, the mole, and the beaver furnish notable illustrations. Some spiders construct their habitation by digging a well in the clay, plastering it up, and closing the entrance by a door hung on veritable hinges, and furnished with internal fastenings. The classical illustration of this instinct, however, is found among the bees. It relates to the structure of their cells, and involves the principles of the higher mathematics. The problem is, to construct a cell with such a basal angle as to give the greatest economy of space with the least expense of work and material. Every mathematician will recognize this at once as the famous problem of Maxima and Minima in Calculus. Maclaurin solved it, measured his angle and found, to his surprise, that the bees had been there before him. We cannot refrain from enquiring, " Who taught the bees Calculus?"

(2) *Instincts for the Preservation of the Species.*

(*a*) Precautions in laying eggs. These are observed most strikingly in animals that never see their young, and therefore could not possibly know either by experience or by reason, the early needs of their offspring. And yet the mother provides food for them, and that, too, often contrary to her own taste and need.

The necrophores, for example, bury the body of a mole and deposit eggs therein, so that the young may find at once a habitation and a larder. The pompiles live on flowers; but their larvæ are carnivorous; and so the mother anticipates their wants, by depositing her eggs beside the bodies of spiders, caterpillars, etc.

(*b*) Nest building. The saya, or bullfinch of India, makes its nest bottle-shaped and suspends it invariably to such slender, flexible branches that apes and squirrels cannot reach it. The sylvia sutoria, or tom-tit, sews leaves together with grass, and lines the nest with cotton. The crested grebe incubates on a miniature raft, constructed for the purpose. If danger impends, she puts her feet out for oars, and paddles her floating island to a place of safety.

(*c*) Park building. This is exhibited by the species of partridge called chlamyderes. They construct a grove some four feet in diameter, beautifully laid out with

hedges, trees, shaded promenades, and well rounded cause-
ways. The whole park is then ornamented with shining
shells, gaudy feathers, knives, watches, rings—any thing,
in short, that these æsthetic birds can steal within their
immediate neighborhood. The newly-mated couple thereupon take possession for the season.

(3) *Social Instincts.*

(*a*) Temporary societies. Such are the hunting expe-
ditions of hyenas and wolves, the migratory companies of
swallows, locusts, and herrings, and the occasional pleasure
parties of some animals who assemble to bathe or play in
some favorite stream. In all these cases, the company
breaks up, after the special purpose of the gathering has
been accomplished.

(*b*) Permanent societies. Among these may be mentioned the often quoted colonies of beavers, bees, ants,
etc. In some of these communities, the body-politic is
accurately organized, and the principles of political and
social science seem to be strictly observed.

Now all these instincts (and they are but a few of the
many cases hitherto observed by naturalists) are plain
tokens of adaptation or design in nature. Nobody pre-
tends for a moment that the skill and forethought displayed in them are evidences of prevision, intelligence,
and reason in the animals themselves. Their source is
evidently farther back, in the constitutions of the animals.
Instincts are implanted, but it required the design of
some marvellous intelligence to construct and implant
them. Their operations are results. These results are
eminently rational and useful. This rationality does not
reside in the animals that perform the operations. Nature is therefore responsible for it. But this is exactly

what is meant by the minor premise in the teleological syllogism.

Thus far, the proofs of this proposition have been drawn exclusively from animated nature. It must not be supposed, however, that no proofs exist in other departments of nature. They do, in fact, exist everywhere. Chemistry and physics are full of them. The prevalence of oxygen and its affinities, the relation of heat to chemical changes, the relative specific gravity of certain gases, the constitution and the qualities of atmospheric air, the functions of water in organic and inorganic nature, the laws of climatology, the action of the tides, and the succession of the seasons—these will readily occur as familiar examples. But I must not dwell upon them ; and indeed I need not. The proof is already strong enough. It is useless to introduce further testimony, when the case is already abundantly established. Surely enough has been said to show that rational and useful results produced by the concurrence of suitable causes, do exist in nature. And this is all that the minor premise in Teleology asserts.

3. THE CONCLUSION.

The legitimate conclusion drawn from this teleological syllogism is, that volition is implied in nature. This has been clearly established. Rational and useful results produced by the concurrence of suitable causes, do always and everywhere imply volition. Such results so produced do exist in nature. The conclusion therefore follows by necessity.

But much more than this has been incidentally reached. We have found that the adaptations of nature are general, widespread and far-reaching. The purpose, the volition which exists in nature must, therefore, be equally widespread and general. Indeed there is good reason to infer that it is universal. And this statement is not in the least contradictory of that made heretofore (page 61) on this subject. Then design was being discussed *subjectively*, as a principle of human thought. Now we are considering it *objectively*, as an existing fact in nature. Manifestly, it may be universal in the latter sense and not in the former. The *principle* of design is one thing, the *law* of design quite another. It is freely admitted that there are many operations of nature in which we can see no purpose whatever. That proves that the idea of design is not intuitive. But it by no means proves the absence of design in those particular operations of nature. Manifestly, it may be there, and we may not see it. The marvellous revelations of modern science have disclosed to our view long vistas of purpose of which the ancients were ignorant. And they will doubtless open wider and still wider views of purpose to future generations. Our posterity may some time be able to establish beyond any peradventure what we already rationally infer; namely, that nature is but one vast system of design and adaptation.

Herein may be noticed a striking parallelism between Eutaxiology and Teleology. I have already remarked that the former is a growing science, that it advances with the discovery of truth and the spread of knowledge in the world. So likewise is it with Teleology. While its general argument is patent and free to all, it is being constantly reinforced by fresh and striking illustrations furnished by every advanced step in the discovery of natural truth.

It will be observed that I have not yet arrived at the proof of Deity. But two important steps toward it have been taken. I have shown the existence in nature of wide-spread intelligence and volitional power. These are certainly necessary attributes of the Deity. Their proof is all that I attempt in presenting what are called the two design arguments, or *physico-teleology*. Other elements there are, and other arguments to prove them. But before proceeding to prove them, a little time must be taken to notice certain serious and fundamental objections which have been urged against all teleologic arguments in general.

SECTION III.

OBJECTIONS.

Teleology has been the battle-field of Theism for ages. Every inch of ground has been disputed, every step of progress contested, and every conceivable weapon of warfare used against it. Nor is the battle ended. The enemy is still in sight. An occasional shot is still heard, and a hostile theory explodes at our feet. These missiles are altogether harmless, however formidable they may seem. To be assured of this fact, it is only necessary to examine a few of them which at first sight may appear most dangerous. They are such only in appearance.

I.   CHANCE COMBINATIONS.

One of the alternatives of design in nature is chance. If there be no purpose in things, they must have happened as they are. That they did happen, has been maintained by many philosophers, both ancient and modern. Prominent among them may be mentioned Aristotle, Spinoza, and Lucretius, representing the Epicurean philosophers in his treatise, " De Rerum Natura." Briefly stated, their theory runs thus:

"The universe, as we see it, is the outcome of the fortuitous concourse of primeval atoms. These atoms, being in a state of ceaseless inter-motion, would perform an endless variety of chance-combinations. These combinations would continue in ceaseless round, until finally all possible combinations would have been exhausted. This would certainly be a long process ; but then, these atoms have had all eternity to experiment in. And time and chance are well matched ; for both are exhaustless. Now the present orderly combination of atoms, out of which the worlds are built, is manifestly one of these possible combinations, for its actual existence proves its possibility. But, having once fallen into these orderly forms, they abide there by reason of their own inherent laws. Hence we have an explanation of the orderly results and seeming contrivances of nature, without any postulate of design whatever."

Now this chance theory breaks down at several points.

(1) It presupposes the eternity of matter—a very violent supposition.

(2) It fails to account for the initial atomic motion. Motion requires a cause.

(3) It gives no evidence of this multiplicity of abortive attempts after the Cosmos. If they had existed, some trace of them ought to be discoverable.

(4) It utterly fails to account for those inherent atomic laws, by whose marvellous constructive agency it is claimed that the order of the world is maintained.

(5) If it could account for these laws, it would only be to show a manifest case of design, and not of chance. For these atoms are evidently adapted to the present orderly combination, and not to the former chaotic ones.

(6) It begs the question altogether. It stupidly as-

sumes that the present orderly combination is a possible *chance-combination*, which is the very thing in dispute. This assumption is a most unpardonable sin against the laws of logic. ˙ The mere existence of the world does not at all prove its fortuitous origin. Westminster Abbey exists. It is therefore possible ; but not possible without the antecedent plan of an architect. No fortuitous throwing of stones into a pile could ever have produced it. So is the order of the universe possible ; but not without an intelligent Author.

A theory, whose only explanation of things needs more explaining than the things themselves, is not a very formidable weapon with which to attack the citadel of teleological truth.

2. MECHANISM AND TELEOLOGY.

The objection to Teleology founded on the principle of mechanism, is somewhat akin to the former, but is of very much later origin.

It is an attempt to explain the universe on the principle of efficient causes. It seeks to trace every thing to its physical antecedents and rest it there. Its present popularity is doubtless due, in large measure, to this intensely physical aspect in which it holds all things.

It claims that this universe is but one huge stream of causes and effects; that each follows its predecessor by unvarying law and of necessity; that in such a system there is no room for volition, purpose, or adaptation ; and that the outflow of things in nature is consequently the necessary mechanism of law, and not the constructive design of intelligence.

This antagonism between the physical scientist and the teleologist results largely from the difference of stand-

point from which they view things. The former is looking backward and calls for law; the latter is looking
forward and inquires after a purpose. One sees in nature
the outcome of causes pushed forward from behind; the
other, the execution of plans led forward from before.
Now both these views of nature, when taken together and
unified, are correct. But either taken alone is misleading.
Here, as everywhere, a half-truth is little better than a lie.
And so the mechanist, seeing but one side of the truth,
puts forth his theory as essentially opposed to Teleology,
and destructive thereof. Let us state his doctrine fully
and fairly.

The apostle of mechanism says : " What all philosophers
desire, is an explanation of phenomena. This must be
found by a study of the phenomena themselves. Studying the facts of nature, I find them all the results of
physical causes. This is so of necessity; for all nature is
one unbroken *nexus* of causes and effects. To-day proceeds from yesterday; yesterday from the day before;
and so on back to eternity. Not to the beginning, for
there never was a beginning. Something must be postulated as always existing. I find that eternal something in
nature and natural law. Nature changes in form, it is
true, but not in force or essence. It is a revolving chain
whose links may vary in length and depth, but not in
essential strength. Cut this cosmical chain in the far
distant nebular period, and you will find the promise and
potency of all things as they now exist. How they came to
assume such *orderly* forms cannot be known. But the calculation of chances must not be urged against it. Chance has
nothing to do with the actual and the necessary. It is
only over the future and the contingent that she has any
power. But the stream of things flows in its necessary

channel, and has always done so.   There is no other possible channel, and so chance has nothing to say.

"Moreover, there is nothing wonderful in this particular
combination of elements which we see in nature.   It is by
no means the best possible combination, as you teleologists are wont to declare.   Nature is very imperfect and
intractable after all.   It is neither the worst nor the best
that can be imagined; a pretty fair average only, and
needs neither chance nor design to explain it."

Against this ingenious and specious statement of doctrine, there are four fatal objections. (1) It explains
nothing. (2) It contradicts experience. (3) It is unscientific. (4) It is nugatory.

(1) *It Explains Nothing.*

The mechanical theory of nature depends upon four
subsidiary theories; the nebular hypothesis, the persistence of force, spontaneous generation, and the development of animal species.   It can explain the course of
things only by establishing these theories.   But neither
of them has yet been established.   Take the nebular
hypothesis, for example.

In stating this famous hypothesis, a reasonable familiarity with it on the part of the reader must be assumed.
In its elements it admits of very simple statement. Given,
the space now occupied by the solar system, filled with
homogeneous, attenuated nebulous matter of any form,
with an initial motion, and the present solar system is
claimed to be built up, *as a necessary result*.   This diffuse
matter contracted upon itself.   In accordance with the
astronomical law that *radii vectores* always describe equal
areas in equal times, it began to revolve more rapidly as
contraction proceeded.   Finally the centrifugal force at

the equator of motion became so great as to throw off rings of matter, out of which planets were successively formed, with their revolutions, rotary motions, and satellites all determined and preserved by immutable laws of celestial mechanics. In like manner all other cosmical systems are formed.

Now this theory seems beautifully simple. But unfortunately it fails altogether to account for the facts, or even to agree with them.

1st. It does not account for nebulous matter.—The atoms of which it is composed are endowed with gravitation, molecular motions, and chemical affinities. These are marvellously potent and constructive in their work. Mechanism allows no intelligence in them, but yet they are extremely intelligent. No God made them. That postulate is unscientific and absurd. And yet they are little gods in themselves, with capacities vastly beyond human intelligence. Is there more absurdity in believing in one great God than in a million little ones? Teleology certainly has the advantage over mechanism at this point.

2d. That initial motion must be explained.—Who started it, and when? If these nebulous atoms were once for a single moment in all past eternity, in a state of rest, they would have remained so forever. But if they were always in motion, the possibility of an *initial* motion is excluded. What then becomes of those immutable laws of celestial mechanics? Either horn of this dilemma makes uncomfortable riding for the mechanist.

3d. The formation of concentric rings is troublesome.—As the mass contracts, the atoms are brought together, and their mutual attractions are thereby strengthened. But the same cause increases the centrifugal force by increasing the rate of rotation. It is shown mathematically that a contraction of one-half must increase this latter force eight times, while it increases the former only four times. No matter, therefore, what their relative strength at first might have been, the time must come when the centrifugal would surpass the centripetal. At that time and ever thereafter matter would be left behind at the equator of motion, and would form an equatorial sheet, and not a series of concentric rings, at immense distances from each other. Prof. Newcomb, realizing this and other difficulties, says: "The nebular hypothesis is not a perfectly established scientific theory," and thinks it impossible "to show how a ring of vapor surrounding the sun could condense into a single planet encircled by satellites."

4th. Orbital periods of the planets are equally troublesome. —The sun rotates in twenty-five days. Apply to its angular velocity the law of equal areas heretofore mentioned, calculate its rotation when it filled the earth's orbit, and you get over 2,200 years. This ought to be the earth's period of revolution, instead of one year, as it actually is. So in the case of Neptune. Instead of 165 years, its period ought to be nearly 3,000,000 years. Here are fearful discrepancies between theory and fact. These unruly planets are most recklessly ahead of time. They must certainly fly the track and wreck the whole celestial train. Mars seems to understand the danger; for he is busily engaged putting on the brakes. He has actually so slacked his motion as to rotate more slowly than his satellites revolve. *Phobos*, his inner moon, revolves in eight hours. Mars ought therefore to rotate in less than fifty minutes. Instead of that he actually rotates in about twenty-five hours. Here is an immense discrepancy on the other side of the ledger.

The satellites of Neptune seem to have left the nebular

track entirely. For they actually revolve at an immense angle and in the opposite direction from what they ought.

Now all these facts thrown directly across the track of the nebular hypothesis are sufficient—not to mention others—to show its inability to dispense with intelligence and design in the formation of the solar system. How then can it be expected to explain the formation of numberless out-lying cosmical systems? Whether it be true or not is no question for the teleologist. Two things seem certain. *First*, it is not established. On the contrary, it is falling into disfavor with mathematical astronomers. The hypothesis of *meteoric agglomeration* threatens to take its place. *Second*, if it were established, it can, by the nature of the case, do nothing whatever toward explaining the universe.

And this is the case with all the theories on which mechanism depends. They are equally tentative and opaque. They explain nothing.

(2) *Mechanism Contradicts Experience.*

It does this in two ways.

1st. By denying the existence of human purpose.—Man is a part of nature. Mechanism assumes that all nature is the simple unfolding of effects from physical causes. That includes man, with his so-called mind and spirit. But, if there is no purpose in nebulosity, then, according to this theory, there can be no purpose in human will, which is nothing but star-dust in another form. But the existence of human purpose is a matter of daily experience with every man. Mechanism denies it, and pulls itself down in the very denial.

2d. By ignoring the function of human purpose.—Every such purpose is executed by the employment of secondary causes. These causes are necessary to it. We very well know that we employ the principle of physical causation to carry out our purposes every day. But mechanism assumes antagonism between this principle and that of design. We know by experience that no such antagonism exists.

The question is not between design and mechanism in nature, as though the admission of the one excludes the other. That alternative may stare the mechanist in the face; but it never troubles the teleologist. He freely admits mechanism in his system. He has steady use for it. He puts it to work executing in orderly and rational manner the designs of an intelligent Creator. In this light all the facts of nature become luminous indeed. Mechanism exists, to be sure. So does intelligence. One is neither a substitute for the other, nor an enemy of it. It is simply a method of execution. Human intelligence carries out purposes by means of physical causes under natural law. So does Divine intelligence. All is perfectly clear and consistent. But mechanism, denying this plain principle, ignores the function of human purpose, contradicts human experience, and at the same time plunges itself into inextricable difficulties.

(3) *Mechanism is Unscientific.*

This is a serious charge. If it came the other way, it might not seem so bad. Mechanism claims to be the quintessence of science itself, and is quite accustomed to charge Teleology with unscientific methods. He who sees in nature any evidences of intelligent design, expects to be ornamented with such complimentary titles as "bundle of prejudices," "relic of barbarism," "exploded supernaturalism," and the like. But this charge is serious indeed, if established against mechanism. It is as if one should prove a clergyman unclerical, a physician unskilful, a mathematician unmathematical, an artist inartistic. The charge can be established, however. Mechanism is unscientific.

1st. *By contradicting experience.* — All science claims to be based on experience. What has been experienced is certain, and the scientist rejects all else as baseless theory. But he must not contradict experience, and claim to be scientific.

2d. *By transcending all experience.*—It basely attempts to pit the atomic theory as a fact against Theism as a theory. The ability to do this requires either great obtuseness of head or great perversity of heart. To say the very least of it, the existence of an atom is not a whit more scientifically certain than the existence of a God. The whole fabric rests on pure speculation.

3d. *By assuming that nothing exists but atoms.*—Their own existence is mere assumption. When they propose to monopolize all possible reality, it becomes downright effrontery, which no science can tolerate.

4th. *By necessitating a hiatus between man and nature, and making all science impossible.* — We study animals by means of their sensitiveness, instinct, and intelligence. These things we learn only from their respective actions. But mechanism steps in and says these actions are merely automatic, the result of organism and unconscious neural tremors. They seem as if intelligent and responsive, but in truth they are not. All is pure physical automatism. The same argument holds even as regards our fellow men. For really we know nothing of them except from certain actions and appearances. So it turns out, according to mechanism,.

that these extensive classifications of men and animals we have been making are huge delusions. And so of all so-called science and knowledge. The assumptions of mechanism, carried to their logical result, undermine scientific principles completely, and render all science impossible.

(4) *Mechanism is Nugatory.*

It avails nothing. Resting solely upon physical causation, it demands the eternity of matter and the persistence of force. This eternity of matter and energy includes every thing now in existence, or that ever will exist. Energy may be kinetic or potential, but the only possible change is in form and combination. Moreover, these changes are but the necessary and inviolable results of inherent properties of matter, existing and working in it from all eternity.

They are as they are, because they must be. Mechanism started out to explain and justify phenomena. She closes up with the astounding and luminous assertion that *they necessarily are*. That is like explaining a rainstorm, by saying *it rains*. It is mere stultification. At the best, it is but an unmeaning truism. Mechanism sets out to solve a problem, and leaves it ten-fold darker than before. How striking the contrast between this phenomenal darkness and the clear light of design in the teleological argument. The eternity of matter must be assumed in order to make the truth of mechanism possible. But this assumption is itself impossible. Material phenomena are cyclical, not eternal. Cosmical forces are in a condition of unrest. They constantly tend to equilibration. When equilibrated they will cease to act. The existing order of things cannot be eternal. It had a beginning and must have an end. The cosmos has its own cycle, beyond which it cannot go. All physical science teaches this truth. The hypothesis that matter is doomed to an eternal alternation of chaotic and cosmic cycles is highly imaginative, immensely improbable, and unsupported by even a shadow of truth. Moreover, it has against it the fact that eternity and mutability are contradictory ideas. Matter as known by its phenomena —and it cannot be otherwise known—is essentially mutable. It cannot, therefore, be eternal. The material universe must, then, depend for its origin upon an un-caused Cause which is immaterial, immutable, and eternal. But this hypothesis leaves no room for mechanism.

3. IMMANENT DESIGN.

This objection lies not against design itself, whose ex-istence it plainly implies, but rather against intelligence in design. It runs thus:

" In nature the efficient cause reaches its end without ever going out of itself. But in the works of man the very contrary of this is true. The end is realized in one object, while the efficient cause resides in a distinct and separate object. Nature works from within, and appar-ently without intelligent purpose. Man works from with-out and evidently with purpose. The forces of nature act after the manner of instinct rather than of intelligence. Hence the analogy between the works of man and of nature will not hold. At the utmost, the latter can show nothing more than a sort of blind intelligence."

Hegel, who emphasizes this doctrine, insists that we need not conceive the final cause in nature as having consciousness, and realizing its ends as a result of choice, foresight, and voluntary activity.

In replying to this statement, it is freely admitted that

the forces of nature act blindly. No one supposes for a moment that gravitation knows what it is doing; that oxygen seeks carbon with the express purpose of forming a certain chemical compound; that crystals of snow take their places as the result of a personal mathematical calculation, or that lightning strikes a building with the malevolent design of destroying human life. These forces are undoubtedly blind, incapable of foreseeing an end, or choosing means appropriate thereto. But for that very reason we are obliged to postulate a conscious and foreseeing wisdom of which they are the mere instruments. To say they have a blind intelligence in them will not do. It is an absolute contradiction in terms. It is using words without thought. The fact is, the intelligence resides not in these forces at all, but in the intelligent Author of nature back of them.

We are forced to trace it thither. Whenever we see a purpose realized, we attribute it to intelligence, no matter whether the agency of its execution acts from within or from without.

The execution of a purpose as seen in the movements of a steam-engine, implies intelligence, whether that intelligence resides in the iron or the coal or the water or the steam, or in all or neither of these combined. If I accomplish a purpose with this valuable machine, it is no more and no less an intelligent purpose than if I had performed it with my own hands.

Thus it is with purposes in nature. They imply intelligent volition. Their source is immanent in nature, but it is not therefore identical with nature. And so their immanence has no bearing whatever upon the question of their intelligence.

But we must not go to the opposite extreme of this

" blind immanence " theory, and say that " marks of design are marks of incessant intervention of the first cause."

Intelligent design does not imply intervention. An astronomical clock is a thing of design, and yet the designer need not be constantly tinkering with it. An incendiary puts the torch to an inflammable building, on a windy night, and burns up half a city ; and yet he need not be incessantly stirring up the fires in order to accomplish his fiendish purpose. A benevolent citizen gives a million dollars for the establishment and sustenance of a university, and when he is laid away to rest, multitudes of ambitious youth receive the benefits of his noble design, and that without any intervention from him whatever. Design does not necessitate interference at all. And so Teleology is not in the least concerned about the question of the Divine interference in the course of nature. There may be other and cogent reasons for believing in these interventions of Deity, but the principle of design does not call for them, and this is not the place to vindicate them.

4. ABUSE OF TELEOLOGY.

Objections heretofore mentioned come from the enemies of design. This one is attributable to its friends. It arises in general from the vain attempt to find design in every thing. This leads men to think they see design where none exists ; or, what is equally fallacious, they attribute a false design instead of the true one. This tendency brings on another error, namely, the explanation of things by sole reference to their design, to the exclusion of their efficient causes. This is extremely unphilosophical, and yet it must be admitted that teleologists have done it time and again.

Now, we must be consistent. We have justly condemned the mechanist for excluding design in favor of mechanism ; we must, with like vigor, condemn our friends if they exclude causation in favor of design. It is doubtless absurd also to suppose that the letters of the alphabet came together *by chance*, and formed the " Iliad " or " Paradise Lost." But these ante-theistic follies will nevertheless justify the teleologist in going to the opposite extreme of folly. What this extreme is will be best illustrated by inserting a few well-known historical examples.

Euler opposed lightning-rods on the ground that lightning is intended as a Divine punishment for our sins, which it would be impious in us to attempt to escape.

When Jenner made his great discovery of the principle of vaccination, Dr. Rowley, a pious English physician, declared it to be " an audacious and sacrilegious violation of our holy religion. These vaccinators appear to defy Heaven itself and the very will of God."

When winnowing machines were introduced into Scotland, certain pious people opposed them and stigmatized their product as the *devil's wind*, because they sacrilegiously usurped the work of Deity, whose prerogative alone it is to raise the wind.

Fénelon insists that the moon is made to give light in the absence of the sun, in which case Providence seems to have partially failed in his beneficent design by reason of his ignorance of the higher mathematics.

Bernardin de Saint-Pierre delivers himself thus : " Wherever fleas are, they jump on white colors. This instinct has been given them that we may the more easily catch them. The melon has been divided into sections by nature, for family eating ; the pumpkin, being larger, can be eaten with one's neighbors."

Buckland confronts the problem of the wolf's devouring the lamb, and solves it thus: "We have here a proof of the goodness of Providence, for thereby it escapes sickness and old age."

In view of such puerilities, it is no wonder that Voltaire sarcastically adds: " Noses are made to bear spectacles; let us therefore wear spectacles." These citations, along with others, are given by M. Janet to illustrate the abuse of Teleology. They are amusing in the extreme, but when put forth in solemn earnest in works on Teleology they strike us as sacrilegious apologies for Providence. Janet well says that they make more atheists than believers.

Let it be remembered, however, that Teleology is not responsible for these absurdities. Its argument does not imply them, its method does not employ them, its conclusion does not involve them.

Because design does not exist in every case, is no reason why it may not exist in any case. The fact that men in their ignorant haste, have made serious or ludicrous blunders in tracing or identifying certain designs, raises no argument, nor even a presumption against the principle of design itself. It simply shows its liability to abuse. But what good and true principle is there, that is not so liable?

Be it further remembered that the teleologist is under no obligation to prove the universality of design in nature. On the hypothesis that there is a God, and that he has made the universe, man ought not to be expected to grasp all the designs of the Infinite intelligence, in his constructive work. If he could, his ability to do so would form a strong presumption against the infinity of God. It is clear, therefore, that his inability to do so cannot make in the least against the hypothesis of a Deity. Neither can it raise an argument against design. On the contrary, it harmonizes perfectly with the principle of teleology.

There is no argument against design that can bear the test of logical scrutiny. Teleology, as an argument for volition in nature, repulses every foe, of ancient or modern attack, and placidly holds the field.

REFERENCES.

Ueberweg's "History of Philosophy."
Janet's "Final Causes."
Bascom's "Natural Theology."
Bowne's "Studies in Theism."
Newcomb's "Popular Astronomy."

CHAPTER III.

THE PERSONALITY OF GOD; OR, THE INTUITIONAL ARGUMENT.

SECTION I.

NATURE OF THE ARGUMENT.

THE arguments hitherto employed, have been inductive and syllogistic. By means of them, we have proved the existence in the universe of a widespread intelligence and volition. The next step in the logic of Theism, is to prove a corresponding personality in the universe. It must be shown that this intelligence and this volition belong to a person, an integral being. For this purpose, an entirely different kind of argument will be used. The personality of God comes to us by intuition, and not by the inductive process heretofore employed in this work. No one need be surprised at this change of method. It is just what might be expected, and is in full accordance with the principle of Theistic proof, as heretofore laid down (page 26).

It will be well to preface this intuitional argument with a brief reference to the essential nature of intuition as a power of the human mind. Clearness and force will thereby be gained. The best thinkers on this subject have recognized certain general principles and definitions which may be epitomized as follows:

I. DEFINITIONS.

(1) Intuition is used in three senses, to designate a mental power, a mental act, or a mental product.

(2) As a power it is innate, as an act, it is immediate, as a product it is primitive and self-evident knowledge.

(3) As power, act, or product, intuition is distinguished as presentative, and rational.

(4) Presentative intuition is of two kinds, external and internal.

(5) External presentative intuition, or *sense-perception* is that intuitive knowledge of material objects which is gained by the senses.

(6) Internal presentative intuition, or *self-consciousness*, is the mind's intuitive knowledge of itself and of its own states and operations.

(7) Rational intuition is the direct, self-evident knowledge of a necessary truth or principle.

(8) That necessary truth may be subjective or objective ; it may be an intuition of knowledge or an intuition of being.

(9) Intuition as a product, is knowledge. It is primary and immediate ; but it is knowledge, no less than are secondary and mediate kinds of knowledge.

(10) Rational intuition is more important in our philosophy than presentative intuition. But it must be remembered that the knowledge gained by perception and consciousness, is immediate and self-evident knowledge ; and that, therefore, any objections raised against rational intuition, on such grounds, must be of equal force against perception and consciousness.

(11) Presentative intuition deals with individual objects and gives material for thought; while rational intuition deals with general principles and regulates thought. They

are counterparts of each other ; and both are necessary to the best products of each.

2. NEGATIVE PROPOSITIONS.

To understand the better what intuition is, it will be useful to consider what it is not ; first to distinguish it carefully from other acts and products that are liable to be confounded with it, and then to state its positive elements. Dr. McCosh employs this method, with results substantially as follows :

(1) *Rational Intuition is not Innate Image-making or Representation.*

What a man has seen, he can picture to his memory afterwards. Products of other senses may, with greater or less vividness, be recalled in like manner. New images, in endless variety of forms, may be constructed by the imagination. There exists in the mind multitudes of elements ready for facile use by this plastic and fanciful power. But these elements are all products of experience. Rational intuition creates no mental images.

(2) *Intuition Furnishes no Innate Concepts.*

Concepts are not innate. They are derived. Of course, they cannot be pictured. I can picture a rose, a lily—a hundred lilies—but I cannot picture a general notion of a rose or lily. That general notion can be formed in the mind, to be sure ; but it must be formed by a process, from materials of experience. The mind is not furnished with original concepts. The newly born infant, for example, knows nothing, in their abstract forms at least, of such ideas as personal identity, time, space, cause and effect, infinity, and the like. Neither has it the concepts of the simplest objects in time and space.

(3) *Intuition does not Impose upon Objects any à Priori Mental Forms.*

This statement will be recognized at once as antagonistic to the doctrine made famous by Kant in his *Critique of Pure Reason*, and somewhat extensively adopted by philosophers since then.

This is not the place to enlarge upon that doctrine. It is sufficient for the present, to remark that any declaration to the effect that the mind in the act of cognition gives to the object cognized what is not in that object already, is to be condemned as unnatural, unwarrantable, and dangerous doctrine. Forms of sense, categories of understanding, and ideas of pure reason may be admitted as necessary to knowledge.

Whether the manifold of sense is united into knowledge in the way Kant declares, may be a question. But one thing is certain. Intuitive powers do not impose forms on things. They simply act as instruments by which we may discover what is in those things. They cognize, but do not create.

(4) *Rational Intuitions are not Always Formally Recognized as Laws of Mental Activity.*

They do indeed constitute the fundamental regulative principles under which the faculties of the mind act. Of individual mental acts, so regulated, we are directly conscious. But we need not always construe to consciousness the principles underlying these acts. Our consciousness of memory, judgment, imagination, or any other original faculty of mind, comes through the acts it performs. So it is with the original principles of intuition. Take the principle of cause and effect, for example. When we see a peculiar and unexpected effect, we know it had a cause, and seek to identify it. But the general principle of causation may never enter our minds, although the search be ever so earnest and protracted. We tacitly recognize it by working under it.

3. POSITIVE PROPOSITIONS.

(1) *Intuitive Principles do Exist in the Mind.*

This statement cannot be elaborated here. It means, however, that the mind must have in it some native elements to start with; that these elements must have laws and properties; that the mind can form original perceptions, and discover necessary and universal truth; that all experience would be impossible without native laws and principles; and that the data of reason itself are not products of reasoning, but are principles which must be assumed as intuitively evident, without any process of proof.

(2) *Intuitions are Immediate.*

They come to us at once, and not as the result of a mental process. They may, in a certain sense, depend upon such a process. But it forms only the occasion of the intuition, not its method or essence. Sense-perception may be taken to illustrate this relation. I see a book, and perceive at once that it occupies space. I see a brutal wretch pitch upon a cripple and demolish him. I condemn the act, say it is wrong, and will see it adequately punished, if possible. Now, the space relation, and the iniquity, in these respective cases, are not products of sense-perception at all. It gives their occasion, but not their cause. Neither are they products of reason. They arise spontaneously, necessarily, and immediately, without the intervention of any process whatever. So of all intui-

tions. They are direct acts of the mind, and not mediate processes.

(3) *Intuitions Depend upon Objects.*

The very nature of intuition presupposes objects. By
this power we discover immediately some quality or
some relation of an object. Were there no objects,
there could be no qualities or relations to discover. In
the utter mental absence of an object, the intuitive perception concerning it becomes meaningless. Of course,
an object of sense-perception may be absent, and even
destroyed ; but memory must furnish a mental transcript
of it for the service of intuition. Intuition, as the term
implies, is a looking into ; and without any thing to
look into, is quite as absurd as vision without any thing
to see.

(4) *Intuitions are Primarily Directed to Individual Objects.*

I first contemplate a certain body as occupying space,
and afterward arrive at the idea of space in general.
I observe a given event as taking place in time, and
pass from that to the idea of time in general. Certain actions strike me as being good, and certain others as
not being good ; and thereupon the abstract idea of
moral goodness arises in my mind. So it is in the history
of every child. His first intuitions pertain to objects of
individual experience.

(5) *Rational Intuitions are Involuntary.*

They do not depend upon the action of the will.
Like respiration, digestion, and circulation in the physical economy, they go on without any voluntary deter-

mination whatever. They fill every moment of our conscious existence, whether we take notice of them or not. They are simple laws of mental activity, enacted in the mind, but not by the mind. By acts of volition we may study them, examine their character, and trace their results, just as we proceed in other cases by the method of induction. But we can neither command their exercise nor forbid it. We cannot go to work purposely to establish an intuition, as we do an argument or mediate judgment. Neither can we shut off its light, as we can that of the sun, by simply closing the eyes.

(6) *Criteria of Intuitions.*

There are certain marks or tests by which intuitive truths may be invariably known. These are three in number. 1st, Self-evidence. 2d, Originality or Necessity. 3d, Universality.

Self-evident truth is such as carries its own conviction, and cannot be proved by any process whatever. It needs no proof and admits none. *Necessary truth* is such as must be believed. It cannot be doubted. Its denial leads to self-contradiction or absurdity.

Universal truth is that which is believed by all men everywhere in their normal state. It may not be clearly recognized by the infant or the savage, but that fact makes nothing against its originality or its universality. The oak must not be judged by the acorn.

These, then, are the certain marks of intuition. Any truth possessing them must be intuitional. It cannot be analyzed, derived, or arrived at in any other way.

I shall hope to show in the following section that personality in God and in man is such a truth.

SECTION II.

PERSONALITY OF GOD AND OF MAN.

Christian Theism insists that God is a person.   He is not merely a Cause or even a Power; he is a Personal Being.   He has power, he originates causes, but these are his attributes and acts, not himself.

Now this doctrine of Theism agrees perfectly with rational intuition.   Indeed, the idea of absolute personal being comes to us invariably in that way.   Rational intuition does not give the knowledge of individual realities, but it does give the necessary relations and general principles under which those realities exist.   It does not give the idea of being, for that is included in self-consciousness, but it does assure us that absolute, uncaused being must exist.   It does not give us our own personality, for that likewise is involved in self-consciousness, but it does give us that absolute personality which is the necessary source of our own.

True, we can form no exhaustive conception of the personality of God, but an image of it can be recognized in human personality.   This image falls short of adequacy because it is subject to limitations.   And yet, though it be finite intelligence, it helps us to understand that which is not finite.   There is a sort of parallelism which is suggestive and useful.

1. ELEMENTS IN COMMON.

The personality of God and of man have some elements in common.   Religious history, the world over, attests the truth of this statement.   Beliefs in these two personalities have always gone hand in hand.   It seems impossible that one should stand or fall without the other. Wherever one is weak or indistinct, the other is correspondingly so. Take the Eastern systems of pantheistic belief, for example. The Brahmin believes in 300,000,000 gods. The Divine personality is badly used used up in such a crowd. But this same Brahmin has a very weak hold on his own personality. This is evident from his easy belief in the doctrines of transmigration and final absorption in Nirvana. He sluggishly contemplates his own soul as an evanescent bubble on the ocean of infinite being, destined to burst in a moment, and disappear forever.

A more recent illustration of the same tendency is furnished by atheistic and deistic philosophers of modern times. Those who postulate uncreated matter, Eternal Energy of the Unknowable, instead of a Personal God, do thereby invariably impair the personality of man. Atheism and Pantheism sweep different arcs of the circle, but they meet at last at the same point of blank impersonality. If God is not a personal spirit, neither is man a personal spirit. And if man is not a personal spirit, we have no sufficient evidence that God is such. Huxley may properly view individual life as the mere display of the necessary properties of organic matter, and Harrison may go on worshipping the "Great Human Being" as the only possible God, and the author and minister of all law. Some such errors as these must result from rejecting the evident truth that man's idea of a personal God arises intuitively out of his perception of his own personal attributes. The inseparable character of these two beliefs depends upon the two essential characteristics of personality, which are *self-consciousness* and *self-determination*. These two elements belong alike to every spiritual being, whether God, angel, or man.

2. SELF-CONSCIOUSNESS.

Perception involves a percipient being. I am conscious of certain fluctuating states of thought, feeling, and volition. But this is not all. I am conscious of myself as the identical and enduring subject of these changing states. Now this knowledge of self is individual knowledge. It is not therefore the product of rational intuition, which gives general knowledge only. It is simply a primitive deliverance of consciousness, without which all other knowledge is impossible.

Prof. Bowne " objects that consciousness does not tell us how we are made." True, but it does tell us *that* we are made ; and the mere fact of a personal ego is the only question here. He further intimates that the ego is rather the " necessary condition of all consciousness." But how are we assured of the existence of this condition ? It comes not by perception, judgment, or reason. There is nothing back of consciousness to give it. We never go through a process of any kind, to convince ourselves of our own being. The conviction is a direct product of consciousness. Moreover, like all other facts of consciousness, it is irresistible—an indubitable conviction of reality.

I may possibly persuade myself into a doubt of external objects ; but my own existence I can never doubt. The existence of the pen in my hand and the paper before me, may be questioned. I may doubt, but I cannot possibly divest myself of the certainty that I am doubting. Doubt implies a doubter as surely as belief implies a believer. The fact is, that every conscious mental act involves the personality of the ego. Take the case of memory. I can think back thirty years to the scenes of my childhood. I recall with a smile the vague and grotesque ideas of those early days of my life. Many things that then seemed real, I have since learned were only phenomenal. But I know that I who now write these words, am the being I was when I had those mistaken thoughts thirty years ago. And I know that thirty years hence I will still be the same being. Through the whole cycle of my conscious being, I do not and cannot part with myself. The conviction of my own personality never leaves me. Philosophers may dispute about it as long as they like, but I know that I am myself.

Herbert Spencer considers it an illusion to suppose " that at each moment the ego is something more than the aggregate of feelings and ideas, actual and nascent, which then exists." Hume says that when he enters intimately into what he calls himself, he finds "nothing but a bundle or collection of different perceptions which succeed each other." Mill speaks of mind as "nothing but a series of our sensations and internal feelings." Prof. Clifford declares : " The perceiving self is reduced to the whole aggregate of feelings linked together and succeeding one another in a certain manner." Huxley insists " that we know nothing more of the mind than that it is a series of perceptions."

Now all such views as these are contrary to the facts of universal consciousness. They must, therefore, be rejected as unphilosophical and untrue. If man cannot believe consciousness of his own personality, he cannot believe any thing. All truth and knowledge are at an end.

But this self-consciousness in man implies a self-conscious God. It arises from certain mental states of knowledge, feeling, or volition. But these mental states depend upon the outer world. Without the *non-ego*, self-consciousness might be potential, but could never become actual;

it would remain an empty faculty. The thing itself exists
in man; but its basis or ground of exercise is not in man;
it inheres in some external object. Now what is its
source? It cannot be in nature. It is true, in the forcible words of another, that " Nature cannot give what she
does not herself possess. She cannot give birth to that
which is *toto genere* different from her. Only like can produce like. Nature can take no such leap. A new beginning on a plane above nature, it is beyond the power of
nature to make. Self-consciousness can only be explained
by self-consciousness in its author and source. It can
have its ground in nothing that is itself void of consciousness. Only that personal Power which is exalted above
nature, the creative principle to which every beginning is
due, can account for self-consciousness in man. It presupposes an original, and unconditioned because original,
self-consciousness. This spark of a divine fire is deposited
in nature; it is in it, but not of it. Thus the consciousness of God enters inseparably into the consciousness of
self, as its hidden background. The descent into our
inmost being, is at the same time an ascent to God."

Our conviction of a self-conscious God is involved in
the consciousness of our own personal being. It is given
to us by rational intuition as the necessary condition
of self-consciousness. The reality of a conscious self, implies the reality of a conscious God. This conviction of
God is not always equally clear and strong. It is doubtless obscured by the presence of moral evil in the soul.
But it is there, nevertheless; and responds to every mani-
festation of God in nature and providence and grace.

3. SELF-DETERMINATION.

This is the second necessary element of personality. It
is implied, indeed, in self-consciousness. Self-action de-

pends upon volition. If I were always the passive prey of objective impressions with no possible experience of self-initiated action, it is difficult to see how I could ever attain consciousness of my selfdom. The two ideas are dependent upon each other.

Fatalism is the alternative of self-determination. Men have ingeniously obscured it, and vainly striven to evade it, but at bottom, this is the sole issue.

Do I originate my own voluntary acts? Or are they the necessary result of some antecedent cause, within or without the mind? This is the question to be decided in self-determination. It touches upon a metaphysical problem, whose elaborate discussion would manifestly not be proper in this place. It is mentioned only in so far as it relates to the argument in hand.

That I do originate my voluntary acts, is a primary datum of consciousness. The only way I know they are voluntary, is by recognizing them as self-originated and self-determined. This conviction is not a negative affair, resulting from my ignorance of certain pre-determining agencies which are at work without my knowledge and back of my will. Acts of will are objects of consciousness, just as much as acts of perception, memory, or reason. If the so-called acts of volition are mere illusions, so likewise are all other acts of the mind. I can initiate action or refrain from it, by an efficiency within me which is neither irresistibly controlled by motives, nor yet determined by an irresistible proneness inherent in the mind itself. And this is the universal conviction of mankind.

Philosophers, indeed, have theoretically ignored this conviction. This course must be expected on the part of those who deny self-consciousness. The two theories are invariably linked together.

Herbert Spencer says: " That every one is at liberty to

do what he desires to do, supposing there are no external hindrances," constitutes personal freedom.   It will be observed that this freedom does not include the control of our desires, and is therefore not freedom at all.   He further states that psychical changes conform to law, and that therefore, "there cannot be any such thing as free-will."

Spinoza, after avowing similar fatalistic sentiments, remarks that "in the state of nature there is nothing done that can be properly characterized as just or unjust—faults, offences, crimes, cannot be conceived."   He adds, quite naturally: "Repentance is not a virtue, or does not arise from reason ; but he who repents of any deed he has done, is twice miserable or. impotent."

Mill persuades himself that his philosophy is not fatalistic, but necessarian.   Its goal is fatalism, however.   He thinks men must do as they do ; and yet punishment is right, both for the restraint of the evil-doer and the protection of society.   On this point he says: "It is just to punish, so far as it is necessary for this purpose, exactly as it is just to put a wild beast to death, for the same object."

In a like manner, Prof. Bowne cites Prof. Tyndall as arguing this social problem with the robber and ravisher, somewhat as follows: "You offend, because you cannot help offending, to the public detriment.   We punish you, because we cannot help punishing, for the public good. The public safety is a matter of more importance than the very limited chance of your moral renovation.   We entertain no malice or hatred against you, but simply with a view to our safety and purification, we are determined that you, and such as you, shall not enjoy liberty of evil action in our midst."   And with that word, the amiable professor gracefully chops off his head. What a beautiful and lucid theory of justice this is! No one is to blame for any thing, according to the learned professor. Public utility is the only standard of morals.

Now, suppose the "robbers and ravishers" should multiply in the land; suppose that, by fiendish methods and the use of fiendish weapons, they should obtain temporary control of society; suppose they should say to Prof. Tyndall, and to all other virtuous citizens: "We entertain no manner of malice against you; but the fact is, the example of your abstemious and fanatical life is damaging to our principles and practices; your presence is the constant occasion of uncomplimentary and annoying comparisons; and simply with a view to our own comfort, we are determined that you shall no longer live in our midst." Is it not clear that the professor's ethics would justify the villains in taking off every virtuous head in the land? Nay, would not his ethics positively require them to do it? The result might seem to be a catastrophe and an iniquity; but, according to fatalism, it can be neither. We have been too hasty, in accusing the professor of erecting public utility into the sole standard of public morals. There is, in truth, no such standard possible. Of course not, for there is no such thing as morality. That word has vanished. The distinction of right and wrong is utterly abolished. And what boots it now, whether Tyndall & Co., or Robin Hood & Co., shall rule in English society, or in English philosophy? Guilt and innocence, praise and blame, justice and injustice, virtue and vice, gratitude and resentment, reward and punishment, hope and fear, are all blotted out. The very basal beliefs and principles of human thought and human living, are forever gone. They, too, have vanished in the light of this fatalistic philosophy.   But we need not lament them ; for man himself is reduced to a mere automaton, and what sort of use has an automaton for principles and beliefs? As well might we ask for the beliefs of a blizzard, or the morals of a mowing machine.   The professor is entirely too timid when he takes pains to disclaim all malice and hatred in beheading the free-booter.   That, surely, is a needless precaution.   These sentiments, so virtuously and strenuously disclaimed, are just as virtuous as any other, and the head comes off with equal promptness and pre-cision, in either case.   Where, then, is the difference? The professor must throw off the old-time prejudices and boldly face the results of his theory.   And what moral distinctions can there be in the limited vocabulary of this destructive philosophy?   But these contradictory and absurd results are the logical out-come of fatalism, and indeed, of every denial of man's self-determination.   The trouble is with the philosophy.   It is essentially untrue, and unsound from top to bottom.   It is a gigantic error, and issues in gigantic follies.

The plain truth is that man is free and self-determined. But this self-determination, as already stated, is the sec-ond essential element of personality.   Man is a free per-sonal spirit.   No absurdity whatever results from the admission of this proposition.   It accords perfectly with the plain common-sense and the universal experience of mankind.   But its denial is beset on all sides, with all manner of adsurdities.   Philosophers should remember that no philosophy is safe which combats common-sense and universal experience.

Ignoring this wholesome precept, extremists have suc-ceeded in the erection and adoption of theories which blot God out of the universe.   But this is by no means all they have done. At the same stroke, they have blotted man out likewise. They have destroyed his personality; they have reduced the pronoun "I" to a collective noun denoting "aggregations of related sensations"; they have abolished mind, and replaced it by physical organism and transmitted neural tremors; they have stifled the rational hopes of life, and obliterated freedom, virtue, merit, reward, gratitude, justice, and morality from the vocabulary of truth; they have undermined the foundations of philosophy itself, by breaking down all distinctions between right and wrong, virtue and vice, truth and error; they have robbed man of himself and his God together, and have made life not worth living, truth not worth seeking, God not worth worshipping. The moral catastrophe is cosmical, universal. Grim fate rules the world; and hope goes out in helpless despair.

But fortunately this murderous philosophy, in destroying all things else, has likewise destroyed itself. In its self-destruction, we find a self-corrective. The voice of its own logic breaks the horrid nightmare, and we behold the harmless phantasm of an ugly fatalistic dream.

It is clear that self-consciousness and self-determination, the two essential elements of personality, do belong to man. They are intuitively perceived, upon the occasion of voluntary, rational acts. The capacity for such acts furnishes unquestionable evidence of personality. But this personality is not original; it is derived. Yesterday it was not; to-day it is. Moreover, it is limited and imperfect. It must have its source in an underived, original personality, whom we are pleased to call God. His is the only unlimited and perfect personality. The being of an underived personal spirit is as certain as the being of derived personal spirits. It is the universal conviction of

rational intuition, as Lotze has well expressed it, that the
realm of highest reality is restricted to the living, personal
spirit of God and the world of personal spirits, which he
has created.   I find within me an inexpugnable conviction that my being is derived, not from a law, or a
process, or a physical cause, but from a personal being,
conscious, intelligent, volitional, and underived.

Now this conviction is purely intuitional.   As such, it
is independent of the principles of induction, deduction,
or causation.   This truth is clearly shown in the religious
history of the world.   Men always learn to pray before
they learn to reason.   Belief in God is spontaneous ; a
thing of immediate cognition and involuntary emotion.
It comes not at the end of a long chain of speculative inquiries concerning the nature and causes of things.   It
comes rather with an intuition of being, an instinct of
worship, an emotion of love and awe, that are quite independent of pure reasoning processes.   Kant has called it
the practical reason ; but the truth seems to be that belief
in God flashes upon the mind at once, without any process
of argument whatever.

This view is not inconsistent with what has heretofore
been said concerning the careful and varied arguments
necessary to the demonstration of Deity.   The truth here
asserted is, that a belief in the existence of an underived
personal spirit involves no process.   But this is not saying that a satisfactory demonstration to others of the being and attributes of the Deity, may not require several
steps of argumentation.

This consideration brings us to a review of the arguments thus far developed.   By the inductive processes of
Eutaxiology and Teleology, we have demonstrated the
existence of intelligence and volition in nature.   These

demonstrations are independent of each other. But that does not prove that the things demonstrated must be mutually independent. Plan shows intelligence, purpose shows volition. Now, if plan and purpose are found in the same thing (as they undoubtedly are, in the structure of the hand and eye, for example) then intelligence and volition are found united there. This much has been learned from a study of nature.

But in the present chapter we have left nature, and turned our gaze inward upon ourselves. We have found within us the self-evident, necessary, and universal conviction of an original, superhuman personal spirit without us. This spirit, of course, is recognized as self-conscious and free.

Now this conviction is independent of the former arguments from nature. It is on another line altogether. It would remain in full force, if material nature were destroyed. The question therefore arises : Are the products of these independent inquiries, independent also, or are they identical? In other words, is the Personal Spirit whom we recognize as the source of human spirits, identical with the intelligence and volition found in nature?

This is by no means an idle question. Lucretius and the Epicureans answered it in the negative. They believed in the existence of personal gods, but held that they had nothing to do with the constitution and phenomena of nature. I unhesitatingly answer in the affirmative. The following truths necessitate this reply :

(1) Intelligence and volition must be united. They cannot exist apart. The one depends upon the other, and is inconceivable without it.

(2) Intelligence and volition are essential to personality. That personal being without us must therefore have them.

(3) The union of these two elements constitutes personality. Nature, then, indicates a personal being.

(4) Our own derived personality is inseparably bound to nature by means of a physical body which is itself a part of nature.

(5) Therefore that Personal Being who is the source of our conscious personality, must be one and the same Being whose intelligence and volition are displayed in the material universe about us.

Thus far I have arrived at the proof of the existence of a superhuman Personal Intelligence. This is not yet the God of Christian Theism. For convenience I shall call him God; but it is freely conceded that certain additional characteristics in the nature of this Being, must be proved, before he can be termed God, in the strictest sense. This proof will be submitted in the following chapters. But before proceeding, it will be well to notice the subject of *Anthropomorphism*, which is closely allied to the theme now in hand.

SECTION III.

ANTHROPOMORPHISM.

This term signifies the representation of God in human form, or as possessed of human attributes. The history of religion shows a strong and almost universal tendency in this direction. As we trace religious history back to the infancy of the race, or of the individual worshipper, we find this anthropomorphic idea stronger, bolder, and grosser in character. The ideas of God entertained by the average child of five years and by the average man of fifty, differ widely in many respects; but perhaps in no other so much as in this one we are now considering.

Childhood is wont to picture God as a being of parts and physical proportions. John Fiske is by no means the only man who, when a boy, imagined the Deity as a great big man, with long, white beard and penetrating eye, standing at the zenith of the heavens, looking ceaselessly down upon the earth, and recording with omniscient accuracy in a ponderous ledger, every peccadillo of every boy and girl in all the world. Some such experience is common. We can all remember childish attempts at practical theology, not a whit less grotesque than this.

And what is true of men personally seems, to some extent at least, to be true of the whole race. The present idea of God has, as a rule, been reached by a process of growth. This growth has been mainly along two lines, which may be distinguished as the anthropomorphic and the cosmical. The former is historically connected with ancestor-worship and hero-worship ; the latter, with nature-worship. The Chinese, Romans, and Zulus illustrate the former phase ; while the Greeks and Hindus are examples of the latter.

Now when Christian Theism came in contact with these pagan ideas it became variously modified and corrupted by them. The Christian Fathers, so-called, were radically divided in this regard. Origen and Athanasius, for example, were cosmical in their views ; while Augustine was decidedly anthropomorphic. And the views of the common people, in the middle ages, as well as in the early days of Christianity, were often gross and grotesque in the extreme. Were it not so, the puerile representations of the mediæval miracle-plays could never have been possible, not to say, popular. Fiske mentions one of them, wherein the crucifixion is portrayed. An angel, who has just witnessed the catastrophe, rushes excitedly into heaven crying : "Wake up, Almighty Father! Here are those beggarly Jews killing your son, and you asleep here like a drunkard!" The Father arouses himself, rubs his eyes, and drowsily replies, "Devil take me, if I knew a thing about it!"

Now this irreverent and blasphemous representation of the Deity was not intended to convey the slightest irreverence. On the contrary, this play was among the few which were approved by the church, on account of the salutary influence they were supposed to exercise upon the laity and the people at large.

In view of such facts as these—and there are many such—it is vain to deny or ignore Anthropomorphism. It is a conspicuous fact in religious history. Atheists are disposed to rejoice over it, and some theists have grown pale with fear and trembling. Much feeble philosophy has been expended on both sides of the line, in order to prove or to disprove the fatal consequences to Theism, which have been supposed to lurk beneath this anthropomorphic tendency of man's religious nature. But it is evident that both parties to the dispute are unwarrantably excited. The struggle is by no means a desperate one. In truth, there is not the slightest ground for any struggle at all. Let it be freely admitted that our idea of God is anthropomorphic. What of that? How else ought it to be? How else, forsooth, could it be? How can religious truth grow in the human mind, except by conformity to the laws of the human mind? How, indeed, can the Divine Spirit be cognized, except by reference to the human spirit, and under the proper similitudes thereof? Knowledge of God is knowledge, and must observe the universal laws of knowledge. There is no other possible medium through which men ever have attained or ever will attain any intelligent idea of Deity. Even the nature-gods of the Greeks and Hindus had a distinctively anthropomorphic element in them. And so must it always be. If there is absolutely nothing in common between God and man, no knowledge of God could ever be possible to man. In revealing this common relation, either man must be raised to the Infinite, or the Infinite must condescend to man. The former is manifestly impossible. If the latter is graciously done, certainly no theist need be alarmed or need apologize for the Infinite condescension.

Concerning this whole subject, two general remarks are to be made.

1. ANTHROPOMORPHISM HAS A TRUTH IN IT.

In believing in God, we must ascribe to him the highest possible perfection. But personality in man is the most exalted fact of which we know, outside of the Deity. If God is impersonal, he is inferior to man, no matter how mighty his cosmical power may be. God must, therefore, be like man in his personality. He is a Spirit, and must have qualities similar to those we find in our own spiritual natures. Or rather we feel—and we cannot rid ourselves of the feeling—that God has made us somewhat like himself. He has put somewhat of his own nature upon us. Rational intuition agrees with the sublime doctrine of Moses, that man is made in the image of God. Intuitive truth calls for the sanction of a spiritual God. It must be that the cognition of right and wrong, for example, which he has made so vital in us, exists in him likewise. If he has made us to follow the good and eschew the evil, it must be because he himself approves the one and hates the other. Human reason calls for a

God who is the Perfect Reason, and the source of all
rationality, wherever and however it may be displayed.
Human conscience calls for a God who is the Perfect
Righteousness, whence emanates all that is holy and good
throughout the universe.   The human heart calls for a
God who is Perfect Love, who pities the distressed, com-
forts the sorrowing, forgives the erring, and desires the
holiness and happiness of his intelligent creatures.   But
such a God as this must have something in common with
man—some adequate ground of knowledge, sympathy,
and communion.   And this is the rational basis of Anthropomorphism.   Surely there is nothing in it that is, in
the smallest degree, damaging to Theism.

God is not degraded by supposing a possible communion with man.   Man's highest elements are not
necessarily imperfections.   Their imperfection in man results from the being of man, and not at all from any
thing inherent in the elements themselves.   It is impossible to conceive that consciousness, volition, personality,
feeling, love, justice, veracity, and moral purity are in
themselves of the nature of frailties.   Man is not rendered
frail by possessing them, but they are rendered frail by
existing in man.   They may all exist in God in illimitable
perfection.   To predicate the perfection of such attributes
in the Divine Being, is not to degrade him, but to exalt
him to the highest place of moral excellence which human
thought is capable of reaching.   It is to make him a Perfect Person—infinitely superior to the cold, impersonal
Deities reached by the speculations of philosophy.   It is
to give him power over the hearts and consciences of
men, to win them into paths of true virtue, to turn their
feet from the slippery ways of vice, and to comfort their
hearts in the hour of darkness and death.   Deism can fur-

nish no such power. Max Müller rightly says: "A mere philosophical system, however true, can never take the place of religious faith." It is not a mighty abstraction, nor an impersonal force, nor a compend of principles that we believe and love and trust and serve. It is a Personal God, who is perfect in purpose, motive, and affection, as well as in intellect and principle. Such a Being, and such alone, could be the adequate source of all that we see in the world without us, and in the soul within us.

2. ANTHROPOMORPHISM IS LIABLE TO TWO ERRORS.

This is not strange. Error is always mixed with truth; and some truth is nearly always mixed with error. Where is the system, or domain, or theme of human thought that can claim entire exemption from error? If such a system were let down from Heaven to-day, to-morrow it would be misinterpreted and corrupted by human thought. There is nothing perfect under the sun. The history of Anthropomorphism is not at all exceptional in this regard. In attempting to construe to their minds and hearts the Divine Personality, men have often fallen into two gross errors:

(1) *They Have Supposed God to Possess Every Attribute of Man.*
This tendency is quite natural and quite prevalent. The irreverent ridiculousness of the old miracle-plays, to which reference has been made, undoubtedly resulted from this error. And the world has not outgrown it yet. The book of Mormon represents God as having the figure of a man, and as being of definite, measurable proportions. No small part of the popularity of that monstrous system is due to this grossness of representation. It brings down Deity to the easy comprehension of ignorant and indolent

minds. And some such gross ideas of God, it is to be feared, exist in the minds of many nominal Christians. John Fiske justly remarks : " If we could cross-question all the men and women we know, we should probably find that, even in this enlightened age, the conceptions of Deity current throughout the civilized world contain much that is in the crudest sense anthropomorphic." Many of us have never developed the embryonic Theism of our childhood.

But it need not be so. It is a natural development abnormally arrested. Because God has some attributes in common with man, it does not follow that he has them all. We do not reason thus concerning one another. Every man is like every other man indeed ; but he is just as truly unlike every other. So in a deeper sense must we suppose God to be unlike all men. If, like man, he have intelligence, it does not follow that, like him, he has also bodily organism. If he have an emotional nature capable of ineffable happiness, we need not therefore conceive him like man in the enjoyment of the ludicrous. Because a hearty laugh is proper in man, the counterpart of it need not be postulated in the nature of God. He may have what is highest in man, without having what is lowest.

(2) *Men Have Limited God to Human Attributes.*

They have sluggishly supposed that God has no qualities except those possessed by man. This likewise is a gross error. No thinking man supposes for a moment that God possesses any attributes whatever *in the exact way* in which he himself possesses them. They differ in degree, being finite in one case and infinite in the other ; they differ in origin, being derived in one case and original in the other ; they differ in scope and method of operation ; and they may differ in many other respects. Take the matter of consciousness as an illustration of this possibility. Man's activity gives him the power, or, at least, the occasion, of self-consciousness ; but it would be a great blunder to prescribe the same condition to God's self-consciousness. Man's knowledge of the *ego* depends upon the existence of the *non-ego*, either material or mental. But God is subject to no such dependence.

If then we must admit that even those Divine attributes which are held in common with man are necessarily unlike the human, what sheer folly is it to deny to Deity the possession of any attributes beyond those which we possess ! It is reasonable to suppose, and unreasonable to deny, that God has perfections differing, both in degree and in kind, from those possessed by his human creatures. He may have put some of himself into man, but it is not at all likely that he exhausted himself.

The crude anthropomorphist will doubtless ask the theist to name, describe, or locate these supra-human elements in the Divine nature. This demand is unreasonable. It cannot be met. But this confession does not militate against the existence of these elements. It only shows them to be in reality supra-human. Having never fallen under our experience, and being without the limited circle of our intuition, we cannot even so much as conceive of them, and still less can we describe or identify them. But this inability, again, is not against their existence, but the rather in favor of it. There is rationality no less than inspiration in the scriptural statement : "Thou art a God that hidest thyself." There is a befitting majesty of mystery about that Divine Being whom we can never find out unto perfection. What innumerable and ineffable perfections may dwell in the nature of God, it is not for man to say or think. But to deny their existence is to act the part of the immodest and the irreverent.

With the proper elimination of the errors just described, there is in Anthropomorphism nothing whatever that is either illogical or damaging to the cause of Theism. It is simply the necessary and suitable form in which we construe to ourselves the personality of God. We have seen that the personality of God is an intuitive truth, that as such it is self-evident, necessary, and universal, and that it involves the personality of man, the foundations of truth, and the most intimate beliefs and hopes of life. If we give it up, all is lost. There is nothing left us, in the bitter irony of fate, but to lift imploring hands to the " Inscrutable Unknown," and, as Harrison sarcastically puts its, to pray " O, X^n, love us, help us, make us one with thee ! "

But we need not give it up. Neither logic, nor true science, nor sound philosophy requires it. We may still rest our hearts and our hopes in the arms of a personal, conscious, intelligent, living, loving God.

REFERENCES.

McCosh's " Intuitions of the Mind."
Fisher's " Grounds of Theistic and Christian Belief."
Fiske's " The Idea of God."
Count d'Alviella's " Evolution of Religious Thought."
Max Müller's " Science of Religion."

CHAPTER IV.

THE GOODNESS OF GOD; OR, THE HISTORICAL ARGUMENT.

SECTION I.

THE PROBLEM STATED.

PREVIOUS arguments have established the existence, in the universe, of a supra-human Being, intelligent, volitional, personal. For convenience, I have called him God; but he is not yet shown, by any means, to be the God of Christian Theism. He might possess all these elements, and be a demon as well as a God. Before deciding this momentous question, his moral character must, in some sense, be ascertained. Is he a wise, holy, just, and good Being; or is he a cunning, malevolent monster? Is the universe the outcome of beneficent wisdom; or is it merely a crazy freak of fiendish passion? Is Righteousness enthroned therein; or does Diabolism bear perpetual sway? This question is vital to the Christian system. If God exists at all, he must be complete in wisdom and in power. And, if he is so complete, he must likewise be perfect in moral goodness. Any lack of goodness carries with it a corresponding lack of wisdom. A malevolent being may be cunning, crafty; but cannot be truly wise. Perfect wisdom and power cannot be rationally accepted apart from perfect goodness. The separation of these elements is mentally incongruous and morally repugnant. Their logical connection has been universally recognized. Rousseau, in vindicating the goodness of God against the supposed evil of an earthquake, puts the matter thus: "All these questions are reducible to that of the existence of God. If God exists, he is perfect; if perfect, he is wise, powerful; if wise and powerful, my soul is immortal; if my soul is immortal, thirty years are nothing to me, and are perhaps necessary to the welfare of the universe."

In all theistic study, therefore, evidence of the goodness of God is no less important than that already adduced in favor of his being and personality. Search for such evidence will lead us somewhat into history. It will be needful to take a look at the past; and to observe the historic trend of things. This argument has therefore been properly termed historical. It will not be confined to history, however; the discussion must necessarily have some range and diversity.

Before arguing the question in detail, it is well to notice some preliminary points concerning the general nature of the problem to be solved, and our own fitness to reach a satisfactory solution of it.

1. THE PROBLEM IS A MOST COMPREHENSIVE ONE.

It is comprehensive in time. It concerns the past, present, and future. We must not decide against God's goodness without taking in the endless reach of duration and being. It is vast in extent. It includes all the manifold of being. It sweeps the universe and the two eternities. It is vast, likewise, in purpose. If God be truly good, he loves goodness in all his created intelligencies, no less than in himself. He therefore desires their voluntary and loving attachment to the eternal principles of righteousness and truth. His perfect goodness can be satisfied with nothing less than their moral perfection. His moral government seeks that perfection, and must be judged after the standard of this high purpose. Any other ground of judgment is manifestly unjust.

2. THE PROBLEM IS STILL UNDEVELOPED.

The moral system of the world is in its infancy. The sovereignty of brute force has largely passed away. Intelligence now rules the civilized world. But righteousness has scarcely yet begun to take the sceptre from the hand of pure intelligence. The world is yet young. Character, and even intelligence itself, are still in their period of tutelage. An immense sweep of growth is before them. What they shall be, when Righteousness shall bear undisputed sway in the earth, doth not yet appear. The era of the universal sovereignty of moral ideas is just beginning to dawn upon the earth. We cannot now judge of the day it shall usher in; for we stand in the uncertain twilight of its first morning hour. The proper discipline of the world is a vast and promising work; so much so, indeed, that its accomplishment may include and justify the entire system of things which we see developing mysteriously before us. And so we ought not to pronounce judgment against it, even though there be in it as yet things which seem to us dark and unfavorable. It is not time to render the verdict; the evidence is not all in. The possibilities of matured and disciplined manhood must not be measured by the foibles and failures of untutored youth.

3. THE PROBLEM TRANSCENDS OUR CAPACITY.

At the best, we are poor judges of moral discipline. The wisest parents often make fatal mistakes in training

their children. Instructors of youth, by profession, are
scarcely less blundering. We set before us a desirable
point in youthful attainment, and we push on with all
possible speed to reach it. But we take such hasty and
ill-judged steps as to miss entirely the goal of our lauda-
ble hopes. Moral discipline is a thing of slow degrees and
short stages; it must not be crowded. Moral growth cannot be forced. Hot-bed plants are never sturdy. Theoretically, we admit these facts; but in practice we strangely forget them. Many a devoted parent has ruined his
child by bringing him up in a moral hot-bed.

Now, if we fail so conspicuously in our little matters of
individual discipline, modesty would suggest extreme
caution, on our part, in criticising God's plan for the
moral discipline of the whole world. Mere kindness of
heart, even in human discipline, is almost sure to fail of
its purpose. Wisdom, sternness, and even hardship, must
frequently be called in, to insure success. The simple
presence of hardship in the world is no argument, therefore, against the goodness of God. We know not how
much of its sturdy discipline may be requisite to establish
a free moral intelligence in a state of voluntary moral
perfection.

4. THE PROBLEM CONCERNS US PERSONALLY.

It so happens that this discipline weighs heavily upon
us ourselves. It often touches us at the tenderest and
weakest points of our being. We reluctantly endure its
hardships, and would escape them if we could. Pangs of
suffering, disappointment, and regret come to ourselves
and our friends; and, quite naturally, we question the
necessity and the propriety of all these things. We
would be quite willing and even ambitious to attain

moral growth in some other way, but we do not relish it in this particular way. It is too hard and unsavory. And then it is not complimentary to us personally. It wounds our pride to admit that we are so very far from moral perfection as to employ extreme rigors in the pruning of our vices and the strengthening of our virtues. Only terrible diseases justify heroic treatment. And so we are tempted to reject the whole system as a thing of unnecessary hardship and cruelty.

We will do well to bear in mind, however, that parties to the suit are plainly disqualified from passing unbiased judgment upon the decision of the Court.

With these facts in view, no man ought to expect a perfectly clear and solid solution of this difficult problem. When he has done his best on it, there will doubtless be some points of darkness and mystery still left. But this should not deter the theist from undertaking the problem and facing the facts in the case.

SECTION II.

THE FACTS.

There are many facts in the world that point distinctively toward the goodness of God, but there are likewise many others that point the other way. At least they occupy debatable ground. Their proper interpretation is a matter of some difficulty and doubt. That is to say, the facts and phenomena of the universe may be divided into two classes, the former of which shall contain all such as are manifestly benevolent in character, while the latter includes any that may be reasonably considered of doubtful significance.

For the sake of brevity, the former class will be entirely omitted from the present discussion. A sufficient reason for this omission will be found in the fact that the goodness of God is established in the general belief of mankind, and that therefore the *onus probandi* is upon the man who denies it. Liebnitz recognized this principle when, without attempting a perfect explanation of the phenomena, he said : " We have explained enough when we have shown that there are cases where some disorder in a part is necessary to the production of the greatest order in the whole." That is, he takes it for granted that the *production of the greatest order in the whole* is the object of creation, and thus practically throws the burden of proof upon him who denies the goodness of God. This is logical and right. Such facts as are relied upon to furnish proof against God's goodness, must be examined, but the discussion need not be burdened with a detailed recital of the facts on the other side. Facts supposed to make against the goodness of God are usually presented in three groups, the *Physical, Social,* and *Moral.*

I. PHYSICAL FACTS.

There are certain purely physical facts in the world that seem to be malevolent. We are told—and we cannot dispute it—that the general aspects of nature are often stern and severe. Her laws are irrevocable and apparently merciless. Men and animals often derive but a meagre support from her unwilling soil. Storms, cyclones, and thunder-bolts sweep over the land and decimate its inhabitants. The sea rises in its anger, and, without a moment's warning, engulfs hundreds of souls and millions of money entrusted to its treacherous waters. Miasma rises from a swamp and depopulates a whole city. Summer drought and winter frost vie with each other in the work of destruction and death. One man dies of sunstroke ; another is found stiff and stark in a blizzard.

The volcano buries a helpless city in sudden ruin and death. Even Mother Earth shakes beneath us, and the strongest human structures crumble and disappear. The very air we breathe, and water we drink, are laden with the seeds of destruction and death, no less than the necessary supplies of life. Human existence is one prolonged struggle with the elements and the environment. Nature must be conquered. She yields but slowly, she struggles persistently, and so the perennial tussle goes on. Physical suffering in the world is immense. Neither men nor the lower animals can escape it. A painless life is the rare exception. Even animals themselves seem bent on injuring and destroying one another. Claws, fangs, poisonous stings, and, indeed, all manner of implements of torture and death are general, familiar, and popular in the operations of the animal creation. Carnivora and parasites have found their way into every part of the animal kingdom. The lesson of physical pain is written in ghastly lines on earth and air and sea and sky.

2. SOCIAL FACTS.

Those who deny the goodness of God have likewise presented numerous facts of Sociology which seem to strengthen their denial. They insist that the relations between man and man are far from being perfect. Society is indefinitely stratified, and the lower orders are continually suffering from the inequalities of their lot: Caste with iron heel treads down the masses to the earth. The great struggling multitude are in perpetual unrest. They are neither willing to endure their fate nor able to overcome it. Ambition and despair sweep alternately across their path and make them doubly miserable.

And then there are the gross injustices of life. One man sows, and another reaps. One toils, and another robs him of his just reward. The shrewd villain impoverishes the honest citizen, the tongue of the slanderer destroys the fair name of the virtuous, and the artful seducer corrupts the heart of the unsuspecting and the innocent. The strong oppress the weak. Abounding wealth turns naked poverty unclothed and unfed from its door. Successful vice sits enthroned at the centre of many a social circle, and stares with brazen face at the retreating form of defeated virtue. The fortunate classes treat with ill-disguised contempt their less fortunate neighbors. Poverty pinches the poor, and the helpless cry of squalor, oppression, and despair goes up from every land.

Then comes war, the final stage of social distress. Men are made savage and brutal. The arts of peace are forsaken, and the instruments of death brought forth. Fraternal love is forgotten, and blood is sweet to every taste. Treasures are wasted and lives poured out like a flood. For some real or fancied wrong, thousands of men are drawn up in stately array for the sole purpose of butchering one another. And when at length the struggle is ended, one side is found crushed by defeat, the other brutalized by victory, and both demonized by unrelenting hate.

This dark picture is no mere fancy. The history of the world is a history of war. There is blood on every page.

3. MORAL FACTS.

The facts just enumerated would seem discouraging, indeed ; and yet they are only surface facts after all.

They do not penetrate to the heart of things. The centre of the disease is further down. Moral evil is the deep-seated sore of the ages. Sin is the unsolved problem of the universe. Its sway is universal. It has passed upon all men. " The slime of the serpent is upon every head ; its loathsome coil in every heart." The consciousness of sin is as broad as the human race and as long as time itself. But whence came it ? and why ? These questions have never been finally answered. Men have always grappled with them and philosophized upon them with great freedom, indeed, but with little success.

And then the transmission of moral evil constitutes another dark problem. Sin reproduces itself. The law of heredity comes in and hands it down from father to son. One generation sins, and a thousand generations inherit the wretched patrimony. The glutton, the drunkard, and the debauchee entail upon their remotest offspring the fatal effects of their loathsome vices. In the fulness of time, each succeeding generation must take up the burden of a father's sins, either to fall beneath it, in physical and moral weakness, into an untimely grave, or transmit it, enlarged and intensified, to the still more unfortunate heir that shall come after him. And so the dreadful entail goes on from one generation to another till the end of time. This perpetual subjection of human hearts to the powers of evil, and this involuntary entailment of hereditary sin, are the bottom problems for Beneficence to solve. I have presented them in the strongest light possible, and in the very words of the pessimist, in order that the difficulties involved may be fairly seen and squarely met. There is no evasion in theistic thought. If God be infinitely good, why are things thus ?

SECTION III.

FALSE ANSWERS.

This question of the ages must be approached in a spirit of modesty and self-distrust. One cannot hope to succeed wherein others have uniformly failed. What has puzzled earnest thinkers hitherto will doubtless remain a puzzle hereafter. The last word on the origin and justification of moral evil in the universe has not been written. Probably it will not be written till the light of a clearer day shall dawn upon human vision. And yet the problem comes legitimately across the pathway of our theistic studies, and it would be sheer cowardice not to attack it.

The many solutions hitherto attempted, as well as those that may follow, can be gathered into three general groups; namely, *Ditheism, Pessimism,* and *Optimism.* For convenience of discussion, this classification will be adopted, and the various theories will be examined in the order indicated. Ditheism and Pessimism will be found weak and unsatisfactory. Optimism stands on the firmest footing.

I. DITHEISM.

By this term is meant the belief in two divine beings, one good and the other evil. It is the dualism of gods. This doctrine is no uncommon thing in the early history of religions. It seems, indeed, to be the first solution men have attempted concerning the problem of sin. Pressed by its cogent facts and direful consequences, they have been forced to ascribe its origin to the will of an evil spirit of vast power and relentless cruelty. But the numberless benefactions of nature have, by a mental necessity, been already ascribed to a good spirit from whom all the blessings of life are supposed to emanate. Hence arises a dualism of antagonistic deities. To these two rival deities is attributed that essential and eternal warfare between good and evil which all men recognize and seek to explain. One god is beneficent, mild, and loving; the other is cruel, hateful, malignant. One seeks the perpetual happiness of man; the other his misery and destruction. There is hostility between them, and eternal war is waged. The progress of the conflict is portrayed in many early religions.

In the Zend-Avesta we find Ormazd and Ahriman, the good and evil spirits, perpetually striving for the mastery of the world. In the Vedic religion the same antagonism is asserted between Brahma and Rudra, the creator and the destroyer. In the pantheon of Scandinavia it is Odin and Loke; in ancient Egyptian mythology it is Osiris and Typhon. As late as the third century of the Christian era this dualism was revived by Mani, who insisted upon the coördination and independence of the good and the evil spirit. Even Augustine and other Christian Fathers, for a time, taught the same doctrine.

In every case there are two great contending powers; the one benign, the other malevolent. It is the Good Spirit and his angels fighting against the Evil Spirit and his angels, and struggling for the supremacy of the universe. This is the warfare of the ages supposed to be carried on throughout all nature, as well as in the hearts and lives of men. It is the duty of all men to ally themselves to the Good Spirit; and it is their privilege, by personal good deeds, to advance his righteous cause.

This dualism, in some form, is likewise taught by many philosophers. Empedocles represented Love and Hate as opposing forces working with the elements of nature. Love at length succeeds in bringing light and beauty out of darkness and death. Pythagoras taught that intelligent spirits are good and free; that there is a divine soul of things, but matter is a perpetual and hurtful incubus upon it ; and that the human soul is in itself a harmony, but rendered discordant by its imprisonment in the body. In our day, J. S. Mill presents a view of Theodicy which is little less than a revival of Pythagorean dualism.

Now this ditheistic solution of the problem of evil is essentially childish and crude.   The coëternity of two fighting deities is an impossible conception.   Arguments for the Unity of God, which will be set forth in the next chapter, and which need not here be anticipated, will amply refute this doctrine.   It is enough for the present to say that it is a passing mode of undeveloped thought, which uniformly recedes before the light of advancing civilization.

2. PESSIMISM.

The pessimist attempts to explain evil by making it dominant, supreme.   He turns his back to the light, and says there is no light ; shuts his eyes to the good, and de-clares all is evil; bars his soul against all hope, and revels in despair. He believes the universe is under the supreme control of evil, and is getting worse and worse.   He re-gards the struggle of right against wrong as hopelessly unequal, and is quite disposed to give it up entirely. With Buddha, he declares existence to be an evil, and longs to be rid of it.   Or, with Schopenhauer, he believes the world is not the best, but the worst, of all possible worlds.   Or, with Hartmann, while admitting that the existing world is the best of all possible worlds, he never-theless regards it as a failure, and thinks it would be far better if no world had ever been made.   As the world exists, he sees it full of pain and cruelty.   All nature is a scene of universal and prolonged misery. If there be a God at all, the pessimist declares him to be a malevolent monster who takes fiendish delight in wantonly torturing the creatures he has made. If he were not a monster, he would stop all this horrid pain and agony of life. A clever stroke of logic is brought in to clinch this pessimistic nail. Epicurus and Lactantius used it. And to this day, pessimists seem never to tire of using it. They say: "If God is almighty, he is able to destroy evil; if he is good, he is disposed to destroy it. But, inasmuch as he does not destroy evil, he is either not almighty or not good." Taking the second alternative, the pessimist declares God to be a malicious demon.

To prove his view, he cites the numerous ills and pains of life. His tongue is dipped in poison, and is voluble of evils. Carnivorous animals, parasites, human suffering, the severities of nature, moral evil and inherited sin, constitute his staple and well-worn arguments. With a depth of pathos equalled only by the height of his indignation, he rings the changes on the dark list of calamities, iniquities, and griefs. Some fair average samples of the list have already been borrowed from him and written down in the second section of this chapter.

As a conclusion of his whole argument, he says: "Scarcely is a happy life worth living, and few, indeed, find that life." And there is a sort of sullen satisfaction in the very ghastliness of his words. He can rejoice in one advantage of his philosophy, at least. It releases him and absolves his conscience from all struggle with the powers of evil in his own soul. If evil sits supreme upon the throne of the universe, it is worse than vanity, and a double folly, to strive against it in the weak and broken citadel of his own heart. And so he gives over the struggle, throws down his arms, and surrenders at discretion to the domination of imperious appetite and passion. Henceforth he may lead an ignoble and vicious life; but he easily persuades himself that it must be so, since evil is supreme in the world, and indolently throws upon God the responsibility of his own misdeeds.

But the pessimist's philosophy is one-sided and weak. It attempts to solve the dark problem of evil; but the solution reached is darker by far than the problem to be solved. Indeed, it is no solution at all. It is the rather a cowardly retreat from the difficulties that confront us. There is a better, braver course.

SECTION IV.

THE TRUE ANSWER—OPTIMISM.

The optimist takes a broad and comprehensive view of the question of morality in the universe. He believes that, on the whole, all things in nature are ordered for the best; that God is just and wise and good; and that these attributes of Deity are increasingly manifested to man, as the ages go by. But he by no means ignores the existence of physical and moral evil in the world, nor the widespread and desolating effects thereof upon the lives and destinies of men. He freely admits both, and seeks to reconcile them with the goodness of God. This attempt his philosophy compels him to make. He sees the goodness of God written everywhere, and cannot question it. He likewise recognizes the presence of evil in the world, and cannot question that. Both exist, and must, therefore, coëxist. But how are they to be reconciled? Herein is the difficult problem. The ditheist evades it at the expense of God's unity, and the pessimist evades it at the expense of God's goodness. The optimist is left to grapple with it unaided and alone.

I. AS TO PHYSICAL EVIL.

Suffering is an obtrusive fact in the world, vast in amount and severe in character. And yet, it is habitually and grossly over-estimated. We waste a great amount of pity, for example, in view of the suffering of animals. The carnivora undoubtedly inflict some pain; but it is probably not a tithe of what we are accustomed to think it. The victims of their rapacity are merely physical beings. As such they are capable of physical delights and sufferings, and nothing more. They have no view of the future. The tenacity of life, the dread of death, and the agonizing uncertainty of the future so natural to man, are, in their case, comparatively nothing. Consciousness means nothing, in strictly organic life. Even sensitiveness is greatly reduced. Every thing is less acute than in the higher organism of man. The head of a dragon-fly will continue to eat after it is severed from the body. A worm may be bisected, and still get along with apparent comfort. It cannot be that there is much pain in these operations. Judged by our own sufferings in such a case, it would be vastly exaggerated. Bearing this in mind, we can better understand that "law of merciless and incessant destruction" among animals, as the pessimist is pleased to term it. Look at the case. An animal has filled up his plenum of physical life and pleasure. He must die in some way. He meets his death by violence; a few well-directed blows at the nervous centres; a brief struggle, in which the excitement of the contest deadens the pain of the wounds; and all is quickly over. A moment ago he en-

joyed the fulness of animal life ; now it is gone, and that
is all. If we lay mere sentiment aside, we can see that
this method of death is no worse than that slow decay and
protracted pain which must otherwise turn into a prolonged burden, a life whose only value is found in its
capacity for physical pleasure. It would seem, at least,
that this famous *carnivorous* argument against the goodness of God must be greatly minimized. It is certainly
true that health and pleasure are predominant among un-
domesticated animals, and that nature inflicts far less pain
upon them than man does upon those that serve him.

But this is not all. We likewise over-estimate human
suffering. We thrust ourselves under other men's burdens. We judge of them by their supposed weight upon our
own shoulders. In so doing we ignore those external and
internal adaptations of life which are constantly at work
reducing the severities of human experience. This is a
great mistake. The truth is that man's versatility is without limit ; he can become accustomed to almost any thing.
Life uniformly and readily adjusts itself to its environment. Every man's burden is fitted to his back, and his
back to his burden. If I wantonly trade burdens with
another man, I destroy the adjustment, and get to myself
an intolerable load which to him may have been as nothing. Nay, it may have been light as air, pleasant as sun-
shine, sweet as honey. The learned savant passes by the
hut of the peasant and greatly pities him in his state of
lowliness, ignorance, and physical toil. But his sympathy
is wasted. For that same peasant is merry at heart and
free from care. He goes singing at his work, and only
wonders how any sane man can deliberately shut himself
up and waste his life over dull and musty books. Such a
life to him would be worse than the prison or the rack.

One man's happiness may be on a lower plane than another's, but it is happiness nevertheless. It would be a great mistake to label it misery simply because it fails to conform to our particular pattern of happiness. But this very mistake we are constantly making.

These considerations will serve to reduce the physical suffering of the world to a point far below our ordinary estimates. The fact of suffering still remains, however, and calls for explanation. The following suggestions are offered in answer to this demand.

(1) *Suffering is Exceptional in the World.*

In the aggregate it may be very great, but proportionately it is extremely small. Most animals are comparatively free from pain. And even man, with all the aches and ills that flesh is heir to, is not subject to much physical suffering. Pain asserts itself, and is more clamorous than pleasure ; but, after all, it occurs but seldom. If the average number of moments of pain that each man now living has suffered during the past year were accurately ascertained, and the average of pleasurable moments likewise computed, and then if these respective averages were multiplied by the whole number of men, and their ratio taken, it would be found that the pain of the world is but a very small *per cent.* of its pleasures. To the most of us there come ten days of health to one of disease—a month of physical pleasure to an hour of physical pain. Health is the rule ; suffering the exception.

(2) *Suffering Ministers to Life and Safety.*

Pain is a monitor. It discloses dangers of body and of mind, and incites us to avoid them in the interest of health and happiness. If its monitions are heeded they are neither severe nor frequent. The first indigestion is not dyspepsia, nor the first cough consumption. But if they are neglected, what rational being can complain of their frequent repetition or of their increased severity? Suffering makes the experience of fools a dear school, and of course the greater the folly is the greater the suffering must be.

(3) *Suffering is a Penalty of Law.*

Law must have penalties, and must be inexorable. But a penalty which involves no suffering is not a penalty. If men will violate law, they must suffer the consequences. If obedience to physical law brings physical pleasure, disobedience must bring physical pain. The laws themselves are beneficent and good; so far as we can see, they are necessary even. But they are not coercive; men may yield to them, work under them, and live by them, or they may totally ignore them to their own misery and destruction. For these painful results the laws themselves are not at all responsible.

(4) *Suffering is Incident to Mental Growth.*

Growth in knowledge and intellectual power is not in itself a painful process. On the contrary, it is positively pleasurable. But, nevertheless, it is subject to conditions and limitations. These are necessary and must be observed. A man must not pursue useful knowledge even, in any manner and to any extent whatever, and it is often the mission of pain to remind him of this fact. A nervous headache is an uncomfortable affair, but it has saved many an ambitious youth from suicide by an over-dose of truth.

And then the very conditions of pleasure and pain furnish every man with a practical problem whose proper solution brings intellectual rewards as well as physical.

(5) *Suffering Increases Happiness.*

This statement is no less true than paradoxical. One moment of pain emphasizes a whole day of physical health, whose pleasure would otherwise scarcely be noticed. Indeed, it has become proverbial that men do not value the joy of health until an occasional pang of disease reminds them of its worth. Monotony is burdensome to most men, and contrast heightens all enjoyments. Pain exists for pleasure's sake, and there seems to be just about enough of it to disclose at their best the general joys of life.

(6) *Suffering Leads to Righteousness.*

Correct and upright living in a world of fierce temptations and angry passions is attained only by struggle and severity. Pain of body often purifies the soul. The problem of the existence of moral evil in the soul will be discussed hereafter. But certain it is that physical pain often becomes the means of its removal. Inasmuch as pain does this, it is a blessing, and not a curse ;—a thing of love, and not of hate. It leads men upward to enlarged and noble living. If the human race were robbed of its inheritance of noble lives made heroic through suffering, it would be morally poor indeed.

(7) *Suffering is Largely Unnecessary.*

The aggregate of suffering actually endured in the world at any given time is greatly in excess of what it need be. It could be readily reduced. Man could diminish it if he would. By far the severest sufferings in the world are matters of voluntary infliction by man himself. Human heedlessness, cruelty, and vice are chargeable with nine tenths of the pains of life. Man is vastly more savage than nature. He has no right to complain of the existence of suffering in the world until, instead of wantonly multiplying it, he has done his utmost to remove it.

2. AS TO SOCIAL EVIL.

The optimist admits the existence of social evils in the world. Wherever man exists, society is found; wherever society exists, social evils abound. This has always been so; and while man is an imperfect being, it will continue to be so. All that the pessimist has said concerning social inequalities, caste, oppression, injustice, tyranny, anarchy, revolution, and war, is literally true. But his inference from these facts is not true.

There are two remarks to be made in explanation of social evils:

(1) They are the direct results of human depravity—the natural outflow of sin. They are simply moral evils in a social setting. The discussion of the next topic will therefore apply with equal force to them.

(2) They are self-corrective. A glance at the pages of history discloses this fact. Oppression breeds anarchy, anarchy breeds war, war brings on revolution, revolution advances liberty and destroys oppression. So universal and proverbial is this tendency, that it has given us the historical aphorism, " Revolutions never go backwards." War is always fruitful of good, as well as of evil; and the good preponderates. The bloodier the war is, the greater the good that flows from it. The great battles of the world have marked the epochs of its progress. This must be so; for the deeper the disease may be in the body politic, the keener must be the lance that probes it.

Social evils are slowly correcting each other. It is true that in the process one extreme continually begets another. The pendulum of progress has still a mighty sweep, but it is steadily approaching the centre of the arc, and is drawing men with it.

3. AS TO MORAL EVIL.

As already intimated, moral evil is at the heart of the problem that the optimist would fain solve. Sin is the dark fact of the universe. In approaching its discussion, I make two stages.

(1) *Suppose its Origin to be Explained.*

Let it be granted, for the present, that moral evil exists, and that its origin in the universe is not incompatible with the goodness of God. On this hypothesis, the whole system of things can easily be justified.

(a) *The existing world is the best possible world.*—To the pessimist's argument that the best possible system of things would be perfect, and that therefore this imperfect world is not the best possible, we reply: The best possible created system *as an end in itself*, is a contradiction ;· for that end, however good, can still be increased in quantity, till it reaches the infinite. But that infinite is God himself. *As a means to an end*, a created system may be the best possible, or the worst possible. All depends upon its fitness to achieve the end desired. Now, if this world is a mediate system, designed for the moral perfection of man, it must be judged by its relation to this moral purpose. That it is so designed, is the common belief of mankind. Kant says: " The most vulgar minds agree that man can be the final end of the creation, only as a moral being." But the rational end of man is not mere animal pleasure. His true happiness cannot be secured apart from the development, regulation, and perfection of his spiritual nature. Granting, then, that the rational purpose of creation is to establish imperfect moral beings in a voluntary state of eternal virtue, it is clear that the existing system is the very best possible for that purpose. But if it is not, let the pessimist propose a better than the present one, or at least an equal to it. When he has done this it will be time enough to entertain his senseless quibble about the best possible system of things.

(*b*) *The so-called cruelty of nature vanishes.*—Mr. Mill confronts the optimist with the statement that nature is cruel, that cosmic forces go straight to their end, and crush men to death on the road. He quotes Pope's famous line, "Shall gravitation cease when you go by?" and plainly intimates that if nature, instead of being a cruel demon, were possessed of common human morality, then gravitation would cease rather than interfere with human life. Now this suggestion would necessitate a perpetual miracle. For there are always some men who are heedless or reckless enough to expose themselves to the dangers of natural law. After rejecting Gospel miracles, whose evident purpose was to make men better, by introducing and establishing a pure and holy religion, Mr. Mill turns around and demands a perpetual miracle whose operation must be baleful in the extreme. Instead of making men wise, law-abiding, and self-helpful, it would dwarf their best powers, and render them incompetent, exacting, and childish. Rousseau, applying this thought to the severities of the famous earthquake at Lisbon, says: "What would such a privilege signify? Would it not mean that the order of the world must change according to our caprices? that nature is subject to our laws? and that to forbid an earthquake in any place, we would only have to build a town there?" Such a disposition of events in nature would be lawless indeed. It is difficult to conceive a more unreasonable and inconsistent suggestion than Mr. Mill has made. Nature is not cruel when viewed as a means to the moral renovation and perfection of man.

(*c*) *The entail of sin is justified.*—The law of heredity is well established. Neither its existence nor its force need be questioned. By this law, evil is transmitted, as well as good. And why not? Ought sin to be protected against itself, and relieved of its own entail? Can it be repressed by coercive enactment? Is there any better method than this very law of inheritance, to display the hideousness of sin, and so deter men from it? Is it not the last link that binds many a man to virtue? The wayward and rebellious soul is often willing to pursue a life of sin, and take the consequences of his own folly; but the last remains of manhood in him rise in revolt against the idea of visiting upon his innocent and helpless child the penalties of his own transgression. And so passions are curbed and iniquity restrained by the reflex action of this very law.

But this is not all. There is another and better side to the question. If this law gives vice its own entail, it gives virtue its own also. It is not altogether destructive, as the pessimist would say; indeed, it is, on the whole, constructive in the highest and best sense. It transmits vastly more good than evil. Were it otherwise, the world would be growing worse and worse every day. The constant improvement of the world is a constant vindication of this law. And so shall it continue, until at length the stream of righteousness, reinforced by gathered ages, shall roll over the earth through the broadening channel of this same beneficent law.

(*d*) *The penalty of sin is likewise justified.*—The religious pessimist is wont to trouble himself about the final punishment of sin. He asks: " How can God be good, if he has created a moral being who he knew would pass his life in sin, and then fall into eternal misery?" Put that way, the question looks dark indeed. But turn the horoscope and look the other way. Let the pessimist say: "God has made me a rational being, and endowed me with conscience and free-will. He has put his love upon me and offered me eternal felicity, if I will only leave the ways of sin. I have spurned the offer, chosen sin rather than holiness, hell rather than heaven, and thereby deliberately shut myself out from the fellowship of the blessed. But, then, God is to blame for it all. He ought not to have given me freedom at all. Or, at least, he ought to have made me a saint, whether I would or not. And because he has not done this, he is a demon and I am clear." Put thus, this pessimistic plea looks childish and unreasonable.

The same question is sometimes proposed in a different form. " Why is temptation in the world? Why am I frail and peccable? Why must I continually resist and struggle? Why is not stainless virtue an inalienable possession, rather than a possible prize of life?" Now all these questions may be hard to answer. But one thing is certain ; the asking of them betrays the moral coward and sluggard. What man, who is a man, would want moral goodness forced upon him? What would such goodness be worth? Indeed, how could it be possible? It might be the goodness of the steam-engine or of an automaton, but not of a man. Virtue cannot be forced upon a free. being. All a true man asks is a fair chance to struggle and win it for himself. If God has given him the power to struggle and the will to decide, that is enough ; he asks no more. Coercive measures would reduce his manhood, and make him a mere machine or a pitiful moral beggar. Character must be free ; and sin must find in the sinner its proper arrest and its righteous punishment.

The discussion thus far has proceeded upon the hypothesis that moral evil exists in the world, and that its origin is consistent with the goodness of God. But the pessimist justly claims that this cannot be taken for granted without begging the main question. Attention must therefore be given to this point in the problem before us. It constitutes the second stage of the discussion.

(2) *The Origin of Moral Evil.*

Although logically first, I have placed this question chronologically last, because of its extreme difficulty. The force of the preceding discussion must be admitted, provided the fact of moral evil can be justified. But the objector may still ask: " Why is sin possible ? Why should it ever have had an existence in God's universe ? If he be omnipotent, why did he not prevent it in the beginning?" These questions are the hardest of all. There are a few suggestions to be made in reply which at least give some light.

(a) *God's omnipotence must not be misunderstood.—* It is not power to do the impossible. There are moral impossibilities which the Divine Omnipotence cannot destroy. Every child, for example, has, at some time, been puzzled to know how God can do every thing, and yet cannot tell a falsehood. But a man will scarcely ask such a question. For he has learned that infinite power cannot do all conceivable things, but only such things as are proper objects of power. Now the mentally impossible, or the rationally contradictory, is not a thing of power. No amount of power can set aside truth or annihilate reason. It is not within the range of God's omnipotence to make two and two five, or to commit any evil deed. And yet this is not cutting down the Deity; to suppose him capable of sin, would be to reduce him fatally. Eternal harmony and moral consistency belong to his character.

Viewed in this light, the famous Epicurean doctrine that if God be omnipotent he can prevent moral evil, must be taken with great allowance. Considerations may be adduced to show that the question of universal moral perfection is not a question of power at all. Before the pessimist is entitled to his conclusion, he must show that moral character is a thing to be determined by mere power. This he can never do.

(b) *Man's freedom must not be destroyed.*—Sin implies law. More than this, it implies righteous law. For the transgression of any other would not be sin. But a righteous law implies a righteous law-giver. A clean thing cannot come out of an unclean. And so the very existence of sin in the creature presupposes righteousness in the Creator.

Now the only remaining question is: " Why does not this righteous, omnipotent God prevent the transgression of his righteous law?" It is evident that he could do this. But so far as we can see, he could do it in no other way than by abridging man's freedom. When he gave that freedom he gave the possibility of sin. This possibility is necessary to moral character. For there can be neither virtue in avoiding that which cannot be done, nor vice in doing that which must be done. But a free moral system is better than a mechanical one.

Horace Bushnell has forcibly expressed this thought. " Is it any impeachment of God that he did not care to reign over an empire of stones? If he has deliberately chosen a kind of empire not to be ruled by force; if he has deliberately set his children beyond that kind of control, that they may be governed by truth, reason, love, want, fear, and the like, acting through their consent; if we find them able to act against the will of God, as stones and vegetables cannot; what more is necessary to vindicate his goodness than to suggest that he has given them, possibly, a capacity to break allegiance, in order that there may be a meaning and a glory in allegiance, when they choose it? There is, then, such a thing inherent in the system of powers as a possibility of wrong; for, given the possibility of right, we have the possibility of wrong."

The question, then, is not one of freedom and possible sin ; but of creation itself. Was it better for the Divine Being to make a world at all? Is its creation a thing of kindness or of cruelty? Is the universe a huge blunder, which ought to be blotted out at once and forever? Nay, would it have been better if, from all eternity, God had dwelt in the solitude of his own being?

These are solemn, earnest questions, and must not be charged with impertinence or sacrilege. They are the utmost push of the soul at the hidden arcana of its own being. We can but sympathize with this unconquerable desire to disclose the secret mysteries within. And yet the attempt to do so may be altogether unwise and vain. In our present state of knowledge it may be impossible to reach the last truth in the problem of being. Indeed, we must suppose that it is impossible. Our vision is too limited to sweep the universe and the two eternities. Our light is too dim to penetrate the inner depths of the

Infinite God.   Our intellect is too sluggish, our heart too
earthly, to reach the highest planes of Divine justice,
purity, and wisdom.

Any attempt to question God's motives in the creation
of the universe must be made with modesty and reverence.
God can be under no possible obligation to reveal his inmost thought.   Even if he should do so man could not
receive the revelation.   The finite cannot hold infinity.   It
is the part of human wisdom to read the truth he has
written out for us, and leave the rest to him in humility
and trust.   In this spirit two lines of thought have been
presented concerning this ultimate problem of created
being.   In the same spirit a third and fourth may be
distinctly and profitably itemized.

(*c*) *Man does not believe the universe to be a failure.*—He
does not regard his own life as such.   In itself it is a
priceless boon.   Although weighted down with inherited
evils and with his own personal sins, he still holds it as his
dearest treasure.   He will not give it up.   Who would
wish to be blotted out of existence forever?   How many
men are there who have found life such an intolerable
evil that they would gladly be rid of it?   A few such
there are, doubtless ; and they are the true, practical
pessimists.   All others are such by profession only.   But
this class of true pessimists is extremely small ; the great
bulk of humanity is not in that list.   Suicides are mentally
or morally deranged.   At least they are so regarded by
men in general.   And this is an unanswerable argument
in favor of human life.   Nothing is clearer than that men
do value existence, and thus practically declare the goodness of God.   The fact that this declaration is not intentional only adds to its force.   Moreover, it is the
greatest and the best among men and among the nations,

who invariably value human life most highly. Unless we are made to be strangely deceived, herein is a sure token of the true worth and sanctity of life, and the essential goodness of its Author.

To be sure it is always easy to assert that God ought to make human life better than it is; but that is not pessimism. It is downright impudence that calls for rebuke rather than argument.

(*d*) *The world is growing better continually.*—This is a plain, historical fact that no pessimist can successfully deny. The trend of things is upward. The stream of human events is clearer, purer, stronger, to-day than ever before. And still the clarifying process goes on. It may be slow and, at times, uneven, but it never stops and is never reversed. Compare with one another the times of Zoroaster, Nebuchadnezzar, Alexander, Cæsar, Charlemagne, Luther, Cromwell, and Gladstone; and no better evidence of the world's progress need be desired. Every thing noble, good, and worthy among men has advanced almost unmeasurably since the beginning of historic time; and every vile and ignoble thing has been correspondingly repressed. War, oppression, tyranny, slavery, abject poverty, and systematic cruelty are passing away from the abodes of civilized men. And civilization is advancing with firm and rapid step. Its present prevailing type is incomparably better than former types now supplanted. The people are happier, society is better, education is cheaper, truth and knowledge are freer, fraternal sympathy is broader, religion is purer, heaven is nearer, and earth is holier, as the centuries go by. What lover of humanity and truth and righteousness could wish the world set back a thousand years? The very mention of such a desire serves to emphasize the fact of its upward progress.

We are on the up grade. There may be steeps to climb ahead of us, but we will not turn back, for the worst of the road is already behind us. To what heights of intellect and soul we shall yet be led, we know not. But one thing is certain : the issue of every struggle hitherto has been righteousness and peace. And this is a pledge of the world's manifest destiny. There is in it a " Power not ourselves that makes for righteousness." That power is not an omnipotent demon. If he were, he would have made things intrinsically bad at the first, and would have sunk them into lower depths of iniquity with every passing year. No, the Author of this world must be a holy God, of infinite justice, purity, and love. We cannot fathom his being, or find out all his ways. " Clouds and darkness are indeed round about him ; but righteousness and judgment are still the habitation of his throne."

Sin still remains as a dark spot in the universe, but light shines all about it, and across its deepest blackness we begin to trace the golden threads of hope and love. The past, indeed, has not given us perfection ; but there are sure prophecies that it still awaits us in the future. To that future we press, and into its clearer light we bring our darkest problems with perfect confidence and hope.

Let the pessimist go on proclaiming his dark gospel of hate and despair, if he must. It is ours to preach the better gospel of love and hope. The bow of promise spans the sky. We will follow the light of its radiant arch till the morning shall dawn and the Day-star of eternal righteousness shall beam upon the earth.

REFERENCES.

Lord's " Natural and Revealed Theology."
Wallace's " Kant," Chapter XIV.
Ueberweg's " History of Philosophy."
Janet's " Final Causes."

CHAPTER V.

THE UNITY OF GOD; OR, THE MONISTIC ARGUMENT.

WHEN the Christian theist speaks of God, he means one Personal Being. The idea includes unity. But it may be questioned whether this Divine Unity is a philosophical necessity in all Theism. At least, the arguments hitherto set forth, may not be sufficient to prove the oneness of God. There may be in nature a single Being, having intelligence, volition, personality, and goodness; or there may be a thousand. There is nothing in the preceding arguments that absolutely forbids a plurality of divine beings. Take the case of design, for example. Suppose one hundred instances of design in nature to be clearly proved. These may be the executed purposes of one God or of one hundred gods; and their simple character as isolated designs can never determine the unity or diversity of their origin. The same is true of order-making in nature, and, to some extent, of the argument for a super-human Personality. At any rate, it is well to bring forward special proofs for the decision of this question. Is there one only God? or are there many? This question has had two answers. Historically, theistic thought has been constantly vibrating between Monotheism and Polytheism. For the establishment of Monotheism, there are three general lines of argument; namely, the *scientific*, the *philosophic*, and the *religious*.

SECTION I.

SCIENTIFIC MONOTHEISM.

A careful study of nature has always led men to the unity of God. This effect has followed in all ages and on all continents alike.   India, Egypt, Europe, and America bear witness to its unvarying certainty.   It is an undoubted historical truth.   Like all other history, it has a philosophical principle beneath it.   And this is the principle ; the unity of nature leads inevitably to the unity of God.   But men must learn to study nature and reason about the cosmos as a whole, before they can be sure of the unity of nature.   The natural facts that we see passing daily before us, are diverse in character and, in many cases, apparently hostile in purpose.   Thus it is that a cursory view of nature is quite as apt to disclose to men the existence of many gods, as of one.   True, there is one great fact in nature that has always given, even to the most indolent observers, a hint of its unity. I refer to the sun.   Its position, its apparent motion, its influence upon the earth, and its part in the sustenance of animal and vegetable life—all serve to suggest the unity and interdependence of nature.   But then there are the other heavenly bodies, somewhat like the sun and yet evidently diverse, independent, and therefore de-structive to cosmical unity.   It is only when men are so advanced in the study of nature as to penetrate to her inner truths, that they recognize in all her varied forms, the phenomena of one immense noumenal unit.   Finding that all nature is one, they are thereby convinced that the God of nature is one.   Natural Science, therefore, tends to Monotheism. The distinctive features of modern science are continually enforcing this truth more and more.   Notice a few of them.

1. GRAVITATION.

This principle has at length been shown to be universal. It is now admitted to be the widest generalization in nature. Newton's famous induction traced it to the moon, and thence to the bounds of the solar system. But its extension to the fixed stars was not demonstrated till more than a century after Newton's death. Indeed, its establishment beyond any peradventure, dates as late as the middle of the present century. This secret of the stellar heavens has been disclosed, without question, by a study of their *binary* and *multiple* systems. It has been demonstrated that the most distant star obeys the same law that controls the nearest planet. That simple but mysterious force which brings to earth the matured fruits of autumn and sends the waters to the sea, reaches out into the distant sky, and keeps a million worlds flying through its measureless depths. Here, then, is an endless chain that binds the universe in one. The God of gravitation cannot be many, he must be one; and that one must be the God of all nature. It must be one single will that employs this universal agency in dominating every atom, and thereby securing and preserving the physical harmonies of the universe. A diversity of gods in nature would mean an inevitable and interminable · conflict of laws ; and this conflict would issue in the destruction of worlds, the dismemberment of systems, and the prevalence of universal chaos. The unity and harmony of nature are rational proofs of the unity of God.

2. INTER-STELLAR ETHER.

Until recently the far-reaching depths of inter-stellar space were thought to be absolutely void. Physicists have now universally rejected this theory. It is conceded that these abysses of space are occupied by luminiferous ether (so-called for the sake of naming it), a substance of peculiar character and wonderful properties. It must be material substance, and yet it defies the tests of weight and measure ordinarily applied to matter. Its light-bearing qualities prove it to be almost infinitely hard and elastic; at the same time its non-resistance to moving bodies indicates its extreme tenuity. It is in a constant state of sensitive and tremulous movement. Morever, that movement is almost inconceivably heterogeneous in origin, direction, and character. Waves of light, heat, actinic power, or electricity are continually advancing in all directions from millions of central spheres. The mode of their motion is a matter of bewildering complexity, and, at the same time, of unerring harmony and certainty. A mass of matter falls into the sun and disturbs the heated currents on its incandescent surface. Thereupon, a stream of electricity sets forth throughout the solar system. Instantly, sooner than its mode of motion can be described, or even the fact recorded, it has reached the earth, convulsed every magnetic needle, disabled every telegraph office, and produced all the well known phe-nomena of an electric storm. And this is but one of the myriad movements constantly going on throughout this luminiferous ether. Still there is not a jar nor a jostle. The numberless interlacing threads of movement, with inconceivable speed, and without disturbance or delay, are pursuing their individual ends. They traverse one broad highway—they are parts of one boundless system. Here, then, is the fathomless ocean of physical being. All worlds and planets and stars are immersed in it; and none can go beyond it.

The God who made it and filled it must be the one God over all; for it includes all.

3. SPECTRUM ANALYSIS.

To the spectroscope all nature is one. The chemical elements of the earth are disclosed in the lines of the solar spectrum. Sodium, calcium, magnesium, potassium, cadmium, chromium, iron, cobalt, nickel, lead, and a dozen other well known chemical elements are prominent in the atmosphere of the sun, no less than in the structure of the earth. Indeed, the spectra of nearly all terrestrial elements have been distinctly traced in the chromosphere. The same is true of the planets, and, so far as observations have been conducted, of the farthest fixed stars also. To whatever celestial body the scientist turns his spectroscope, he finds the same unmistakable lines of oxygen, hydrogen, sodium, and iron. As the new and wonderful science of spectrology advances, doubtless other stellar elements will, from time to time, be identified with those of the earth. Already stars, planets, nebulæ, and even erratic comets have been interviewed by this most persistent questioner of the sky, and all have told the same story of their chemical composition. Worlds in apparent formation, incandescent worlds, worlds partially cooled, like Jupiter and Saturn ; planets like the Earth and Mars, with cooled atmosphere and solid surface—all yield up to the spectroscope the same chemical secrets. Even the cold, rigid, and airless moon tells the same story—a voice from the cosmical tomb declaring the unity of nature and of God.

The spectroscopist has far outstripped the marvels of telegraphy. He has practically annihilated inter-stellar space with the same ease with which the electrician has annihilated terrestrial space. With perfect confidence he sends his message to the most distant star, receives instantaneous returns at pleasure, and sits at his desk leisurely computing the movements and examining the chemistry of celestial bodies billions upon billions of miles away. As the result of this cosmical catechism, far-reaching and almost limitless as it is, he announces to us that the whole physical universe is bound in one, composed everywhere of the same elements—an absolute constitutional unit.

4. TERRESTRIAL LIFE AND MOVEMENT.

The unity of nature is forcibly displayed in the development of life upon the earth. The functions and phases of life are indeed many and various, but the life-principle is the same in them all and through them all. It has the same uniform physical basis to start with. Albuminous compounds are found in every organism, high or low, simple or complex. And then there is the same development and support of the life-germs. Processes of selection, appropriation, and assimilation are common to all forms of life. Still further, the same life-cycle is disclosed everywhere. Each life has its successive periods of growth, maturity, and decay. Each life depends upon a preceding life, and in like manner bequeaths itself to the future. The individual dies that the species may live. The law of descent has passed upon all animate nature.

These truths have become so familiar to modern science that their force is often lost. But they do certainly point to the unity of nature and of its Author.

The movement of organism upon the earth, from year to year and from age to age, discloses an evident unity of purpose and end. In the busy laboratory of nature all tends to the production of one final compound. Crass matter is first organized into vegetable growth. Vegetable life is destroyed for the support of animal life. Animals die that man may live. Cosmic history is not equally complete at every moment. It moves on to a certain end. It is difficult to doubt that the earth is expressly fitted up for man's residence upon it. More than this. It is manifestly adapted to man's development, growth, and indefinite progress in intelligence and righteousness. Under this one guiding purpose, modern science traces cosmical movements all the way backward, as far as phenomena can carry them. From the very start, man seems to have been the intended outcome of creation. At every succeeding age lengthening vistas of purpose open to the view, all finding alike their focus, their explanation, and their justification in the final development of one being—man.

But this movement is by no means confined to animal and vegetable life. It pervades inanimate nature as well. Absolute rest is nowhere to be found. Every atom is in motion. The more nature is studied the more striking becomes the fact of universal and unceasing energy. Motion implies force; force, in its constant activity, implies an animating principle that is both absolute and eternal. How shall we describe this eternal source of all phenomena? It will not do to call it simple force; considered apart, there is no meaning in that term. It may satisfy the scientist who seeks only for facts and laws. It is useful, indeed, as an abstract symbol by which to designate conveniently a universality of fact. But it cannot satisfy the philosopher, whose proper search is after the nature and causes of things. Neither can this source of phenomena be regarded as in any wise a material thing. It is the source of matter, and therefore cannot be matter itself. Matter, after all, is but the recognized seat of external phenomena. But this eternal source of things is the ultimate reality of the universe, back of all phenomena and back of all matter. What is it like? In answering this question we are forced to the one only reality that every man knows directly for himself; and that is his own conscious intellect. His own selfdom is the form of being and of knowledge in which he is bound to conceive of that Eternal Reality, whose manifestations of power he sees everywhere throughout the material universe. That Being cannot, then, be material. He must be psychical, personal, moral. And this is the one only eternal and living God.

On this subject John Fiske has expressed his thought most beautifully: "When from the dawn of life we see all things working together for the evolution of the highest spiritual attributes of Man, we know, however the words may stumble in which we try to say it, that God is in the deepest sense a moral Being. The everlasting source of phenomena is none other than the infinite Power that makes for righteousness. Thou canst not by searching find Him out; yet put thy trust in Him, and against thee the gates of hell shall not prevail; for there is neither wisdom nor understanding nor counsel against the Eternal."

SECTION II.

PHILOSOPHIC MONOTHEISM.

The view of God's eternal unity, as thus far given, arises from a practical study of nature. It remains to be shown that pure philosophical inquiries lead to the same belief. The philosophic form of Monotheism is quite as prevalent as the scientific. It is the belief in one perfect, self-existent Being. He is conceived of as the ultimate, intelligent cause of all nature, and therefore as superior to it, yet not separate from it ; as the foundation of its substance, and therefore as beneath it, yet not merged into it ; as the constant source of its energy, life, and harmony, and therefore as within it, yet not restrained by it. He is absolute, sovereign, infinite. He is independent of creation, and is removed from it by all the lengths and depths of infinity ; and yet he is bound to it by the voluntary bands of his own creative energy. He is forever one ; and yet is the vital source of all existing things. Nearly all the great thinkers, of all ages and all countries, have been led, by the simple force of their philosophy, to some such monotheistic view of the Deity.

The most ancient philosophy in India taught the existence of such a Being. One of its writers says: " An omniscient and indestructible being is to be proved from the existence of effects, from the combination of atoms, from the sustained order of the universe, and from the traditional arts among men."

The *Hindu Vedanta* is in the same line, declaring: " Brahma is the all-knowing, all-powerful cause, from which come the production, continuance, and dissolution of the universe. Every soul is evolved from him and returns to him. He consists of joy. He is creator and creature, actor and act. He has neither beginning nor end, parts nor qualities ; he is immutable, and the only real substance." This sublime passage certainly has an odor of pantheism about it. But it teaches monotheism, beyond any sort of doubt.

So much for India. Let us now turn to Greece, and we shall find the same tokens of philosophic monotheism in the early history of that classic land.

Ecphantus taught the doctrine of an absolute world-ordering spirit, which was doubtless developed from the famous Pythagorean doctrine of the original "Monad."

Philolaus believed that "The director and ruler of all things is God; he is one and eternal, enduring and immovable, ever like himself, and different from all things beside him."

Xenophanes and the Eleatics taught that "God is eternal, one, spherical, neither bounded nor unbounded, neither moved nor unmoved."

Euclid of Megara declared: "The good is one, although called by many names, as intelligence, God, reason. The good remains ever immutable and like itself." Socrates was a teleologist, and asserted that good men are inspired by a supreme and Divine intelligence. Aristotle recognized God as the source of all motion, energy, and life. The Stoics likewise held to the unity of God. They argued that force is inseparably joined with matter; that the power which joins them is God; that the universe is a thing of general unity, as well as of individual variety; that its beauty and adaptation must have come from a thinking mind, and, therefore, prove the existence of Deity; that it contains parts endowed with consciousness, and therefore the whole, which must be more perfect than any of its parts, cannot be unconscious; and that this universal consciousness is the Deity himself. Cleanthes one of their number, indites a beautiful prayer to Jupiter, which begins thus: "O thou who hast various names, but whose essence is one and infinite! O Jupiter! first of immortals, sovereign of nature, who governest all, who subjectest all to one law, I salute thee."

But perhaps Plato, who, by reason of his continual and devout meditation concerning the Deity, has been called the "Divine Plato," has left us the strongest evidence of non-christian, philosophic Monotheism. From often-quoted passages in his writings, almost numberless terms have been taken, which describe the one only God. Among them are these: "Maker and Father of the universe," "God over all," "Creator of nature," "Architect of the world," "Cause of all things, whom it is hard to find out and impossible to declare," "The first God who always is, and never was made," "Always good, never evil," "Who cannot change for the better, and who will not change for the worse."

Thus far our quotations are all from philosophers of ancient times, and non-christian countries. They could not therefore have been influenced by the pure Monotheism of Christ and his Apostles. Moreover, scarcely any two of them can be said to be of the same school of philosophy. Selections have purposely been made from those who differ most radically in their general philosophical doctrines. And yet their belief in one Supreme Deity is wonderfully unanimous and striking. Quotations from the ancients might be indefinitely multiplied with the same result.

The annals of modern philosophy disclose the same unanimity on this subject, and that even more positive and striking than before. Nearly all the great thinkers of modern times, of whatever school of thought, have been forced to admit the existence of one supreme, perfect Being, who is the uncreated source of all things that exist. The names of Bacon, Descartes, Spinoza, Leibnitz, Kant, Schilling, Fichte, Hegel, Locke, Hamilton, Darwin, and Max Müller, will readily occur in this connection. Numerous quotations from their works could be brought forward to establish the fact of their belief in one Supreme Being. The general reader's familiarity with their views, however, renders such formal quotations unnecessary. With remarkable unanimity the philosophic thought of the day leads all thinkers to the unity of God. There are apparently a few notable exceptions. But they are such in appearance only. Herbert Spencer, for example, and the entire school of agnostics, do not deny the existence of such a Supreme Being. It is only the possibility of knowing and characterizing him that is questioned. In truth, his existence is almost universally conceded. And every advance in philosophy serves only to emphasize the unalterable conviction of mankind, that there is one supreme and eternal God.

SECTION III.

RELIGIOUS MONOTHEISM.

All religion refers to God in some form. It is the binding link between Deity and humanity. Neither the ancient Buddhist nor the modern atheist has succeeded in rendering worship without a God. Man is compelled by nature to seek after some great, superior Being above himself, and when he has found him, to worship him. Thus far, religion is natural to man. If there be a God, therefore, and he be one, this truth addresses man as a religious being, no less than as a scientist or a philosopher. Nay more, for it must concern him more profoundly and vitally by far, as a religious being, than in any other capacity whatever. In this way, and in this only, it concerns him universally. Few men are scientists or philosophers; but all men are religionists. The faith-faculty is universal; and may be justly expected to lead to one only God, provided there be one only God. In this just expectation, the student of religious history is not disappointed. An examination of the great religions of the earth gives convincing proofs of monistic tendencies in nearly all of them. As a matter of fact religious Monotheism has been almost world-wide. It exists in various types and various degrees of clearness, which may, in general, be divided into two classes : *Pure Monotheism* and *Imperfect Monotheism.*

I. PURE MONOTHEISM.

By Pure Monotheism is meant the worship of only one God, who is recognized as infinite and eternal, and as separated by this vastness of infinity, from any and all other beings whatsoever. It is the worship of God not as *a* God, but as *the* God—the one only God. He is not merely one among many Gods, nor even the supreme Source and Sovereign of Gods ; but he is absolutely the only God actual or possible. Moreover, he is an intelligent, personal Being. Pure religious Monotheism avoids the two extremes of polytheism and pantheism.

There are just three great religions that teach this true unity of God. They are Judaism, Christianity, and Mohammedanism. It is worthy of note that these three monotheistic religions, and these alone, have laid claim to universality among men. Others are narrow, tribal, ethnic, designed for one race or one country alone. Even Buddhism, which in some respects seems otherwise, is confined to the Mongolian race. These three alone have been missionary religions, striving to be universal—aiming at catholicity in some sort. But Judaism is but an arrested form of Christianity, and has fallen from its high aim. Mohammedanism likewise has failed to fulfil its early promise, and becomes more and more local. So that

Christianity remains the only consistent cosmopolitan religion upon the earth. It teaches the unity and Fatherhood of God, and the unity and brotherhood of man. But Mohammedanism is equally emphatic as to the unity of God. The Koran repeatedly avers that there is one God only, and Mohammed is his Prophet.

2. IMPERFECT MONOTHEISM.

It is quite true that pure monotheism is confined to three religions. But to stop with this statement would be to make a gross misrepresentation of monistic tendencies in the religious world. By far the greater amount and wider sweep of this tendency is to be found in what may be called Imperfect Monotheism. This term designates any and every adequate recognition of a Supreme Being in the universe. Along with this idea may be found polytheistic or pantheistic tendencies of every possible shade. But through it all, from the nature-worship of India to the anthropomorphism of Western Europe, runs this inconquerable belief in the existence of one Supreme God. Polytheism seems to be an after-growth, a sort of religious makeshift. Imperfect men, oppressed by their own guilt, and awed in the presence of a pure and perfect God, are prone to find relief by peopling the sky with beings midway between themselves and the Deity. Added to this religious exigency there is a purely philosophical speculation, which seems not unreasonable. It runs thus. If God has made, upon this gross, material earth, such an exalted spiritual being as man, why may he not have made, in the higher realm of spirits, beings immeasurably superior to man? Indeed, is it not very probable that he has made such beings? and that, too, ages upon ages before the first man stood upon the earth? And if there are such beings, may they not have some agency in the lives and destinies of men ? And if so, is it not the dictate of reason as well as of religion, to propitiate their favor and engage their support by acts of worship? Manifestly it is but a short and easy step from these philosophic queries, to the grossest polytheism. Where monistic religions stop with angels, paganism goes on to heroes, gods, and demi-gods innumerable. This is, indeed, a grievous mistake; but it is merely a natural corruption of monotheism, due to the weakness, ignorance, and indolence of men. James Freeman Clarke, in his book entitled, " Ten Great Religions," has called attention to the facts just recited, and, with great patience of scholarship, has traversed the entire field of imperfect religious Monotheism.

The results of his investigations agree substantially with those of other workers in the same field. He finds traces of Monotheism everywhere. This truth may be enforced by selecting from his list some religions that are ancient, some that are modern, and designating them geographically.

(1) *Persian Religion.*

The ditheism of the Zend-Avesta has been mentioned in another connection. We must now inquire whether monotheism, or pure dualism is, after all, the doctrine of that sacred book. It is quite true that Ormazd and Ahriman are represented as coëqual and rival deities, and that the presence of evil in the world is thus explained. But this is not the whole truth of the matter. We find, upon further examination, that " Infinite Time " or " All-embracing Time " is the Creator of both Ormazd and Ahriman ; and there are distinct intimations that, behind these two opposing powers of good and evil, there remains the measureless background of ultimate being, from which

both have proceeded and into which both shall finally
return. And then the sovereign restorer or savior, under
the name of Sosioçh, is expected by all devout Parsî to
come at the consummation of all things, accomplish the
resurrection, and introduce a kingdom of unalloyed happiness and peace forever. There are several undoubted
passages in the Avesta which refer to this coming resurrection.

But this means the destruction of Ahriman and the
immortal coronation of Ormazd. So this troublesome
ditheism, however long and persistent, is not eternal,
after all. It is finally dissolved in a sort of pantheistic
monotheism—a belief in one infinite and eternal Being.
According to the Zend-Avesta good shall at last prevail
over evil, and God shall be all in all.

(2) *The Religion of China.*

Nearly five thousand years ago the Chinese, we are told,
had associated the idea of a Supreme Being with that of
the visible heavens. One word was used to designate
them both. That word was Ti, the name of God and the
name óf the sky. Shang-ti was the Supreme God or the
Supreme Heaven.

A little reflection will convince any one of the eminent
naturalness of this connection. The contemplative China-
man early recognized, and learned to worship, the powers
of nature around and above him. But he perceived that
they were all changeable, conditioned, and finite. Even
the all-producing sun suffered the nightly eclipse of his
glory. But this vast, unbounded sky, surrounding all
things, containing all things, conditioning all things, un-
fathomable, unbroken, unconditioned, unchanging, and
infinite—seemed to him the fittest emblem of the infinite

and eternal God ; and so he used the same terms to indi-
cate both. Dr. Legge, a profound Oriental scholar, in
speaking on this subject says : " These characters show us
that the religion of the Chinese, five thousand years ago,
was a monotheism ; and these two names have kept the
monotheistic element prominent in the prevailing religion
of China, down to the present time.

(3) *The Religion of Egypt.*

More than twenty-three centuries ago, Herodotus travelled in Egypt, and, according to his custom everywhere,
studied carefully the civilization of that ancient country,
with special reference to the habits, customs, character,
and religion of the people. As a result of his observations, he declared that the Egyptians of Thebes, one of
the oldest and grandest cities, worshipped one Supreme
God who had neither beginning nor end of existence.
Several centuries later, another writer quotes from an old
Hermitic book as follows : " Before all the things that
actually exist, and before all beginnings, there is one God,
prior even to the first God and King, remaining unmoved
in the singleness of his own unity."

De Rougé, a distinguished Egyptologist, in describing
the Egyptian doctrine of God, the world, and man, says :
" I said ' God,' not ' The Gods.' The first characteristic
of the Religion is the unity of God,—God, one, sole, and
only, no others with him. He is the only being—living in
truth. He has made every thing."

A further proof of ancient Egyptian monotheism may
be found in their religious hymns and sacred formulas. In
one of these hymns, addressed to Amun-Ra, the supreme
God of Thebes, and said to have originated not less than
five thousand years ago, we find the following words : " Hail

to Thee, Amun-Ra, Lord of the thrones of the earth, the oldest existence, ancient of heaven, support of all things; chief of the gods, father of the gods, lord of truth. Thou art the one, maker of all that is, the one; the only one; maker of gods and men; giving food to all. Welcome to thee, father of the father of the gods; we worship thy spirit which is in us."

It matters not if Egypt did worship lords many and gods many; no one can deny that such a hymn as this breathes the prayer of the true monotheist.

(4) *The Religion of India.*

At first sight it would seem that the original Vedic religion was utterly devoid of the monotheistic idea. There is no Supreme Deity of definite name and nature. As heretofore noticed, the divine supremacy is amiably passed around among the gods. It is attributed variously to Varuna, the heavens; Surya, the sun; Indra, the atmosphere; Agni, fire; and to many others. This would seem to obliterate all monotheism. Two reflections, however, will show that it does no such thing.

(*a*) *The character ascribed in turn to these gods is supreme and monistic.*—Varuna, for instance, is described in the Rig-Veda as " universal king, divine, omniscient, who has made heaven and the earth, who embraces within himself the three worlds; who causes the sun to shine and the winds to blow; who, by marvellous skill, makes the rivers to run forever into the sea, but never fill it; who is unchanging and unchangeable; from whom no one can escape, even if he flee beyond the sky; who can drive away evil, and purify the soul from sin, preserve life, forgive transgression and bestow eternal happiness upon the good."

Now this is clearly the description of one supreme God. The only trouble is that Agni and Indra and all the rest have the same attributes bestowed upon them in turn. This is the puzzle ; but it is cleared up by a further consideration. It is this.

(*b*) *These gods, though differently named, were believed to be one.*—They were all the same in identity and essential being. This truth might be inferred from the fact that these various prayers and sacred hymns were all contained in the same book ; and, without the slightest feeling of incongruity, were actually used by the same worshippers. But fortunately we are not left to mere conjecture in the matter. This identity of being is expressly stated in several passages. Take the following from the Rig-Veda : " They call him Indra, Mitra, Varuna, Agni. Sages name variously that which is but one. Agni becomes Varuna in the evening ; rising in the morning, he becomes Mitra ; as Savitri, he moves through the air ; becoming Indra, he glows in the middle of the sky."

And so it turns out that even these extreme polytheistic vagaries of the Vedas have beneath them the same spirit of monotheism which pervades the religious world everywhere.

(5) *Scandinavian Religion.*

The Norsemen worshipped twelve principal gods. Odin and Loke were evident leaders among them. The former embodied the principle of good, the latter that of evil. Herein there might seem to be an irreconcilable dualism. And yet we need not seek far in the mythological lore of their pantheon to discover traces of that same inevitable, underlying monotheism which we find at the roots of so many other religions. A single passage will be sufficient to establish this statement.   It is taken from one of their sacred books called the prose " Edda."

"' I must now ask thee,' said Gangler, ' who are the gods that men are bound to believe in ? '   ' There are twelve gods,' replied Har, ' to whom divine honors ought to be rendered.'   ' Nor are the goddesses,' added Jafnhar, ' less divine and mighty.'   ' The first and eldest of the Aesir,' continued Thridi, ' is Odin.   He governs all things, and although the other deities are powerful, they all serve and obey him as children do their father.   Frigga is his wife. Frigga alone knoweth the destinies of all, though she telleth them never.' "   " Odin is named Alfadir (All-Father), because he is the father of all gods ; and also Valfadir (Choosing Father), because he chooses for his sons those who fall in combat.   For their abode he has prepared Valhalla and Vingólf, where they are called heroes. He hath formed heaven and earth and the air, and all things thereunto belonging."

It is clear that this passage points back to a time when the Norsemen were monotheists.   If Odin was father of the gods, there was certainly a time when as yet none of his divine offspring were born, and he himself was the only god in the universe.

(6) *Religions among Savages.*

The lowest tribes of savages could not reasonably be expected to rise to the lofty conception of one only and infinite God.   Indeed, it is boldly asserted, in certain quarters, that some of these tribes have no religion whatever, and never had any.   This is a serious mistake.   The statement, heretofore made in this work, that religion is universal, is capable of abundant proof ; and this is the proper place to verify it.

1st. RELIGION IS UNIVERSAL.

To prove this statement it will be necessary to show that the very lowest and most brute-like men are religious beings. But here a difficulty meets us. It is quite uncertain who are the lowest types of men. Specialists, who have devoted themselves to ethnic studies, are not at all agreed as to their estimates. There are several races, widely scattered geographically, to each of which the bottom place has been assigned by learned ethnologists. Fortunately, this disputed question need not be decided here. If it can be shown that every one of these disputed tribes has some religion, the point of the present discussion will be gained without puzzling ourselves over their relative rank. But this can easily be done. The evidence is both abundant and credible.

The principal tribes to whom reference has been made, together with the respective authorities by whom they have been assigned to the bottom of the scale, are as follows :

LOWEST TRIBES.	AUTHORITIES.
Australians, Bushmen, Hottentots, and Terra del Fuegans . . .	Waitz.
Australians	D'Urville.
Terra del Fuegans	Darwin and Wallis.
Bushmen	Burchell.
Lapps and North American Indians .	Lubbock.
Andaman Islanders . . .	Owen.

Now all these tribes have been found to have religious ideas both distinct and positive.

(*a*) *Australians.*—Dr. Lang says concerning them : " They have nothing whatever of the character of religion or religious observance to distinguish them from the beasts that perish." This is certainly damaging testimony, if true. But it is not true. Mr. Ridley, who travelled largely among these tribes, says that he found everywhere among them traditions concerning divine beings ; and that in truth they are ditheists, worshipping two principal Gods, one the creator of the world, and the other the source of all evil. Indeed, the learned Dr. Lang himself has rendered his own testimony nugatory by stating that these same tribes attribute small-pox to the power of an evil spirit, whom they propitiate with offerings of honey, and, in extreme cases, even with human sacrifices. The Australians are certainly religionists.

(*b*) *Bushmen and Hottentots.*—Sir John Lubbock thinks these tribes have nothing which approaches the idea of an avenging or rewarding deity. But Livingstone was convinced that they worship a male and a female deity. Waitz declares that they have a religion ; that they worship the moon with dances and songs. Kolb says that they believe in a divine creator and ruler, and call him " the great Captain." The moon is their visible God ; but they believe in an invisible Deity whom they call " Jouma Tik-quoa," or " God of Gods."

(*c*) *Terra del Fuegans.*—Mr. Darwin distinctly declares that these people have no religion whatever. Now, Mr. Darwin is high authority on questions of fact, and he visited these people personally. But, unfortunately for his testimony in this regard, he himself indiscreetly mentions the fact that these same people are accustomed to blow into the air, in order to keep away evil spirits. Phillips, a missionary among them, was once complaining of the heat of the sun ; whereupon a native exclaimed : " Do not say that ; or he will hide himself, and it will be cold." Verily they believe in the sun-god.

(*d*) *The Lapps.*—Some authors have supposed these tribes to be entirely without religion. But Klemm, a learned writer, declares this to be a mistake, and describes their religion thus: " They have gods of the sky, of the thunder, and other elementary deities. They also worship the sun and water."

(*e*) *North American Indians.*—Sir John Lubbock says that these savages " have no religion, nor any idea of God." It is worthy of remark, in passing, that Sir John has found quite a list of these non-religious peoples. He has an evident relish in discovering them ; and, in his own opinion, has attained some success in such discovery. In truth, this distinguished gentleman has either been strangely unfortunate in his sources of information, or else strangely obtuse in the recognition of religious facts. Certain it is, at any rate, that where other men see abundant tokens of religion, he sees none at all.

In regard to these Indians, it is certain that the Esquimaux and Greenlanders worship spirits of the sea, spirits of the mountains, spirits of the fire, spirits of the battle, and above all a mighty wind-spirit. Even the " Root-digger " Indians have objects of worship. Missionaries and United States Government Agents have repeatedly testified to this fact.

(*f*) *The Andaman Islanders.*—The inhabitants of these islands in the Bay of Bengal, have also been declared to have no trace of religion. They are said to be indescribably low and brutish ; and yet they have quite a complicated religion. Day describes it from personal observation. He states that they worship the sun and moon, principally ; and also genii of the waters, forests, and mountains whom they suppose to be the agents of the deities. They also believe in an evil spirit who sends the storms, and in a future life. Captain Hockoe gives substantially the same report concerning them.

From this brief reference to the very lowest types of men yet discovered on the earth, it is manifest that not one of them is without religion. And yet, at some time or other, this utter absence of religion has been boldly asserted concerning every one of them. Upon better acquaintance with the language, character, and customs of these tribes, this assertion has invariably been shown to be false. And what has been, in this respect, doubtless will continue to be in the future. As new tribes are discovered, some men will continue their hasty and reckless statements, to the effect that these new tribes have no religion among them. But all such statements, by whomsoever made, must hereafter be received with a tremendous discount. We must not believe them, until the most exact knowledge of the tribes concerned shall enable us to judge intelligently of their truth or falsity. In the light of that clearer knowledge, they may justly be expected to dissolve and disappear, as their predecessors have invariably done.

Meanwhile it is perfectly safe to assert that religion is universal—that man always and everywhere is a religious being. Modern discoveries, instead of unsettling this belief, have given the most remarkable and unexpected testimonies in its favor. But before leaving this subject of the universality of religion, a final remark remains to be made.

(*g*) *The highest races of men are likewise religious.—* Religion encompasses the earth. Like a chain with numberless and diverse links, it binds together the whole human race. There are men, however, who seem bent on breaking the chain, at whatever cost. Having been completely foiled in their attempt at the lower end, they have traversed the entire chain, and are now tussling away vigorously at the upper end. Forced to admit that the *lowest* men have religion, they now assert that the *highest* men have none ; that religion belongs to the dark ages and the uncivilized types; that men outgrow it as they do any other superstition ; and that as general knowledge advances among men, religion recedes.

Let us examine this statement. If it be true anywhere, it will certainly hold in the United States. For of all countries on earth, this is certainly the one where intelligence among the masses has been carried the furthest, where the force of religious traditions is the weakest, and where there is absolute freedom from all restraint, either political or moral, by any church establishment whatsoever. If advancing civilization tends to repress the religious spirit, surely this tendency must be most manifest in a country like this. But how stands the case ? In 1850 there were in the United States, 38,000 churches, with 14,000,000 sittings ; in 1870, there were 63,000 churches, with 21,000,000 sittings. During these twenty years, the value of church property increased from $87,-000,000 to $354,000,000. It must be borne in mind that this immense outlay was not in any sense a tax upon the people, but every dollar of it was contributed as a free-will offering to the cause of religion. And this increase of 400 per cent. in these contributions, corresponds to an increase in general population of less than 80 per cent. The entire population at the close of this period was 39,000,000. Making proper deduction for invalids, infants, the aged, and such other persons as could not attend church, these accommodations were amply sufficient for 80 per cent. of the population. But again, take another line of facts. The relative percentages of increase among church members and the entire population show steady gains in religion. Since 1800, this relative increase has been constant, until now there are not far from 15,000,000 church members in this country. That means not less than 40,000,000 adherents to the cause of religion. From 1850 to 1880, the population of the United States increased 116 per cent. During the same period, church members increased 226 per cent., the number of churches 240 per cent., and of ministers 241 per cent. Dr. Dorchester, Dr. Strong, and others have brought out these facts with great force. And, indeed, there is no surer method of disclosing the religious condition and trend of any country, than by an appeal to just such facts. Their testimony is convincing; and it gives no hint of the decadence of religion in this country. On the contrary, it proves its continual and remarkable growth. And the same is true of other civilized countries. From the highest to the lowest of men, religion is universal. Its forms may change; but its vital power remains and grows continually.

2d. MONOTHEISM AMONG SAVAGES.

(a) *African tribes.*—Waitz speaks as follows of the African tribes: "The religion of the negro is usually considered as of a peculiar crude form of polytheism, and marked with the special name of Fetichism. A closer inspection shows that it is neither very peculiar nor exceptionally crude. A profounder investigation, such as has recently been made with success by several eminent scholars, leads to the surprising result that several negro tribes, who have not been influenced from the outside, have developed their religious ideas so far that, if we do not call them monotheists, we must admit that they have come very near the boundaries of true monotheism."

Max Müller declares that the tribes of West Africa worship a Supreme God, whom they believe to be a good being.

Cruickshank and other missionaries give the same testimony concerning the negroes of the Gold Coast. These negroes worship thousands of fetiches, but they believe in a Supreme Being, of whom they say, "God is the old one, he is the greatest, he sees me."

(*b*) *Central American tribes.*—In the ancient religion of Central America, there is the same tendency to Monotheism. Dr. Brinton states that he discovered it in prayers dedicated to the great Creator of the world. Some of the documents recording these prayers, date back many centuries. The following extract is from a translation of his.

"We bring forward the revelation of that which was hidden, the knowledge sent to us by him who creates. Speak his name ; honor your mother and father ; call him *Hurakan*, Soul of the earth, Soul of the sky, Creator, Maker ; . . . call on him and salute him. Hail! O Creator, Maker! thou seest and hearest us. Do not leave us, do not desert us!"

(*c*) *Other savage tribes.*—Examples might be multiplied. Australians, Polynesians, Esquimaux, South American Indians, and in fact all the tribes mentioned in the preceding argument for the universality of religion, might be called upon with equal success to testify concerning this widespread and persistent tendency toward Monotheism. But it is not necessary to dwell further on this point.

The argument for the unity of God is an argument of fact, than which nothing can be stronger. It is a threefold cord that cannot be broken. Science, Philosophy, and Religion, however discordant on other subjects, clasp hands here, and unite their voices in proclaiming the one only God.

Now if these three powerful factors in the world's history are actually coöperating in the interest of Monotheism, it is reasonable to infer that the aggregate of their results should be great and constantly increasing. That such is the case is susceptible of abundant proof.

Nearly one half the entire population of the globe are to-day under the control of pure Monotheism. A glance at the religious statistics of the world will verify this statement. There are 1,392,000,000 people now living upon the earth. Of these, nearly 400,000,000 are Christians and 200,000,000 Mohammedans. But both these religions teach the purest monotheism. Among the remainder, 175,000,000 Brahmins, 340,000,000 Buddhists, 80,000,000 Confucianists, and 100,000,000 Pagans or heathen, some form of imperfect Monotheism is widely prevalent.

A further fact must not be overlooked. Progress in knowledge, thought, science, culture, and civilization tends uniformly to the advancement of Monotheism. As a general rule, its strength is found among the foremost nations of the earth. Polytheism cannot stand before the conquering car of truth and progress. The world is rapidly advancing toward the universal belief in one only eternal and omnipotent God.

References :

Clarke's " Ten Great Religions."
Max Müller's " Science of Religion."
Fiske's " The Idea of God."
Darwin's " Descent of Man."
Loomis' " Astronomy.".
Strong's " Our Country."

CHAPTER VI.

INFINITY OF GOD; OR, THE CAUSAL ARGUMENT.

SECTION I.

NATURE OF THE INFINITE.

CONCERNING the general nature and the apprehension of the infinite, metaphysicians have disputed for forty centuries. Conflicting theories have long struggled for the mastery, and the struggle will doubtless go on. It is no part of the present purpose to enter that arena. Let the able contestants therein fight out their own battles. With one point in the conflict, however, this argument is vitally concerned. And that is, the infinity of God. Christian Theism has always insisted that God is a being of infinite perfections. In maintaining this claim, it will be necessary to touch briefly upon the nature of the infinite. We must first construe to our minds as clearly as possible, what we mean by infinity. McCosh, Porter, Harris, and other recent writers, have given special attention to this subject. A brief digest of their views is all that need be presented here.

1. THE INFINITE CANNOT BE KNOWN BY IMAGINATION.

The imagination always forms a picture of its object. But infinity is an abstraction and cannot be pictured. No abstraction can. Who can form an image, for example, of virtue, love, or truth? The infinite is a quality, and, like other qualities, is likewise incapable of being imaged. Softness, hardness, transparency, elasticity can never be pictured to the mind. Neither can infinity.

This is certainly true, but it is not all the truth on this subject. If it were, it need not have been mentioned. There is a peculiarity in the case. The infinite cannot be pictured *even in its object.* We can form distinct images of a hard, soft, or transparent substance; but we can have no such image of an infinite object. For whenever we image a thing, we mentally assign to it some definite form, extent, and boundaries. And in this very act we destroy its infinity. To picture infinite space, for instance, is to give it limitations. And however vast the picture may be, it falls far short of infinity. We sometimes represent infinite duration by a right line. But this representation is utterly inadequate; for any right line is limited. It may be conceived as billions upon billions of miles in length; but still it is limited and measurable. It is no nearer the infinite than if it were a single inch in length. The infinite can never be pictured to the mind, either as an abstraction, an attribute, or an object. The attempt to do this impossible thing has led to numberless errors in philosophy, among which may be mentioned the *antinomies* of Kant and the *necessary contradictions* of Hamilton.

2. THE INFINITE GIVES NO CONCEPT.

The concept is a purely mental product—the result of certain definite mental processes. It arises from the combined action of analysis, abstraction, and generalization. Now it is evident that the infinite cannot be analyzed; for if so, it could be measured, and would therefore be finite. Neither can we reach the infinite by abstraction ; for that is a drawing away, a diminishing process. Infinity so reached would be a negative affair indeed, a mere negation, and nothing more, as Hobbes puts it. It is equally certain that generalization cannot lead to the infinite ; for generalization merely groups objects in accordance with certain known attributes. If, therefore, there is no infinity among the elements of the first individuals, there can be none in the general class at which we arrive.

But, again, the infinite is not a mental product arising from processes of reasoning. Deduction depends upon induction, and induction depends upon the intuitions of time and space, which, in themselves, involve the infinite. In other words, if there is nothing infinite in either of the premises, there can be nothing infinite in the conclusion. No new term can be introduced in the third proposition. It is safe to conclude that the infinite is not derived from a process, and that we can form no general concept of it.

3. MENTAL APPREHENSION INCLUDES MORE THAN THE IMAGE AND THE CONCEPT.

In some cases the mind is compelled to believe in existences beyond either of these products. But this compulsion is not universal. The unmeasured is not necessarily the infinite. Let us illustrate. The geologist digs into the earth and finds stratum upon stratum, however far down he goes ; but he is by no means forced to believe that mundane stratification is infinite. The mariner lets down his sounding-line hundreds of fathoms into the deep sea, and finds no bottom ; but he never once dreams that the ocean is therefore bottomless. The astronomer first counts the visible stars, our nearest cosmical neighbors. He then sweeps the sky with his telescope, and adds many thousands to the list.   Finally he scans the distant depths of the Milky Way, and finds therein signs of stellar bodies still more immensely remote.   And yet he is by no means compelled to believe that throughout the measureless void of infinite space there must be star after star forever.

But he is compelled to believe that wherever the remotest star may be there is still space beyond it ; that whenever the first star was made, there was still duration before it.   And in general with all men, he must admit that whatever is farthest out in space does not end it, and whatever is farthest back in duration does not begin it.

Whence arises this belief in the infinity of time and space?   It is in the mind, and native to it.   It must be accounted for ; and yet it brooks no limitations and submits to no analysis.   There is no other conviction, either to which we can reduce it, or from which we can derive it.

This fact suggests that it must be original and intuitive in character.   Upon examination it bears the tests of intuition.   It is self-evident.   By no combination of arguments can we prove that space is infinite ; and yet we know it without proof.   It is necessary.   We are forced to the conviction, and cannot successfully resist it.   Conceive yourself at the centre of a sphere whose radius is a billion billion miles, and there is still space beyond it. Now raise this number to the billionth billionth power, and upon the new radius thus formed, construct another sphere.   And yet this sphere, however immense, does not and cannot exhaust space.   You must believe that if placed on the surface thereof, you could still peer into the depths of space beyond, even as we do now from the surface of the earth. Moreover, it is universal. True, it does not apply universally. The conviction of the infinite may not exist with equal clearness and definiteness in all men. The child or the savage may never have thought himself very far out into space ; but so far as he has gone, he has still found the "infinite beyond." And the farther you may succeed in leading his thought, the wider still becomes to him the inner surface of this infinite. Rightly interpreted, this conviction is universal, no less than self-evident and necessary. It is therefore an intuition of the mind, and neither its existence nor its character can be reasonably questioned or ignored.

4. INFINITE OBJECTS ARE INCAPABLE OF INCREASE.

These objects are time, space, and Deity. Of course, in dealing with them, the imagining power of the mind fails us completely. It is true that any attempt to picture them does give an object that can be increased. The sphere in space, the line representing duration, and the anthropomorphic attributes ascribed to the Deity are all of this character. But it is equally true that all these things fall far short of the infinite. Space is larger than any sphere, time is longer than any line, and the perfections of God are felt to be infinitely beyond the attributes of man or his powers of comprehension. Nothing whatever can in anywise be added to them. And this inability is not a mere negation, arising, as Hamilton insists, from the impotence of human faculties. It is the rather a positive thing, due to the inherent nature of the infinite itself. This infinite perfection of God is the universal claim of Christian Theism. Nor is it confined to Christianity alone. The most thoughtful devotees to systems of pagan worship insist that their supreme deity, in nearly every case, has these same illimitable and unincreasable perfections. This is the universal characteristic of the infinite, wherever we perceive it, and however we may attempt to construe it to our minds.

5. THE INFINITE IS AN ATTRIBUTE.

I have just spoken of it as a quality. But it must not be forgotten that this quality, like any other, must always belong to some object. It has no separate or independent existence. True, it is an abstraction, but as such it has a mental existence only. However we may think it apart, it must not be supposed that infinity can actually be separated from its object, any more than beauty or truth or love can. There is quite a tendency among metaphysicians to overlook this truth, and to speak of infinity as though it were an abstraction having an existence in the universe, independent of any object or personal being. This is certainly a false view. Infinity exists. That is not denied. On the contrary, I insist upon its reality. But it has that reality simply and only as an attribute of some existing object. Theism deals with it solely as an attribute of a Personal Being whom we call God. There is here no occasion to view it in any other aspect. The infinity of God is the theme of the present discussion.

SECTION II.

THE INFINITE BEING.

A vast amount of false philosophy and fruitless speculation has been expended upon the question of God's infinitude. To avoid this error, let us first of all ask ourselves what we mean when we ascribe infinity to any being. We simply mean that the being of which we thus speak has attributes without limit. When we affirm the infinity of space, for instance, we mean to assert that no bounds can be fixed to determine space, and that this impossibility arises not from any weakness or defect in our powers of comprehension, but from the inherent nature of space itself. When we say that duration is infinite, we are affirming not our inability to conceive its limits, but our conviction that it has no limits—that it is absolutely without beginning and without end. When we assert that God is infinite in power, we simply mean that this attribute of his is so great that it cannot be increased. No possible addition can make it greater. He can now and always do all things which are proper objects of power.

God is likewise infinite in wisdom. He knows all things, and so no addition can be made to his knowledge. Moreover, his use of that infinite knowledge is perfect; that is, any conceivable change therein would be folly, and not wisdom at all. And this is what is meant by asserting the infinity of God's wisdom. The same is true of all his attributes. Whatever element exists at all in the Divine Being exists there not in degree, but in illimitable perfection. It cannot be measured, analyzed, or increased. And the infinity of God consists in this infinity of attributes. God is a being whose personality involves infinite perfections. This is the exact truth and the whole truth that I mean to assert and to maintain on this vexed question. God is not infinite in the sense that he includes in his character every element, actual, possible, or conceivable. He is not a huge complex of contradictories and self-destructive incompatibilities. His character is one of unity, harmony, and moral consistency, with which no opposite elements can possibly interfere.

Any other view of it involves the *pseudo-infinite* and not the true infinite at all.   There are two forms of this pseudo-infinite which are quite prevalent among agnostic and atheistic philosophers.   The first makes the infinite the sum of all things.   It is reached *mathematically* by adding together all finite beings.   The second views the infinite as the *summum genus*, the widest possible concept.   It is reached *logically* by magnifying the extent, and so mini-fying the content, of the concept.   Finally a concept is developed which includes all reality in its extent, and thereby excludes all qualities from its content.   This is the zero of being, rather than infinity.

Many of the popular philosophical sophisms concerning the infinity of God, with which skeptics are wont to amuse themselves and puzzle their antagonists, are founded on one or the other of these false ideas of the infinite.   Thus, starting out with the assumption that the infinite is the sum of all existence, they proceed to some such inquiries as the following :

" How can the infinite and the finite coëxist ? for the infinite is necessarily all-embracing.   How can evil be ex-cluded from the Divine Being without cancelling his in-finity ?   How can weakness, folly, and sin be shut out of a nature that must include every thing?   As Hegel puts it : ' What kind of an Absolute Being is that which does not contain in itself all that is actual, even evil included?' How can God ever be known ? for to know is to distin-guish, and to distinguish is to limit.   How can God know himself even, or be self-conscious? since the knowledge of the ego depends on the non-ego.   How can God have any positive existence at all ?   For the positive must be definite and determined, and therefore limited.   The infinite must then be the negative, the indeterminate, the non-existent, the unknowable. How can the Deity sustain any relation whatever to the universe? since the infinite is the unconditioned, the absolute ; and the absolute, being *the thing in itself*, is of necessity out of all relations possible or conceivable."

Such foolish and impertinent questions as these constitute the staple arguments with which the average philosophical atheist entertains himself and his readers.

They all proceed upon a palpable falsehood. The infinite is not the sum of all existence. The finite exists and must be recognized in order to affirm the infinite. It is true that logically the infinite precedes the finite ; but psychologically the converse of this is true. In the realm of human consciousness the finite always antedates the infinite. Neither is the infinite all-embracing. Time is infinite, but it does not embrace space. Space is infinite, but it by no means necessitates the infinity of time. It is not a whit less infinite for a single instant than for an eternity.

Neither is the Infinite Being the sum of all existence. Rational intuition does not require such a postulate. We know that he is the source of all finite being—its creating and controlling power. And that is enough. We know that his perfections are illimitable. His power, wisdom, and goodness are perfect. But the infinity of these attributes does not imply the possession of an infinite number of attributes. There is in God no weakness, folly, or unrighteousness whatever. These qualities may exist in finite beings, but not in the infinite. The very infinity of the opposite qualities just named excludes them altogether.

The proposition that the infinite is negative and unknowable depends upon the same false assumption. True, we cannot know God to perfection. If we could, that fact would prove either that God is finite or that man is infinite. The finite cannot exhaust infinity. But, in some important sense, we can know him, for we can plainly distinguish him from ourselves, from other intelligences like ourselves, and from the sum of finite existences in the universe. Our knowledge of the Infinite is certainly not exhaustive; but it is real and fundamental in the truest sense possible. There is no philosophical barrier in the way of our knowing God, of whom we may continue to learn more and more, if we will.

The question of self-consciousness in the Deity is a most profound one, and should be approached with the greatest modesty. The exact mode in which the self-directive freedom of the Infinite Being acts may not be comprehensible by the finite. One thing, however, can be stated with positive assurance. Self-consciousness is not, and cannot be, in any being, a token of weakness, finiteness, or imperfection. Those who hold to the contrary derive their doctrine from the self-consciousness of man, which they say is necessarily finite and imperfect. It is not the *fact* of self-consciousness in man that makes him finite, but rather the *method of its origin*. It may be admitted that the knowledge of the *ego* could never have been awakened without the *non-ego*. But when once awakened it is thenceforth independent of every thing other than the being in whom it exists. I may never have known myself without the agency of external things; but, now that I know myself, I would continue in that knowledge, even though the whole universe besides me were blotted out forever. And this law of self-consciousness is not exceptional in the mental economy. The same is true of all the intuitions of the mind. Contact with externality served to awaken every one of them at the first ; but once awakened, they are thenceforth independent of all externality. Derived consciousness does, indeed, imply the non-ego ; but because of this fact it by no means follows that original consciousness implies any such thing. The evidence is to the contrary. Be it remembered that it is the *origination* of consciousness in man, and that alone, that depends upon externality. Its subsequent and continuous exercise is absolutely independent thereof.

Now, God is an uncreated, self-existent personality. What he now is he always was. A just view of his own *aseity* demands this. God was never made. He did not make himself. His personality never began to be. His self-consciousness, therefore, unlike that of man, was not originated at all ; it always existed even as now. Hence it follows that at no single moment of past eternity could the exercise of the Divine self-consciousness have depended upon the external or the finite. It would have been as it now is, even if no Cosmos had ever been created. And so this impious question about God's ability to know himself is as illogical as it is impious.

But, again, God's knowledge of the finite is also arrayed against his infinity. Let us see about this. Intuitive knowledge is the highest, noblest, and most valuable kind of which man is capable. It is the basis of all other knowledge whatsoever, from which it is derived, and without which it would be impossible. Without the unifying power of intuition, the manifold of sense could never be aggregated into knowledge. But intuition acts at once and without conscious effort, while other knowledge comes slowly and by means of laborious processes. Can it be supposed for a moment that the existence of intuitive power in man is a sign of imperfection? Is it not indeed, the thing in him that makes him most like God? What intuitive knowledge he has, is perfect. The lack of it is what brings imperfection. Man's knowledge is finite simply because his intuitions are few, and limited in their application. Only remove these limitations, and we would at once know every thing by simple intuition, our knowledge would become perfect and infinite. But this is precisely what God does. He sees the end from the beginning. He never learns, remembers, or forgets any thing, in the human sense of those terms. Past, present, and future are one eternal present with him. All things are constantly within the realm of his cognition, without any effort or any process whatever.

This is the Divine intuition, which includes what we call self-consciousness. In what conceivable sense can this power make God finite? Would its absence make him any the more perfect or infinite? The very thought is absurd in the extreme.

The only remaining quibble is that which questions the possibility of God's sustaining any relation whatever to the universe. Upon careful examination it will be found equally vain and frivolous. It arises from a strange entanglement of the *unconditioned* and the *unrelated*. The infinite, being absolute, is necessarily unconditioned, but it is not necessarily unrelated. The infinity of space does not prevent its bearing relations to all the objects that exist within it. Time is infinite, and still it is related to every event that ever occurred. Even so God may be infinite, and may still bear to his creatures the tenderest relations of mercy, truth, and love. It is true that the Deity is absolute and unconditioned, in the sense of being utterly independent of all things, in his being, character, purpose, and action. That means that his existence is in no wise conditioned upon the universe; but it does not mean conversely, that the existence of the universe is in no wise conditioned upon God. He may assume voluntary relations, if he so chooses. Indeed, his very absoluteness carries this possibility with it. The fact that he has so chosen, in becoming the Creator and Sustainer of the universe, makes nothing whatever against his independence or his infinity. The infinite cannot be diminished by the creation of the finite. Of his own choice he may have imposed certain relations and conditions upon himself, and certain limitations, if you please to put it so, upon his own activity. In the creation, endowment, and sustenance of free moral intelligences, for instance, he may have so conditioned himself as not in any way to abridge their freedom or to prevent its proper exercise. He may maintain of choice the eternal consistency of his own acts of choice. And yet in so doing he has not abridged his infinity, independence, or absoluteness. A self-assumed relation accords with all these elements. Indeed, the ability to assume relations belongs to his own free personality, if not as well to his very infinity. It is the mere exercise of free personal choice. That would be a strange kind of independence indeed, which would confine the Deity himself to a state of eternal isolation! It is not so. Myriads of beings may exist in the relation of dependence upon him; but the divine acts by which he creates and sustains them do not in any way interfere with his own independence. On the contrary, they fall in with the plainest tokens of that independence.

But it is further objected that even this voluntary exercise of intelligence destroys infinity—that intelligence itself is a limitation—that if we attribute intelligence to·

the Deity, we thereby exclude other qualities. This blunder results from a mistaken use of the disjunctive syllogism. When I attribute intelligence to God, I certainly exclude non-intelligence. But that is all I do exclude. It is a plain case of dichotomy. He may have also the qualities of goodness, justice, veracity, power, and all others indeed that are not logical contradictories of intelligence. There is therefore nothing at all in this argument for the necessary mutual exclusion of infinite perfections assigned to the Deity.

But surely it will not be soberly asserted that intelligence in itself is a weakness—an infirmity. The power to know, is certainly power, and not weakness. It is not intelligence in man, but the lack of it, that tends to make him imperfect. Would he approach perfection, by losing his intelligence? Is human perfection to be found by escaping from intelligence, or is it rather by escaping from the limitations of intelligence? To ask these questions is to answer them.

Now the Divine intelligence has no limitations. His apprehension of truth is immediate, spontaneous, absolute, unlimited. To call such a power as this a limitation or an imperfection of being, is to use words with reckless folly, or to violate the very regulative principles of human thought. And so this logical quibble turns out to be as empty and illogical as all the others.

There are no logical or philosophical objections of any weight against the existence of the infinite or of the Infinite Being. But the Infinite Being must be a person. Essential Reason, realizing its ideals in the Cosmos, must be absolute, unconditioned, and free. The accidents of creation cannot conditionate the essence of intelligent, all-embracing Reason. But reason and free-will are elements of personality. Absolute reason and absolute free-will constitute the infinite personality of God. That can account adequately for the existing universe. Nothing less than that can. If God be infinite, no absurdity follows, either as to his personality or as to his relations. But is he infinite? There may be an Infinite Being; and if there is, nature shows that he must be a personality. But, does nature prove that there must be an Infinite Being? This is still an open question. In other words, proof may still be demanded to show that God is actually infinite. Let us examine and answer this demand.

SECTION III.

PROOF OF GOD'S INFINITY.

It has already been asserted that the infinite is appre-hended by intuition, and that all intuitions being self-evident, are incapable of proof by any mental process. How then can the infinity of God be made in anywise a matter of proof? Is there not here a plain contradiction of terms? Let us see. Observe the nature of our intu-itions. We feel that, so far as they go, they are infalli-ble. What we know by intuition we recognize as certain truth, and likewise as *necessary* truth. It could not be otherwise. But, then, human intuition is by no means unlimited or universal. It tells us the truth, and nothing but the truth, but it is not sworn to tell us the whole truth on any particular subject. It gives us certain ideas which we could never get in any other way, but it does not, of necessity, connect these ideas with every individ-ual fact and being to which they may be applicable. In this way, without doubt, the idea of the infinite comes to

us. It is a quality or attribute which we apprehend by
intuition. It belongs not in the sphere of the physical
senses, the judgment, or the reason. We apprehend it directly whenever and wherever we apprehend it at all. But
that is far from saying that we must apprehend it universally. It does not necessarily apply to every object of
thought. Cases of infinity may exist without our knowledge. Indeed, there must be an appropriate occasion,
upon the occurrence of which we first apprehend the infinite in regard to any object. It is thus, undoubtedly,
that the capacity of space to be occupied by finite bodies
leads originally to a view of its infinity. In the case of
duration, the occurrence of known and remembered events
forms the like occasion. To be sure, there is an impassable gulf between space occupancy and events on the one
hand, and the infinity of space and time on the other.
The transcendent idea cannot be accounted for by the
occasion which it transcends. It is the product of pure
intuition. Even so is our idea of God. His independent
and original personality, as we have already seen, is a
matter of intuition. If he has infinity, that likewise is
intuitive. But has he infinity? Is this intuitive idea of
the infinite applicable to this Personal Being, of whose
existence we are assured upon other and independent considerations? If his infinity is not involved in his independent personality, then it is manifestly proper to adduce
further considerations in favor of his infinity. And this
is not proving the infinite. It is simply connecting it
with a certain object of thought. It is, in short, stating
the occasion upon which the apprehension of the infinite
must certainly take place.

Now this is what I shall attempt to do concerning the
Deity. And this is all that is meant by proving his in-

finity. Is our idea of God such that it must include the infinite? This question I shall try to answer.

I have already stated that nothing less than an Infinite Personality can adequately account for the existing universe. The personality of this Being has already been discussed. Now let his infinity be established and the proof will be complete. For this purpose I employ the Causal argument. And in doing so I do not conceal from myself the opinions to the contrary, expressed by able theistic philosophers, as well as by atheists. They have declared, time and again, that the infinity of God cannot be established by the Causal argument. They admit that the principle of causation leads ultimately and inevitably to God, but they deny that it involves his infinity. It may be hazardous to affirm what the highest authorities deny. And yet I am constrained to take the contrary view, and to insist that the infinity of God is involved in the principle of causation.

Every event must have a cause. This belief is ultimate, simple, intuitive. But it is universal and inexorable as well as simple. It exhausts all the phenomena we know. It transcends our personal knowledge, and leads us through all the numberless and diverse phenomena that are taking place all over the earth. It carries us into the heavens and holds in its grasp the stupendous action of suns and planets and comets and stars. It insists that each one of these must have a definite and adequate cause. And this is not all. That is a false view of causation which restricts it to the physical universe. It enters likewise the realm of rationality, and with the same exactitude requires a sufficient cause for every event that takes place there. Every thought, feeling, and purpose in existence must be explained by it, as

well as every physical fact. It asks an adequate cause
for the Iliad and the Paradise Lost, the Lord's Prayer
and the Vedic Hymns no less than the rings of Saturn
and moons of Jupiter. There is no discrimination here.
The demand is universal. It embraces the utmost sweep
of material and rational phenomena throughout the entire
universe. But rational phenomena presuppose the spon-
taneity of free-will. Events are caused by self-determined
action of mind quite as much as by pre-determined action
of physical force.

But the principle of causation does not stop even here.
Not satisfied with present phenomena, it runs back into
the past. It challenges every cosmical change that ever
occurred, and demands its cause. If a preceding phenomenon is assigned as the cause of the existing one, it
insists upon knowing the cause of that preceding phenomenon. And so on, back into the depths of eternity.
There is and must be an everlasting source of all phenomena. That source of phenomena must be a free Personal
Being, for rationality is involved in the phenomena. And
that Being must be infinite in duration at least, for he is
the source of the first phenomenon, and therefore could
not have been created. If otherwise, his creation would
have been a stupendous event, requiring a cause for itself,
which cause must, by hypothesis, reside in the Being
created. To intimate such a thing is sheer nonsense.
God did not make himself. Nothing can be clearer than
that the ultimate source of phenomena must be an uncreated Personal Being. But an uncreated Being is eternal, and therefore infinite in duration. It is thus that the
causal principle leads directly to one element at least, in
which God is infinite. This statement is not inconsistent
with that made elsewhere (page 60) that design, purpose,

or end is not a cause of rational action in God or in man. The two principles articulate perfectly. Self-determined volition is the cause of purely rational phenomena. The absolute self-determination of the Divine Will is the ultimate cause of all things. The creation of the Cosmos was determined by the Divine Will. But the Divine Volition was not *caused* by certain purposes, ends, or motives set before it. Otherwise it was not self-determined or free. It is thus that the Divine Volition is the first cause of all things. Before it was put forth it remained in the infinite realm of God's potentiality. When put forth, it came into the finite realm of actual causation, and like all other causes, produced its inevitable results in the creation of the Cosmos. It is the ultimate rest of Causation upon the bosom of Divine Potentiality. But that rest demands the infinite duration of the Divine Potentiality. And so, I repeat, the Causal argument brings us directly to one element of infinity in God.

Now, it might be fair to infer that if God be infinite in one attribute, he must be in all. I do not insist on this inference, however. If its fairness is questioned, the infinity of other attributes of the Deity, such as *wisdom* and *power*, for example, can be independently established. The same causal argument compels us to believe that God is infinite in wisdom and power, as well as in duration.

Let us take the attribute of power in God, and apply the principle of causation to the question of its infinity. It is admitted that the constitution of the universe is the outcome of God's power. And inasmuch as the universe is an immense affair, its creation implies the exertion of immense power. But the objector insists that immensity is not infinity, and that a great thing is no nearer the infinite than a small thing.   And hence he concludes that infinity can never be reached by causation.

The truth of these statements must be granted.   The immense is not the infinite.   And yet the conclusion drawn does not follow.   Its error arises from a failure to distinguish between the *principle* of causation, and the *law* of causation.   The former is a subjective thing, existing in the human mind.   The latter is objective, and exists in the universe without us.   The former insists that every event must have a cause.   The latter connects every existing event with its own cause.   If existing events are all finite, then the law of causation is also finite.   But that does not prove that the principle of causation is finite.   True, we feel that of necessity the fact of causation without us must correspond to the principle of causation within us.   But it may not be coëxtensive.   The principle may transcend the law.   The last word has not yet been written concerning this whole question of causation.   Doubtless it will remain unwritten for years to come.   But there are at least three truths in it, which those who deny that causation leads to the infinite, seem to have overlooked.

I. THE CAUSAL EVIDENCE OF INFINITE POWER IS AS GREAT AS, IN THE NATURE OF THE CASE, IT CAN BE.

It is quite true that the universe is not known to be infinite ; and yet it is known to be as vast as finite beings can possibly comprehend.   It is even more so.   It utterly transcends the grasp of our comprehension.   Between its extremes of immeasurable greatness and infinitesimal littleness which are constantly forced upon our thought, there are stretches of being quite beyond the limits of our loftiest faculties.

Contrast an immense star, so far away that its light, travelling millions of miles a minute, requires many years to reach us, with one of those minute organisms so small that numbers of them can float in a drop of water, and then try to picture to your mind the probable size of one of the immeasurable blood-discs in circulation through the veins of each one of these microscopic creatures, and you get some faint idea of the bewildering stretch of being between the extremes of the created universe. If the Author of all this is not infinite in power, one thing is certain: his finiteness is of such character and extent as to baffle all finite calculation. Another thing is equally certain. He could give no more convincing proof of his infinity than he has given. If the existing universe were multiplied indefinitely, we could never know that fact. There is already vastly more of it than we can cognize. The argument for God's infinite power is now so great that no addition could make it greater. It need not have been so. This unutterable and inconceivable vastness is not essential to the Cosmos. It might have been made of moderate and measurable proportions. The solar system, for example, might have constituted the entire creation. There is no logical necessity of its being greater. And surely God could have stopped the outflow of creative energy at one point as well as another. But he did not stop it until such immeasurable immensities were reached as to make the *suggestion* of the infinite as strong as a finite universe could possibly furnish.

2. THE CAUSAL PRINCIPLE IS NOT SATISFIED WITH THE ACTUAL, IT INCLUDES THE POSSIBLE AND THE CONCEIVABLE.

We know that the existing universe has a cause, and that cause is God. We know that, in some way, it is an

outflow of his potentiality.   Now this universe is as great
as possible, or else it is not.   If it is as great as possible,
its creation must have exhausted the Divine potentiality.
But in that case the resultant impotence of the Deity
would have left the universe to its own destruction. That
which must be created must likewise be sustained. The
continued and constructive existence of the universe is
therefore a certain proof that the Divine power was not
exhausted in its creation.   It is therefore true that the
universe is not the greatest possible.   It might have been
duplicated. Suppose it had been.   That second copy
must have had the same creative source as the first. Suppose a dozen or a million copies made.   Still we are compelled, by this same principle of causation within us, to
believe that each one of these systems must have had an
adequate cause, and that that cause, then even as now,
must have been the same everlasting source of all phenomena.

Now let this million of universes be all merged into
one, and let another be conceived possible, so much greater
than this as the ocean is greater than a drop of water ; and
yet this new universe cannot be conceived as causeless,
it must still be the outflow of the same Divine potentiality.

And so we might go on till we reach the limit of possible finite being.   But still God's potentiality is not exhausted.   It covers all actual being ; but it just as surely
covers all possible being.   Whatever is actual must have
an actual cause.   Whatever is possible must have a possible cause.   Nay, more.   Whatever is conceivable must
have a conceivable cause.   This is the final push of the
necessary Principle of Causation within the human mind.
But since the cause of the actual is himself absolute and

underived, he must also be the cause of the possible and the conceivable. Now, the power which creates and sustains, is of necessity greater than the thing created. The power of God is therefore greater than any creation, actual, possible, or conceivable. How much, then, does that power lack of infinity? Being greater than any conceivable quantity, it is certainly beyond all possible increase or interference. It is absolute and supreme. Nothing can ever exist without it. No other power can ever interfere with it. A God of such power as that is strong enough to satisfy both the religion and the philosophy of the Christian Theist.

To this argument it may be objected that, though the creation of the existing Cosmos has not exhausted the Divine potentiality, yet the creation of some small addition thereto, might so exhaust it.

My answer still is, that the power to create implies the power to sustain, and so is necessarily greater than the thing created. God's power is therefore greater than any possible Cosmos, however vast or small it may be conceived to be. But no exhibition of power not derived from him can ever be possible ; for his own independence and absoluteness forbid it. Neither can any addition ever be made to his own power ; for there is no being to make it. Whatever potentiality there is, or ever can be, must belong to him. He has, then, that which is greater than any possible finite creation, and, at the same time, that to which nothing can be added. But to be greater than the limits of the finite, and to be incapable of increase, is to have the tokens of the infinite. Power like that is certainly beyond all finite power, and is all that the rational intuition of the Theist can demand, either for Divine dignity or for human security.

3. THE EXISTING COSMOS INVOLVES INFINITE POWER.

I have admitted that if all existing events are finite, then the law of causation is also finite. But I now deny that all existing events are finite. It has just been shown that the *principle* of causation leads to the infinite. It remains to be shown that the *law* of causation does the same.

The existing Cosmos is finite. It exists in space. It must, therefore, be posited in space or projected through space. But space is infinite. It is likewise homogeneous. There can be no particular portion of it adapted to occupancy, any more than all other portions. Neither can the Cosmos be adapted to occupy any one part of space to the exclusion of all others. If, therefore, one part of space is void, and at the same time another part is occupied by the Cosmos, there is nothing either in space itself, or in the Cosmos, to determine what part shall be void, and what shall be filled.

Now if the Cosmos is posited in space, some particular part has been filled, and all the rest has been void, ever since the creation. But, if the Cosmos is projected through space, some constantly variable portion has been occupied, and the reciprocally varying residue has been void, ever since the creation.

But, in either case, the question of the location of the Cosmos in space, involves the absolute control, not only of the Cosmos, but also of space itself. He who can put the universe into space, can put it anywhere in space. When he made it, there was none other than himself to determine where, in all the infinitude of space, it should be. He determined that question, and thereby showed his unlimited control of unlimited space. If, in all the trackless depths of space, there is a single corner or cranny over which the Creator has no control, who shall determine whether that corner is to be occupied, or remain void forever? But that question must be determined for every point in space, as much as for any point. Moreover, it must be determined for all time, and for every moment of all time. In other words, the constant restraint of the finite Cosmos within its place in infinite space, and the consequent constant determination of every point in infinite space, as world-void or occupied, is a constant event which, by the law of causation, requires a constant cause. But this event involves the control of infinite space. Its Cause must, therefore, be infinite in power. Here, then, is one existing event that is not finite. It is no less infinite than space itself.

But every existing event calls for the law of causation, as well as the principle of causation. So that the one, no less than the other, leads us of necessity to the infinite.

There is only one conceivable objection to this argument. It may be urged that, after all, the Creator of the finite Cosmos may be only a *Demiurgos* of some sort ; that he may have a certain finite portion of space assigned to him, in which to create and sustain his universe ; and that the infinite envelope of surrounding space is under the control of another Being superior to himself.

This objection involves the finiteness of the Demiurgos, to be sure. But it likewise involves the infinity of that Superior Being who controls infinite space. It merely shifts the question, and throws it one step further back. That Superior Being is the God of Christian Theism. His will is the ultimate cause of the universe, no matter how many Demiurgi may be supposed to figure in its development.

Put it in whatever shape you may, it comes to the same thing at last. He who is the Cause of the Cosmos must dominate infinite space. And it is thus that the existing Cosmos involves Infinite Power.

Herein, then, according to promise, I have found an independent argument for the infinity of God's power. God is infinite in duration and in power. In like manner, the infinity of other Divine attributes, such as intelligence and wisdom, can be established. But surely it is not necessary to go further in this line of argument. A Being who is infinite in two attributes, is certainly an Infinite Being. It is presumed that no one will deny his infinity. Now the argument here employed is purely causal. But some one may say that it depends upon the infinity of space, which is an intuitive idea. Grant it. And yet the intuition of an infinite void does not involve the infinite power of a Personal Being. It is only when the *causal* idea, involved in the Cosmos, is applied to the *intuitive* idea of infinite space, that the necessary infinity of God's power is disclosed. The argument is, therefore, essentially causal.

The Infinite God is the ultimate rest of reason. But he is equally the ultimate rest of intuition. Time and space are certainly intuitive ideas. But infinite time without an event, and infinite space devoid of all being, are ideas of a most unsatisfying and perturbing character. They lack equipoise. They must be equilibrated by the idea of the Infinite God. Then, and only then, they give mental rest. He whose power fills all space, and whose being occupies all time, is the ultimate resort of intellect no less than of sentiment. The Infinite God is the necessary correlate of all being and of all thought.

Unless I am strangely deceived, we have reached the close of a legitimate argument for the being and character of God. The proof answers to just such a Being as meets the demands of Christian Theism. It will be remembered that the Christian's idea of God, as set forth at the outset of this work, includes intelligence, volition, personality, goodness, unity, and infinity. All these attributes were to be established. This obligation of the theist has not been discharged at a single stroke. We could not reach God at one philosophic leap, and did not try. That could be done only by taking step after step. These steps we have tried to take with due care and patience.

We have proved the intelligence of God by the existence of order, plan, and harmony in the universe. His exercise of volition has been disclosed in the widespread purpose and design that exist in nature. His personality has been reached by a necessary and undeniable intuition of the human mind. We have established the goodness of God from the history of the world and the evident trend of all things therein. We have demonstrated his unity by arguments drawn from science, philosophy, and religion. And, finally, the necessary and universal principle of causation has brought us to the infinity of God. This is the last link in the chain of theistic proof. It completes the cumulative argument for the being and character of God. And surely this kind of argument is a thing of superior strength. One line of reasoning might possibly mislead ; but when six independent lines all focalize at the same point, they make that point luminous indeed. The white light of eternal truth itself cannot be brighter. There is a Personal God, infinite, holy, and perfect in all his attributes. To this supreme conviction our theistic arguments have brought us. With it, their constructive work is done.

There is a piece of criticism, however, that still remains. Anti-theistic errors have been advanced with ability and mental vigor, in both ancient and modern times. The most important of these must be reviewed. The two following chapters will be devoted to this necessary work.

REFERENCES:

Harris' " Philosophic Basis of Theism."
McCosh's " Intuitions."
Bownes " Studies in Theism."
Porter's " Intellectual Science."

CHAPTER VII.

ANTI-THEISTIC ERRORS.

EVERY denial of Theism involves a positive error. What the form of that error shall be depends upon the particular standpoint from which Theism is rejected. As these points of view continually vary, the resultant forms of error continually multiply. Truth is one ; errors are many. Their name is legion. Theories contradictory to Theism have assumed numerous forms and shades of belief. They cannot all be here discussed. Attention will be given to four of them, viz.: Materialism, Pantheism, Positivism, and Agnosticism. These four theories will be recognized as the boldest of all, and as, in some sense, involving all.

SECTION I.

MATERIALISM.

Materialism is not a new form of philosophic error. It is more than twenty-two centuries old. Its origin can be distinctly traced to Democritus and the Atomists. Through various forms of hylozoism, skepticism, and naturalistic atheism, it has come down unimpaired and largely unchanged to the present day. In general, one distinction must be noted between ancient and modern Materialism. Anciently, matter was considered as cold, dead, passive, inert. In modern times this view has given way to a general belief in the immanence of force and the universality of motion. Matter is now viewed as instinct with activity, if not indeed with life. With this single exception, the doctrines of Materialism, and the grounds on which they rest, are essentially the same as in the days of old.

I. MATERIALISM STATED.

Materialism is the doctrine that the mind has no existence, except as a function of the body; it is a mere product of the physical organism. There is no such thing as an independent, immaterial entity. Thought is not a product of mind. It is a secretion of the brain, just as tears are of the lachrymal gland. The best and fairest statement of materialistic doctrine can be made in the words of its own distinguished advocates.

(1) *Greek Materialism.*

Perhaps no better representative of the ancient Greek school of materialists can be taken than Democritus, leader of the so-called Atomists. His view, given substantially in his own words, is as follows:

The cause of atoms must not be asked for; they are eternal. Motion, likewise, is primordial and eternal. The earth was formed, not by the agency of an overruling Intelligence, but by means of certain rotary motions of atoms, and in obedience to a natural necessity. . . . Organized beings came from the moist earth. . . . The brain is the seat of thought; the heart, of anger; the liver, of desire. The soul is made up of small round atoms of fire, which atoms are inhaled from the air, and variously disposed of throughout the body. . . . Thought results from symmetrical motions of the soul-atoms.

(2) *German Materialism.*

Quite a number of modern German philosophers have revived and somewhat modified the old theories of Materialism. They agree in rejecting all belief in a super-sensible world, profess themselves measurably satisfied with the existing world of sense, and declare, in the words of Carl Vogt, that "Physiology pronounces definitely and categorically against the idea of individual immortality, as, indeed, against all notions founded upon that of the independent existence of the soul; physiology sees in psychical activities nothing but functions of the brain, the material substratum of those activities." Carl Vogt and Louis Büchner are perhaps the foremost champions of German Materialism in the present century. The former became distinguished by his controversial papers; the latter by his systematic work entitled "Force and Matter." Writers of this school tend somewhat toward Pantheism, and speak freely about the "world-soul," and the eternity of the earth, as well as of all other astronomical bodies which contain organized and psychically endowed beings.

(3) *English Materialism.*

England and America have produced many prominent materialistic philosophers within the present century. Among them all perhaps no one has developed more thoroughly the psychological aspects of Materialism than the late G. H. Lewes. For this reason it will be well to let him stand as a representative of his English-speaking contemporaries, and state his theory in his own words. He says: "We must set aside the traditional conception of the mind as an agent apart from the organism. To many thinkers the contrast of

objective and subjective seems far more than that of
aspects ; it is that of agents.   But what we know is, that
the living organism has among its manifestations the class
called sentient, and states of consciousness.   There is no
evidence to suggest that one of these classes is due to the
activity of the organism, the other to the activity of another agent.   The only agent is the organism.   When we
seek the agent of which all the phenomena are the actions,
we get the organism."   " All psychological processes are
organic processes ; their mechanism may be expressed in
objective or subjective terms, at will, sensorial changes
being equivalent to sentient changes."   " A sensation· or
a thought is alternately viewed as a physical change or as
a mental change.   Mechanical and logical are only two
contrasted aspects of one and the same fact."   " States of
consciousness are separable from states of the organism
only in our mode of apprehending them."   " Knowledge
is partly connate, partly acquired, partly the evolved
product of the accumulated experiences of ancestors, and
partly of the accumulated experiences of the individual.
This theory maintains that the individual inherits what
may be called *a priori* conditions of knowledge, and even
a priori experiences, which must determine the result of
our *a posteriori* experiences."   " Every phenomenon is the
product of two factors, external and internal, impersonal
and personal, objective and subjective.   Viewing the external factor solely in the light of feeling, we may say that
the sentient material out of which all the forms of consciousness are evolved, is the psychoplasm, instantly
fluctuating, instantly renewed.   Viewing this on the
physiological side, it is the succession of neural tremors,
variously combining into neural groups.   But experience
is the registration of feeling, and hence the cosmos which

arises in consciousness is a product of the individual organism, as related to surrounding cosmical forces."

In view of these quotations, and such like others as may be readily gathered from current materialistic writers, the following definition given by John Fiske may be accepted as both just and lucid: " A materialist is one who regards the story of the universe as completely and satisfactorily told, when it is wholly told in terms of matter and motion without reference to any ultimate underlying existence of which matter and motion are only the phenomenal manifestations."

2. MATERIALISM EXAMINED.

The theory thus stated is one of the oldest, boldest, and strongest among the antagonists of Christian Theism. And yet, upon examination, it is found to contain a number of fatal weaknesses which serve to mark it as a form of false philosophy. Without stopping to distinguish its various phases, let us note a few of the points at which all Materialism fails.

(1) *It Proceeds upon a Fundamental Error.*

All materialists suppose the mind and the brain to be identical. Certain biological facts are set forth to justify this belief. We are told that the brain is the undoubted seat of mental activity, that movements in the tissue of the brain correspond to mental acts, that these movements are sectional, and that a paralysis or lesion of certain portions of the brain interferes with the operations of certain faculties of the mind and of no others. From such facts as these the materialist concludes that the brain and the mind, so-called, are one and the same thing. This is a great mistake. All that the facts can possibly prove is the dependence of the mind upon the brain. But dependence is not identity. A king may depend upon a cook, but the king and the cook are not the same. To conclude that they are would involve a logical leap not a whit more dangerous than that the materialist is constantly making.

This connection between mind and brain may, indeed, be mysterious. But all the materialist has to say about " organism," " physiological function," " brain-tissue," and " neural tremor," can neither increase nor diminish the mystery. The mere multiplication of points of connection between mental and physical phenomena has no effect upon this problem. One such point is quite as inexplicable as a thousand. The possibility of any connection at all between mind and body constitutes the only mystery in the case. And the materialist does nothing whatever toward explaining the mystery. His denial of the existence of mind is an evasion, not an explanation. He might as well deny the existence of brain and body. Such a denial would be no less logical, and much less at variance with human consciousness and universal experience. It is highly illogical to deny either. This rejection of the reality of mind is the basis of all Materialism. But it involves the rejection of all reality, since no other can give stronger evidence than that of mental reality. Upon this huge error is the whole system of materialistic philosophy based—an error which is little short of philosophic suicide.

(2) *Materialism Contradicts Physical Law.*

It declares that physical force is transmuted into thought. What begins in organism and nerve-motion, ends in consciousness, thought, feeling. This is plainly against physical law. What is once physical force must be always physical force. Motion is one thing, thought another. The former is physical, the latter is not. Mr. Spencer and others have attempted to get the one out of the other, by noting the fact that strong mental activity induces movements of blood, which produce flushing of the face, congestion of the brain, and the like. But these phenomena only serve to disprove the theory they are designed to prove. For, in so far as physical force is transmuted into thought, it ought evidently to disappear in its ordinary form of motion. As thought increases, blood-movements ought to diminish ; and the contrary facts disprove the very principle of Materialism which they are brought forward to establish. Professor Newcomb calls attention to this fallacy and says : " All experiments tend to prove that all the force taken into the body in the form of food is expended in the production of heat and muscular action ; and if this be so, there is nothing left to be transformed into thought. In every case we have reason to believe that, at each moment the total amount of force which has been put into the body from all external sources whatever, is exactly represented by the chemical changes and molecular motions going on among the molecules of the body."

These statements are certainly scientific. All science agrees that heat and motion are correlates of force. All are physical, spatial, measurable. But thought is not a correlate of force. It is neither physical, nor spatial, nor measurable. Force, in every known form, can be brought to a strict mathematical test. The materialist assumes that thought is a form of force. When he has successfully submitted thought to the rules of mathematical measurement, and shown that physical force in other forms does

invariably and proportionately disappear as thought proceeds, his assumption will then have some show of truth
and reason.   Until then it must be rejected as contrary to
the nature of physical force and the law under which it
invariably operates.   Force is neither convertible into
thought, nor deducible from it.

(3) *Materialism Fails to Account for the Existence of Living
Beings.*

We are told that the " organism " is the sole agent of all
the phenomena of life, whether sensorial or sentient.   But
we are not told how life originated in the organism.   Life
must have had a beginning.   This is evident from the fact
that every individual life depends upon a preceding life.
This is clearly seen in the chemical analysis and molecular
structure of life-germs.   Professor Newcomb says : " In
every thing which constitutes a material quality they are
identical.   Yet they differ as widely as a clam, an oak tree,
or a philosopher.   Since this difference does not consist in
the arrangement of their molecules, we may properly call
it *hyper-material.*"   Dr. Harris emphasizes this truth and
justly concludes that " Life, then, is the *cause* of organization, not its product. . . . It is the power of life which
organizes matter, and in and through the organization re-
veals itself."   Manifestly the difference between organized
and unorganized matter is due to the fact that the one is
subject to life, while the other is not.   Whence comes this
life ?   The materialist must account for its origin.   This
he never has done and never can do.   Admitting no life-
giving Creator, he must introduce life through some other
channel.   But no other channel can be found.   Out of
lifeless matter—his only postulate—no life can come.
" *Ex nihilo, nihil fit.*"

(4) Materialism Makes the Origin of Consciousness Impossible.

The materialist begins with crass matter and ends with the organism. In the outcome he tries to show how the "Cosmos arises in consciousness." He overlooks the fact that a knowing subject is presupposed in crass matter, quite as much as in its organized forms. Schopenhauer says : "' No object without subject,' is the principle which forever renders all Materialism impossible." The truth is that all beginnings are spiritual, not material. And conscious spirit must control unconscious matter. Ulrici has shown, " on the basis of firmly established facts, that to the soul, in contradistinction from the body, to spirit, in contradistinction from nature, not simply independent existence, but also the supremacy belongs, both of right and in fact."

Philosophy ought then to begin with supreme spirit, and not with subordinate matter. But Materialism reverses this order, and proposes to get consciousness out of organism. It cannot be done. Every attempt to do this impossible thing has plunged materialistic philosophy into fathomless absurdities. Take the effort of Mr. Lewes as an example. He begins by claiming that a neural tremor corresponds to every feeling. Then he proceeds to assert that these two corresponding things are one and the same thing. This is the first absurdity. A little further on, he declares that states of consciousness are separable from states of the organism. But, according to Materialism, consciousness itself is nothing but a state of the organism. We have here, then, the states of the state of a thing separable from the states of the same thing. A second absurdity. But these states are said to be separable only in our mode of apprehending them. Now this cautionary statement only adds to the obscurity

of the former.   For one naturally asks : Mode of apprehending what ?   Mr. Lewes evidently means states of
consciousness.   But consciousness itself is the apprehension of mental states.   Now as states of consciousness
must evidently *exist*, before any mode of apprehension
can be applied to them, we have here a thing existing and
apprehending itself in order to be apprehended by a mode
of itself.   A third absurdity.

But again, he is forced to make a purely physical organism perform acts of feeling, willing, and thinking.
Matter, simple matter, and nothing more, finds itself some
day in a state of consciousness.   Yesterday it was not
conscious ; to-day it is.   And this remarkable feat has
been accomplished simply by organism.   But this organism itself is the work of unconscious matter.   It seems,
then, that unconscious matter, without any extraneous
power or purpose, goes deliberately and patiently to work
to organize itself into a state of consciousness.   A fourth
absurdity.   Indeed, Mr. Lewes, in common with all
materialists, falls into fatal errors, by applying the language of physiology to the facts of psychology, and supposing that he has thereby identified the two.   They
cannot be identified.   Consciousness and the organism
are not, in any sense, the same ; and Materialism makes
the origin of consciousness impossible, and its plainest
facts inexplicable.

(5) *Materialism Makes All Knowledge Impossible.*

Knowledge implies the fact of a knowing agent.   But
Materialism rejects this implication in two ways.

(*a*) *It denies the knowing agent.*—The personal, conscious being which all knowledge presupposes, is resolved
by Materialism into an aggregation of highly organized

material atoms, thrown into successive and peculiar states of motion. But it is evident that these successive states of motion can never know any thing of one another. Neither can the material organism connect them in consciousness. There is no personal spirit to gather up and unify them, and so they must remain forever separated as isolated phenomena of the organism. From such phenomena, no such thing as knowledge could ever result. There is no more knowledge in " neural tremors " and " states of organism," than there is in ocean currents and states of the atmosphere. The materialist cannot, by any possibility, get the first ray of mental light into the darkness of his bioplasmic organism. The simple truth is that, without a unifying agent, the manifold of sense can never produce any knowledge whatever. Physical organism is not such an agent. Materialism denies any other agent, and thereby destroys the very foundation on which all knowledge rests.

(*b*) *It impairs every act of knowledge.*—This is done by its unthinkable doctrine of inherited experiences. According to Mr. Lewes, every individual inherits "*a priori* conditions of knowledge, and even *a priori* experiences which must determine the result of our individual *a posteriori* experiences." In plain language, this doctrine runs thus: My father's nerves, for some special and adequate reason, took to trembling in a certain way. At length, by frequent repetition, a neural habit was formed which resulted in the "establishment of definite paths" among the nerves. Thereupon neural tremors travelled more readily along these paths and produced the prevailing sensations, feelings, experiences in my father's life. Thus far the theory is comparatively lucid. But next comes the puzzle. It is this: my father transmitted to me, not only those peculiar neural pathways of his, but actually a portion of his feeling, sensation, knowledge, and experience.   How could sensation be transmitted? Even in his own organism, each sensation was constantly and irrecoverably displaced by another.   How then could he propagate a single one of them?   But if he could, what became of it before the dawn of personal consciousness in me?   It must have been preserved *ad interim*, by some materialistic lotion of whose nature and potency I can form no conception.

And then how can knowledge be transmitted by inheritance?   It was not apprehended by me for years after I must have had it.   But how can one have knowledge and not know it?   And, strangest of all, how can a man inherit experience?   Certainly it would be the last of all things to fall into a legacy.   Notice also that this experience is unconscious and *a priori*.   But *a priori* means before experience, or it means nothing.   Now by insisting that such impossible experience as this "must determine the result of our individual *a posteriori* experiences," Materialism undermines all experience and makes every act of knowledge invalid.

(6) *Materialism is Self-Destructive.*

Its self-destructive character appears from two considerations.

(*a*) *It reduces itself to nothing.*—Materialism is a theory in philosophy.   It is put forth for the sole purpose of explaining the existing facts of the universe.   Its value depends entirely upon its ability to explain admitted facts.   But, by denying the existence of mind, it renders itself incompetent to explain the undoubted facts of human personality, and the equally undoubted facts of cosmic development. It thereby stands discredited as a nullity in philosophy—a philosophic zero.

(*b*) *It renders itself impossible.*—According to Materialism, thought is only nerve-motion. Every opinion, every theory must, therefore, be a combination of nerve-motions, nothing more. Who can say, then, that one theory is right, another wrong, one true, another false? There is no possible standard of discrimination among neural motions. It will not do to say that truth results from normal, symmetrical movements of brain tissue, while error arises from the abnormal and unsymmetrical. Motion is motion; and, according to Materialism, any opinion or judgment concerning the relative value of molecular motions among the nerves, must itself be only a matter of molecular motions among those same nerves. It can have no power to arbitrate. There being no standard of truth, there is no truth. There being no truth, there is no philosophy. There being no philosophy, there is no such thing as Materialism. In pulling down all philosophy and discrediting all theory, Materialism has rendered its own existence impossible. A more completely suicidal theory cannot be imagined.

The truth of the whole matter seems to be that Materialism gets into trouble by taking a one-sided view of the manifest facts of human experience. It is true, on the one hand, that the body does influence the mind in numerous and various ways. "Fatigue dulls the attention, narcotics stupefy the powers of thought and emotion, fever may produce delirium, and a blow on the head may suspend consciousness." But, on the other hand, it is equally true that the mind affects the physical organism. And this influence is varied and potent, no less than the other. Fear blanches the face and convulses the limbs,

modesty mantles the cheek in crimson, love and hate
gleam through the eye, grief opens the secret fountain of
tears, the will dominates the muscular and nervous systems,
and even the moral lineaments of the heart fasten themselves upon the face in characters that are both sure and
abiding.

Now Materialism, emphasizing this first truth and
ignoring the second, falls into the error of supposing that
there is no mind, but all is physical. Idealism, on the
other hand, gazing intently upon the second truth and
overlooking the first, embraces the opposite error, and
asserts that all is mind and there is no matter. Both are
manifestly wrong. Matter exists and so does mind.
Moreover they coëxist and coöperate in all human experience. This is the only sound philosophy.

SECTION II.

PANTHEISM.

Pantheism is essentially an Oriental system of philosophy. It is found in the most ancient books of the East,
both philosophic and religious. In the Vedas, Uphani-
shads, and the Taoistic writings, the most positive pantheistic doctrines are expressed. Such doctrines have
been largely dominant in Eastern thought for forty
centuries. Their growth in the soil of Western Europe
is a thing of comparatively recent date. It is only since
the time of Spinoza that Pantheism has taken root in
Europe, England, and America. Within the present
century it has attained a vigorous growth, and has
placed itself across the philosophic path of Christian
Theism. The intelligent theist must meet and answer
its argument.

This doctrine, as its name implies, assumes that every thing is God and God is every thing. Pantheism is not Atheism, for it admits the existence of the Infinite. It is not Deism, for it asserts the immanence of God in the universe. It is not Theism, for it denies the consciousness and intelligent volition of God. Among the many shades of pantheistic writings, the doctrines of two leading schools may be distinguished; namely, the Pure Pantheists and the Ideal Pantheists.

(1) *Pure Pantheism.*

Of the former, Spinoza may be taken as one of the ablest and most distinguished representatives. He insists that there is and can be but one substance—"una et unica substantia," and defines it thus : " By substance, I understand that which exists in itself and is conceived by itself ; that is, that, the conception of which is not due to the conception of any thing else from which it must be formed." He further says : " One substance cannot be produced by another substance nor by any thing else. Substance must, therefore, be the cause of itself." " All substance is necessarily infinite." "God is the immanent, but not the transcendent, cause of all things." " God is a thinking thing and an extended thing ; thought and extension are attributes of God." " The human mind is a part of the infinite divine intellect." " The absolutely infinite is infinite in respect to all attributes." But of all these attributes of Deity, Spinoza asserts that we are capable of discovering only two—thought and extension. Even these attributes are of the same essence and are distinguishable only in our mode of perceiving them. In reality there is an absolute parallelism between them. Individual things must not be regarded as real entities; they are but the passing modes of that everlasting substance which is, at the same time, both the *one* and the *all.*

(2) *Ideal Pantheism.*

This school is of a different order entirely. It asserts the existence of finite spirits and of an infinite spirit, and declares 'there is nothing else besides. The material universe is not an entity at all; it is simply a mysterious energizing of the divine, under the form of time and space.

J. G. Fichte and Hegel may be taken as fair representatives of this school.

The former begins his philosophy with the assumption of what he terms " the universal Ego," from which all individual minds, so-called, and all external objects flow in ceaseless round as mere phenomenal products. This inconceivable universal Ego, this ultimate rational Being, is not an individual, because all individuality is taken away by the universal laws under which the ego is developed. He holds that the moral order of the world is not caused by a personal Being, and declares that " The living and operative moral order is itself God; we need no other God and can comprehend no other."

Hegel's philosophy is absolute Idealism. He begins with the absolute Idea, and traces its development, through the varied forms of nature, to its culminating point in the consciousness of the individual ego. This development is reached by a sort of self-movement in three stages: first, abstract thought; second, nature; third, spirit. The idea emits nature from itself by a species of self-alienation, passing over into something other than itself. Nature is constantly striving to overcome this estrangement and restore itself to its former union with the Idea. This restoration is accomplished at the point of self-consciousness in the human spirit. Hence the human spirit is the outcome of nature, and the ultimate form of the absolute Idea.

2. PANTHEISM EXAMINED.

All schools of Pantheism hold that in some sense things are a part of God, that they are inseparable from him and he is equally inseparable from them, and that therefore the infinite is the sum-total of the finite. They likewise agree in denying an act of creation, the existence of design in nature, and the freedom of the individual human spirit. Insomuch as Pantheism involves any of these errors, it is subject to the strictures concerning them which have been presented in former portions of this work, and need not be here repeated. But there are some special and fatal weaknesses in pantheistic philosophy which must be carefully noticed. This becomes the more necessary in view of the fact that Pantheism has gathered about it a certain air of profound philosophy, superior wisdom, and absolute truth, which tends to hide the most glaring defects, and so impose itself upon the understanding.

(1) *Spinoza's One-Substance Theory.*

This philosopher professes to explain the universe by a strictly deductive method. He lays down definitions, states axioms, and deduces propositions in a manner which is rigorously logical. His fundamental error lies in defining things that are ideal and not real, and in supposing that by defining them he has made them real, or at least shown their reality. All that his logic can possibly do is to prove what might be under certain hypotheses; it is utterly silent as to what actually is. This material fallacy betrays him into many errors.

(*a*) He fails to show that only one infinite substance can exist. Other substances, finite and dependent in their origin and existence, might be brought into being, and, so long as they exist, might be self-active.

(*b*) Granting that one single infinite substance does exist, he fails to show why or how it should have any modes whatever. A diversity of modes in one substance is quite as inexplicable as a diversity of substances.

(*c*) He does not show how, among an infinite number of modes in this one infinite substance, the two modes of thought and extension, and these only, are discoverable.

(*d*) He asserts the parallelism of thought and extension, but utterly fails to prove it. On the contrary, his own philosophy disproves it. He accounts for so-called "acts of will" by effects produced upon the body "from without, under mechanical and mathematical laws." But he has already formally renounced the *nexus* of cause and effect. Here must be a case, then, in which modes of extension act upon modes of thought. Their independent parellelism is therefore impossible.

(*e*) Spinoza likewise fails to explain how this one indivisible substance ramifies itself into an infinite variety of forms, embracing suns and stars, planets and animals, minds and bodies, thoughts, affections, and purposes. At this point, all Pantheism utterly breaks down. The theory of *one in many and many in one*, is beyond its powers of explanation. Having no self-conscious, creating God, Pantheism cannot secure the unity of created things as Theism can by their dynamic connection with their creative source. Neither can Pantheism secure plurality by created atoms, since its doctrine admits of but one substance. How this mysterious, indeterminate, unconscious unity of the pantheist could ever succeed in dividing itself up into the multiform existences of the universe, passes all comprehension. And if it could, that would only be to cancel unity and lapse into atheistic plurality. To assert the contrary is to defy both mathematics and philosophy, by saying that one is many and many are one. Between this childish doctrine and blank atheism, the one-substance theory is forced to choose.

(2) *Ideal Pantheism.*

This system is less revolting than the one just considered. Indeed there is something poetic and attractive about it. There is doubtless a sort of inspiration to be drawn from a doctrine which brings all created spirits into everlasting communion with the uncreated spirit, even though it be an unconscious communion. Idealism does not leave man, as pure Pantheism does, in a state of dreary and hopeless orphanage. Considered from the standpoint of sentiment, ideal Pantheism has the decided advantage. Philosophically, however, it is open to objections equally serious.

(*a*) Fichte derives all our knowledge of the world from our own self-consciousness, without any empirical basis whatever. He asserts that the universal Ego is alone truly existent; and that he has by his own absolute thought placed external nature, as an unreal non-Ego, over against himself. This is a most self-destructive theory. If there is no reality in the universe, there can be neither truth nor knowledge in it; and all philosophy is at an end. There remains in existence nothing but

Fichte's Universal Ego, which is helplessly unconscious and impersonal.

(*b*) Hegel's philosophy is likewise faulty. He attempts the impossibility of deriving the Absolute by *a priori* methods. This is a mistake. The conditioned is the evidence of the Absolute; the creation shows forth the Creator. Ignoring this fact, Hegel quite naturally arrives at an Absolute, which is zero. Supposing this zero to mean the content of universal being, rather than the cessation of human thought—as it does—he proceeds to found his philosophy upon it, and derive his universe from it. In doing so he is forced to posit unconscious thought, which is absurd; to develop the Idea by self-motion, which is impossible; and to make God the sum of all things (evil included), which is both unphilosophical and immoral. By these and other questionable assumptions, he has succeeded in erecting an ideal universe, without any actual existence—a sort of cosmical palace on paper, fair enough to look at, a pretty picture, but having existence as a palace only in the brain of the architect. However commendable his work may be as a product of pure philosophic imagination, whenever he attempts to pass it off as the only actual existing universe, all sober philosophy must seriously demur.

(3) *The Identity of God and the Universe.*

This postulate is, in some form, found in all Pantheism alike. The fallacy of assuming that God is the sum of existence has been shown in the former chapter. But it is equally fallacious to assume that God diminished himself in order to make the world. Infinity can neither be increased nor diminished. The pantheistic emanation theory is therefore absurd. There is one truth, indeed, which the pantheist properly emphasizes. He insists that God is in the universe, and not removed to a distance from it. In this he is right, and Christian Theism approves. As Carlyle puts it, God is not " an absentee God, sitting idle, ever since the first Sabbath', at the outside of his universe, and seeing it go." This immanence of God in nature is a mystery-explaining, God-honoring doctrine. But when the pantheist goes on to add that God is not only in the universe, but is confined to it, inseparable from it, he degrades Deity, dwarfs infinity, and becomes a practical atheist.

(4) *Pantheism Rejects the Doctrine of Design in Nature.*

This is done apparently in the interest of the Divine omnipotence. The pantheist asserts that design means contrivance, contrivance means necessity, necessity means a limitation of power. He reminds us that man resorts to *means* only when he cannot compass his ends otherwise ; that one will not employ a machine to raise his arm if he can do it without ; that God must be supposed to act in the same way ; and that therefore the theistic doctrine of design is destructive of infinite power in the Designer. This specious doctrine is essentially unsound. The theist does not limit God's power, nor restrict him to any method of creation. He could have created all things as they now exist by a single fiat. Moreover, he could have created them without any rational relation of parts, a mere jumble of chaotic confusion. But would that kind of creation show any more power than the existing harmonious and purposeful relations show ? God's doing a thing by the use of means does not prove that he could not do the same thing otherwise. This is not true, even with man. The Instructor may raise

his arm by mechanical means to illustrate before his class
the force of muscular action.   But that does not prove
the paralysis of his arm.   Even so, God may have, in the
employment of design in nature, some other and higher
purposes than the mere exhibition of power.   Among
such possible purposes, a worthy one might be to teach
his human children the beautiful and inspiring lesson of
his own wisdom, truth, and love.   But evidently no such
lesson of God's moral attributes could ever be learned
from a fiat universe, without change, progress, or relation
of parts.   To this undesirable method of creation, the
pantheist would restrict the Deity, under the specious
pretence of preserving his omnipotence against the attacks
of the teleologists.   But who shall protect God's volition,
intelligence, freedom, and moral attributes against the
doctrines of the pantheist?   All these are destroyed and
no power is gained.

(5) *Pantheism is Fatalistic.*

It makes man either a passing mode of an unreal non-
ego, or a necessary product of a divine energizing.   In
either case he has no such personality as gives him true
freedom of action.   He is what he must be, he does what
he must do.   Whether the pantheist asserts with Forberg
that he needs no faith, since death " will be for him a
total end," or hopes with Fichte that " no Ego which has
become real shall ever perish," it matters not ; for, at all
events, he must believe that his destiny, whatever it may
be, is forever fixed and utterly beyond his own control.

Nothing need here be added to what has heretofore
been said on this subject, further than the simple statement that fatalism is essentially the same, whether pantheistic, atheistic, materialistic, or agnostic in its origin.

It is everywhere subversive of sound philosophy, pure religion, and virtuous living.

(6) *Pantheism Denies an Act of Creation.*

It declares that nothing has ever been made. Whatever is, always was. Either matter exists, or it does not. If it does not, all the absurdities of idealism result. If it does exist, then it always existed. It is therefore eternal, and is at the least a part of God. God, then, is both material and finite. The pantheist must choose between these equally absurd extremes; for there is no other course open to him. He usually chooses the latter, makes nature in some way synonymous with God, and interprets natural phenomena as the developments of Deity himself. The God of the pantheist starts with unconscious impersonality, proceeds by a sort of inconceivable self-motion, through all the forms of material existence, and finally arrives at human intelligence—the end of his long journey. This view of the case exalts man, but it degrades the Deity. It makes of God an unconscious force, until he secures his own consciousness in the developed consciousness of man. But human intelligence is superior to any amount of mere force. It therefore follows either that man is superior to God, or that he is very God himself.

But, again, Pantheism is forced to bring something out of nothing. It teaches that there was a time when, in the whole universe, there was no conscious being. Now there are millions of conscious beings; and yet nothing was ever created. The theist may pertinently ask: " Whence cometh this consciousness?" Unphilosophical and immoral as these conclusions are, no pantheist can avoid them; for they are the logical outcome of his doctrine.   Having palpably violated the law of his own consciousness, he cannot expect to escape its just penalty.   It is far better to admit the evident distinctions between subject and object, matter and mind, the finite and the infinite, the created and the uncreated, God and the universe.   These distinctions are fundamental in the consciousness and intuitive powers of every man.   Pantheism, in all its forms, ignores these plain distinctions, and thereby involves itself in fatal errors, for which no amount of profound philosophical speculation can ever be able to atone.

SECTION III.

POSITIVISM.

I. POSITIVISM STATED.

This theory is the very opposite of Pantheism.   Instead of rejecting empirical knowledge, Positivism declares that "experience is the only foundation of truth."   Instead of tracing things from their beginning as the pantheist does, the positivist disclaims all knowledge of the beginning or end of things, the nature or essence of things, the cause or connection of things.   He rejects all Metaphysics and Theology as absurd.   He denies Causation, for fear it will lead to Theology.   For the same reason, he rejects both Pantheism and Atheism.   Indeed, he may be termed a philosophical know-nothing; for his philosophy is mostly engaged in declaring man's necessary ignorance of all philosophy.   He knows what his senses tell him, nothing more.   Even the physical facts of the universe have no connection, order, or relation of parts.   All is segregated, isolated, independent.

Science is confined to the senses. Its only legitimate business is to observe the phenomena of sense and to classify them under the authoritative relations of similarity and sequence. All religion is rejected as an absurd delusion. A certain form of Altruism is indeed allowed —a worship of Humanity, a reverence for the Grand-Etre, of which every worshipper is permitted to recognize himself as a part. But all knowledge of any Superior Being or dependence upon him, is strictly eliminated. The constructive part of this system depends upon the statement that human thought passes through three stages—the theological, the metaphysical, and the positive,—and that these stages are necessarily successive.

Such in brief is the doctrine of Positivism. Augustè Comte must be regarded as the founder of this school of thought. Prominent among its adherents are Littré, Harrison, Ferrari, and the younger Mill.

2. POSITIVISM EXAMINED.

Only a very brief review of this system need be made. No other is necessary to show its essential weakness and self-contradiction.

(1) *It Contradicts its own Principles.*

This it does at the very outset by asserting the relation of sequence. Whence comes this relation? The senses certainly do not give it. That inconceivably short instant of duration which we call the present, is all they can command. Of the past or future, the senses give no knowledge. The positivist must therefore go beyond his senses to get his first idea of sequence, or succession in time. But in so doing he violates the basal principle of his own philosophy, and so makes it self-destructive.

(2) *Positivism Contradicts the Facts of Psychology.*

The positivist must admit the existence of what we call mental phenomena. If not, he tears down his own doctrine, in the denial. On his own principle of similarity, he must likewise admit that these phenomena are distinctively alike in character, and unlike all others. They must belong, therefore, to an entity which is distinct from matter, or to matter itself. If he takes the former view, he postulates mind and ceases to be a positivist. If the latter, he becomes a materialist, and assumes to answer for all the doctrines of that false system.

(3) *Positivism Contradicts History.*

Its boasted " historic conception " is untrue. Human thought does not pass through three distinct and successive stages, in the first of which phenomena are referred to supernatural causes ; in the second, to occult, cosmic causes, and in the third, to no causes at all. Men have believed in creative design, in efficient causation, and in the truths of empirical science, at one and the same time. As a matter of fact, the greatest thinkers do now believe in all these truths. They are coördinate truths growing together. When the positivist asserts that they are successive and mutually exclusive ideas, he thereby contradicts the history of human thought.

(4) *Positivism Contradicts Logic.*

There is in it a vicious specimen of what the logician calls *circulus in probando.* In the first place, the positivist confines his knowledge to the testimony of his senses. This of course excludes all knowledge of himself, except as a physical being. He loses the ego in the non-ego. In the second place, he defines a material object as an object of sense. It exists only as a sensation. Its relation to a percipient being is all there is of it. He declares : " This world which I perceive, is my perception, and nothing more." Now he loses the non-ego in the ego. So both are lost, and all is gone. The last remains of Positivism have disappeared in the vortex of its own false logic.

SECTION IV.

AGNOSTICISM.

I. AGNOSTICISM STATED.

This philosophy is an ingenious combination and modification of the three systems just considered,—Materialism, Pantheism, and Positivism. It differs from them all, indeed ; but it affiliates more than it disagrees with them. In its present phase, it has taken shape and name from the works of Herbert Spencer, the great Agnostic of modern times. Its elements can be briefly stated in Mr. Spencer's own words.

He says: "What we are conscious of as properties of matter, even down to its weight and resistance, are but subjective affections produced by objective agencies which are unknown and unknowable." "A Power of which the nature remains inconceivable, and to which no limits in time or space can be imagined, works in us certain effects. These effects have certain likenesses of kind, the most general of which we class togetner under the names of Matter, Motion, and Force. The interpretation of all phenomena in terms of Matter, Motion, and Force, is nothing more than the reduction of our complex symbols of thought to the simplest symbols; and when the equation has been brought to its lowest terms, the symbols remain symbols still." He speaks of "the consciousness of a universal causal agency which cannot be conceived," and says: "The connection between the conditioned forms of being and the unconditioned form of being is forever inscrutable." Concerning this unconditioned being, he declares that is the "Unknown and the Unknowable," the "Infinite and Eternal Energy," and the Source of all phenomena," and that the human mind must, in "some dim mode of consciousness, posit a non-relative, and in some similar dim mode of consciousness, a relation between it and the relative." As to the subjective and the objective, he says it is "consciousness of a difference transcending all other differences." "Belief in the reality of self, is a belief which no hypothesis enables us to escape." "The force by which we ourselves produce changes, and which serves to symbolize the cause of changes in general, is the final disclosure of analysis . . . the original datum of consciousness." That there is nothing in existence but the impressions and ideas "which constitute consciousness," is declared to be really "unthinkable."

These extracts from Mr. Spencer disclose the foundation elements of agnostic philosophy. If we combine with them a most universal, exhaustive, and ingenious application of the principles of Evolution, we have a fair general idea of the whole system of Spencerian Agnosticism.

2. AGNOSTICISM EXAMINED.

A study of Mr. Spencer's works produces a profound conviction of his depth and patience of thought, his breadth and profundity of scholarship, his fertility of imagination, and his frankness and earnestness of purpose. His admirers are certainly extravagant in claiming that he is "the greatest analytical philosopher the world has ever seen"; and yet he is certainly *facile princeps* among anti-theistic writers of the present day. But this opinion does not require an adoption of his system of philosophy. Neither does it forbid an earnest protest against the immense and fatal errors which it contains. And it is scarcely more than a protest that can be offered here. Any thing like a presentation and discussion of Spencerian philosophy would require a volume in itself. A few strokes at its most fundamental errors, gathered in part from works already written, must suffice for the present purpose.

(1) *Concerning God.*

Mr. Spencer everywhere admits the existence of a Being above man and back of nature. But there is great confusion, not to say contradiction, in his statements concerning this Being.

(*a*) *The knowableness of God.*—He is declared to be the "unknown and unknowable." Here is an inconsistency. That which is now unknown, may hereafter become known. To declare it unknowable is to deny this possibility. But to justify this denial, two things at least must be known about the being in question. 1st, That it exists. 2d, That its nature, etc., cannot be discovered. Thus much, therefore, Mr. Spencer knows about a Being whom he declares to be unknown. And much more; for he describes this Being as "Absolute," "Infinite," "Persistent," "Omnipotent," as "Cause," "Power," as "Source of phenomena," and as "acting upon us." He cannot, then, be in the category of the unknown. It would be more consistent for Mr. Spencer to say: "God cannot be adequately or fully known."

(*b*) *The absoluteness of God.*—At one breath the agnostic calls God the "non-relative," and at the next talks
about "a relation between him and the relative." Now
it may be proper to inquire: How can the non-relative
have any relation whatever to any thing whatever? The
assertion that any being is non-relative, is a self-destructive statement. Such a being might exist; but if Mr.
Spencer knows that fact, his knowledge involves a relation between that being and himself. If he does not
know the fact, he cannot afford to state it as a fact.
There is certainly a dilemma of confusions in this statement.

(*c*) *The moral nature of God.*—Mr. Spencer is careful
not to state or imply that "The Absolute" is in any
sense a moral, or even a spiritual being. He expressly
states, on the contrary, that his doctrines "are no more
materialistic than they are spiritualistic; and no more
spiritualistic than they are materialistic." And yet he
declares that man's religious sentiment will always continue to exist, and will "have for its object of contem-
plation the Infinite Unknowable." Now, this means
nothing more nor less than the worship of a mere Force.
For, while the "Infinite Unknowable" may be a holy
spirit, or may be a senseless fetich, it can be *known* only
as Force, and, therefore, worshipped only as Force. It
would be just as rational and just as comforting to
worship Gravitation or Electricity or any other force.
One might as well pray to a volcano, or offer sacrifices
to a cyclone.

(2) *Concerning Man.*

It is declared that "no hypothesis enables us to escape
a belief in the reality of self." Herein the agnostic
seems to recognize the self-destructive tendencies of his

own principles, and to utter a positive warning against them. It is of no use. The citadel of "self" is already in ruins. Agnostic fires have had their full sweep over it, and it is quite useless now to gather up the ashes. No phœnix need ever be expected to arise therefrom.

The agnostic has told us that we know nothing but symbols, that we know them only by experience, and that experience is confined to consciousness. Two perplexing results must follow.

(a) *Our personal identity is destroyed.*—Consciousness relates only to the present moment. I may remember the past, but I cannot be conscious of it. If knowledge is confined to experience, and experience is confined to consciousness, then, manifestly, I can know nothing of the past. I cannot credit my own memory. I cannot be assured of my own past existence. Indeed, I cannot know that there is any past. If I trust my memory, I transcend experience, and thereby abandon Agnosticism. If I do not, I confine my knowledge of self to the feeling of the present moment, lose all idea of persistent existence, and thereby abandon my selfdom. An absent symbol has neither significance nor existence for me.

(b) *Our knowledge of our fellow-men is lost.*—Agnosticism gives no adequate ground to believe in the existence or the rationality of our fellow-men. It is true, we daily observe daily motions and appearances about us which we are irresistibly prone to attribute to beings like ourselves. But then, this universal proneness may be only a universal delusion. For these phenomena are nothing but symbols, after all. What they may symbolize, remains forever "unknown and unknowable." We may *infer* that they belong to intelligences, but that inference transcends experience, and must be rejected. According to the agnostic, it is quite as unsafe to infer the existence of intelligent beings about us whom we call our fellow-men, as it is to infer our own past existence, or the existence of an intelligent Creator of the universe. If his philosophy is true, all such inferences must be alike untrue.

(3) *Concerning the Universe.*

On this subject Mr. Spencer utters another caveat. He declares that to suppose there is no existence other than our own consciousness, is "unthinkable." This term, "unthinkable," is a great favorite with the great agnostic. It seems to be one of his strongest weapons—a veritable Medusa head, at sight of which he confidently expects any troublesome and belligerent proposition to drop into utter destruction. For Mr. Spencer to declare a thing "unthinkable" or "inconceivable" seems to him the most legitimate and effectual method of making a final disposition of it.

But why should he declare the non-existence of the universe unthinkable? His philosophy does not lead to such a result. He expressly and emphatically asserts that all we know or can know of the universe is in symbols. Now symbols may be of two kinds, pictorial or algebraic. Pictorial symbols represent the known, and bear some resemblance to it. Algebraic symbols represent the unknown, and have no likeness whatever to the thing symbolized. Of this latter class are Mr. Spencer's cosmic symbols. They are algebraic formulas. The equation in which they stand may be reduced to its lowest terms, but it can never be verified in any conceivable way. It is still symbolic language and nothing more.

Now Mr. Spencer himself must admit that algebraic symbols can stand for any thing or for nothing. " X " may be a million, or it may be zero. To deny this is to destroy its symbolic character. Any algebraic quantity may reach its vanishing point. And so this mysterious " X " and " Y " of consciousness may evidently stand for zero. In that case, Mr. Spencer's universe has vanished, past all possible recovery.

It is true he places among these symbols matter, motion, and force. But this avails him nothing, since these terms are all used figuratively without the least knowledge of the realities for which they stand. Even the so-called atoms which are supposed to be their seat of action, are themselves past finding out. These realities may therefore reduce to zero, and still Mr. Spencer's universe is a possible nonentity.

(4) *Concerning Knowledge.*

Agnosticism is a system of philosophy. But all philosophy implies the possibility of knowledge. Mr. Spencer recognizes this fact, and says that the postulate of Absolute Being " is the foundation of any possible system of positive knowledge." Now, since this foundation is the " unknown and unknowable," any system of knowledge erected upon it must be untrustworthy and illusory. Nay, it must be self-contradictory. For if the agnostic knows nothing of the Absolute, he can base no system upon it. But if he knows any thing of the Absolute, then the Absolute is not the unknown. If Agnosticism is true, its foundation is false. To say that one's knowledge is defective, or is confined to phenomena, is to admit that he has knowledge. Hegel says: " No one is aware that any thing is a limit or defect until at the same time he is above and beyond it." When the agnostic declares that he has no faculty by which he can know God, he thereby discloses the fact that he does know God. But, on the other hand, if the Absolute is the unknown, the non-relative, it follows that we cannot know the existence even of the Absolute. We cannot know that it is, any more than what it is. The agnostic, in order to be logical, must join hands with the positivist, and disclaim all knowledge of the existence of any thing but phenomena. Dr. Harris has well said : " There is no half-way house of Spencerian Agnosticism, between complete Positivism, which involves complete Agnosticism and Theism."

All knowledge is impossible. This statement embodies the necessary logical outcome of Agnosticism. If the statement be true, Agnosticism is impossible. If not true, Agnosticism is false. But this is philosophic suicide. Either horn of the dilemma is fatal.

Agnosticism set out to destroy Christian Theism. Its great Apostle declared that under his analysis revealed religion or scientific theology is no longer possible. But the whole system proves to be self-destructive. Haman-like, it has erected a gallows full " fifty cubits high " ; and, Haman-like, it hangs on its own gallows.

REFERENCES.

Wilson's " Kant and his English Critics."
Harris' " Philosophic Basis of Theism."
Clarke's " Ten Great Religions."
Fisher's " Grounds of Theistic and Christian Belief."

CHAPTER VIII.

EVOLUTION AND CHRISTIAN THEISM.

THE doctrine of Evolution is the philosophic specialty of the nineteenth century. But it is not a new doctrine. For more than twenty-five centuries it has, in some form, engaged the earnest thought of philosophers. In ancient Greece, both the Ionics and the Atomists held to it. Thales, Anaximander, Heraclitus, Leucippus and Democritus were evolutionists. Among modern philosophers prior to the present century, Descartes, Leibnitz, Goethe, Kant, and Lamarck, were inclined to some phase of evolutionary thought. It is only recently, however, that this theory has gained extensive recognition, and sought to hold in its grasp the entire circle of human thought and knowledge. Because of this attempt, which must involve Theology, no less than the physical and social sciences, it becomes proper, if not indeed necessary, for the Christian Theist to examine Evolution, as to its philosophic character and its bearing upon Theism.

SECTION I.

IS EVOLUTION TRUE?

There are four distinct types of Evolution. Only one of them, which may be called the Mechanical Type, need be discussed here. By Mechanical Evolution is meant that system of philosophy which holds that the existing universe has been developed from primordial star-dust without any interposition of extraneous power. It makes matter, motion, and force, the sole agents in all cosmical action. Haeckel, Huxley, and Spencer hold this view, and stand in the front among its able advocates. Their arguments in its favor may be grouped under six heads: (1) Spontaneous Generation; (2) Embryology; (3) Natural Selection and Breeding; (4) Reversions and Rudimentary Organs; (5) Anatomical Resemblances; (6) Geological Deposits. In examining these arguments, two cautions must be observed: *First*, a problem of such extreme difficulty, on which great men differ, must be approached with that candor and modesty which will free its discussion from prejudice, self-conceit, and the use of offensive epithets. Mere dogmatism avails nothing. *Second*, Evolution is not a power, but a process. If true, it establishes the fact of a certain process in nature; but it throws no light upon the ultimate cause, the origin or the end of that process.

I. SPONTANEOUS GENERATION.

Professor Haeckel says: "We can assume no supernatural act of creation for simplest original forms, but only a coming into existence by spontaneous generation," and intimates that naturalists who believe otherwise must "renounce their own reason." This original form of life he calls the monern. It came by mechanical processes, from plasson or "primitive slime," and that, in turn, from inorganic carbon combinations. He thinks this plasson still lives in the deep sea, under the name of Bathybius. "The oldest monera originated in the sea by spontaneous generation, just as crystals form in the matrix."

There are insuperable difficulties in the way of this theory.

(1) *As to This Bathybius.*

It has been chemically tested and found to consist of crystalline substance, with the débris of living organisms, but having in itself no evidence of life, past or present. This far-famed protoplasm, the only surviving witness to Professor Haeckel's theory, has failed him, and left his doctrine of *pangenesis* without support.

(2) *Spontaneous Generation does Not Now Take Place.*

In 1870, Dr. Bastian performed an experiment by which the fact of spontaneous generation was supposed to be established. Some ten years later, Professor Tyndall submitted the experiment to sixty careful tests ; and as a result declared : "The evidence in favor of spontaneous generation crumbles in the grasp of the competent inquirer." Indeed, there is now no such evidence worth examining.

(3) *Spontaneous Generation is Contrary to the Analogy of Nature.*

It is declared to be the product of physical force, acting under physical law. Now if such force produced life a thousand or a million years ago, it must continue to produce life. This statement cannot be questioned by the evolutionist, for his whole doctrine demands the eternal persistence of force without increase or diminution. But inasmuch as life now invariably originates from an antecedent life, analogy teaches that it always so originated. Those who think otherwise, have strangely forgotten their favorite motto : "The uniformity of nature."

(4) *Spontaneous Generation is Unphilosophical and Unscientific.*

It claims that dead matter made itself alive. It assigns no adequate cause for life, and tries to get out of matter that which is not in it. This is unphilosophical. Furthermore, it is based upon a mere assumption—an improbable guess, without a fact, an analogy, or even a probability in its favor. This is unscientific; for science is truth, observed and classified. No amount of persistent guessing can transform assumption into truth.

2. EMBRYOLOGY.

There are striking resemblances among the embryonic forms of all animals, and particularly of all vertebrates. Professor Haeckel forcibly exhibits this fact by illustration, in the plates given in the " History of Creation," Vol. I., p. 306. From this fact, evolutionists infer that Ontogeny, or individual development, is a recapitulation of Phylogeny, or tribal development—a sort of historic microcosm. That is to say, because, at certain stages, the human embryo, like that of the tortoise, the chicken, and the dog, shows gill-arches and a tail, it is inferred that these animals must have a common ancestry, having all descended from fishes and from tail-bearing mammals. There are three troublesome difficulties in the way of this inference.

(1) *It Assumes Too Much.*

It claims that because two things are alike in some respects, they must therefore be identical in origin. This will not do. For the same things differ in other respects, and thus, by parity of reasoning, show their difference of origin. One inference is as rational as the other. Embryonic similarities do not prove identity of species now, why should they be thought to prove such identity in the past? The argument is only an analogy at best, and has all the present facts of Phylogeny against it.

(2) *This Inference is Self-Destructive.*

It proves too much. If the existence of a tail in the human embryo proves the far-off descent of man from a tailed vertebrate, then the like appendage in the embryo of the fish and the tortoise must likewise prove the far-off descent of these animals from a tailed vertebrate. This would be evolution backwards. But if all embryonic elements are not phylogenic, there is no evidence that any of them are.

(3) *Even the Facts from Which This Inference is Drawn, are Themselves Questionable.*

Much of this embryonic similarity is such in appearance only, and not at all in fact. Take Professor Haeckel's far-famed gill-arch argument as an example. The embryo of man, at four weeks, shows certain wrinkles or folds in front of the neck; so does that of other animals. At eight weeks, these folds have disappeared. Haeckel argues that these marks, which in the fish are developed into gills, are arrested in man, and show his descent from the fish.

Now this is one supposition. Let it be matched with another. In the early fœtal period, from the form of the embryo and the great relative weight of the head, the neck is necessarily curved forward. But nature, intent on making man erect, deposits life-cells about the trunk symmetrically, in front as fast as behind. Those in front having less room, quietly enfold themselves and await further development. Later, when the abdomen and

lower limbs are formed, this curvature is partially relieved, the demands of growth are largely in front and
below the head, and these folds are absorbed and so disappear. They are not gill-arches at all, and never were. They
are simple neck-folds. They are not historic, pointing to
the past, but prophetic, pointing to the future. This supposition is quite as good as Professor Haeckel's. It is even
better; for the markings in question are *in front* of the
neck, just where they ought to be if neck-folds, and not
on the sides, where they ought to be if gill-arches. Both
gravitation and geometry are against the gill-arch argument. In like manner, other supposed embryonic likenesses, such as chemical identity, the human tail, etc., can
be shown to be equally illusive. The science of Embryology furnishes no good evidence of the animal descent
of man.

3. NATURAL SELECTION AND BREEDING.

The stronghold of philosophic Evolution is Natural
Selection. It bears the burden of the entire system. It
is relied upon to show how, by the most minute changes,
all present forms of animal and vegetable life have been
developed from crass matter. Evolutionists hold that
man has come from protoplasm under the guidance of
natural selection and the law of the survival of the fittest.

As Mr. Darwin is the father of this theory, and as his
views have been largely adopted by evolutionists, it will
be well to let him state them in his own words. He says:
"Slight individual differences, however, suffice for the
work, and are probably the sole differences which are
effective in the production of new species." "Natural
selection acts only by taking advantage of slight successive variations; she can never take a sudden leap; but

must advance by short and sure, though slow steps." "Some have imagined that natural selection induces variability; whereas it implies only the preservation of such variations as arise and are beneficial to the being under its conditions of life." "If it could be demonstrated that any complex organ existed, which could not possibly have been formed by numerous successive slight modifications, my theory would absolutely break down." "If it could be proved that any part of the structure of any species has been formed for the exclusive good of another species, it would annihilate my theory."

Professor Haeckel substantially adopts this view of natural selection. Only a single passage on this subject need be quoted from him. He says: "The adaptability of every organism is limited to the type of its tribe or phylum. No vertebrate can acquire the ventral nerve-cord of articulate animals. Within this inalienable type, adaptability is unlimited."

No one can study this Darwinian theory without a certain feeling of admiration, both for the boldness and beauty of the theory itself, and for the ingenuity and candor of its author. And yet, a careful examination discloses the fact that natural selection, however original and beautiful, is utterly unable to do the immense work so confidently assigned to it by evolutionists.

(1) *It Fails to Account for Variability.*

Both Darwin and Haeckel distinctly assert that natural selection produces no changes. It simply preserves such of them as may be beneficial. Whence arise these changes? The evolutionist says it is from adaptability to environment. But how came any organism to have such adaptability? Nay, more, how came these changes of environment even? If the universe was once an aggregation of homogeneous atoms, why did it not forever remain such? Whence came heterogeneity? For this great and wonderful effect, what is the cause? These questions, natural selection—as, indeed, all evolutionary philosophy—is powerless to answer.

(2) *Natural Selection is Contrary to Existing Facts.*

It declares that all genera and species now existing have been evolved from a common source by infinitesimal inherent modifications. But it neither gives proof that this evolution of species is now taking place, nor assigns any adequate cause of its occurrence, which might serve in the absence of empirical proof.

Now, what are the facts? We see all inorganic elements remaining unchangeably the same. Carbon, oxygen, nitrogen are now what they always were. Forms of organic life seem equally fixed. All animals seek the companionship of their own kind, and invariably propagate their own species. This is nature's universal law ; and the sterility of hybrids is her continual protest against its violation. No mutation of species has ever been known to be produced by nature. The mummy cats and ibisses of Egypt are just the same as the cats and ibisses of the present day. Four thousand years have wrought no change in species. Suppose it were otherwise. Suppose nature were originating new species before our eyes continually and abundantly. Would not such a fact be a powerful argument for evolution by natural selection? And is not the contrary fact an equally powerful argument against it? Professor Agassiz was not speaking without reason when he said : " I cannot admit the transformation of species."

(3) *Natural Selection Requires Too Much Time.*

This demand is twofold : first, to give a rational inference of its existence ; and second, to enable it to do its
work. During historic times, it has given no evidence of
its existence. But the evolutionist asserts that this period
is too short to form a judgment. He insists that if we
had a philosophic microscope of a million million diame-
ters, we could catch a glimpse of some slight mutation of
species in a sweep of a few thousand years. Not having
such an instrument, he protests that we must not decide
against mutation, and solemnly avers that the evidence is
there, if we could only see it. But we cannot see it, and,
by the very nature of the case, never can. Such an argument is unworthy of an earnest, candid truth-seeker.
Indeed, it has the appearance of a mere makeshift.

But, again, natural selection requires too much time to
perform its work. A thousand years is but an hour in its
calendar. It must have taken millions of years to pass,
for instance, from any one of Professor Haeckel's twenty-
one development steps to the next succeeding one. But
astronomers and physicists tell us that the habitable period
of the earth cannot have exceeded 10,000,000 or 12,000,000
years. And their conclusions, based upon the earth's internal heat, the tidal retardation, and the temperature of
the sun, must be approximately correct. But this period
is far too short for natural selection. Physical astronomy
has stubbornly set itself in the very pathway of terrestial
evolution.

(4) *Natural Selection is Inconsistent with Itself.*

Darwin and others insist that natural selection preserves beneficial variations, and just as surely "destroys
needless and injurious variations." Let it be granted

that natural selection has the wisdom to discover and the power to preserve every useful variation,—it matters not how. Even then, organic changes would be impossible. For every new organ would be a useless thing, and natural selection must promptly strangle it in its infancy, when as yet it was millions of years away from that stage of development which would enable it to be of any service. Take the organ of vision for example. At first it is a mere localized chemical disturbance. And then a faint sensitiveness to the light, but giving no vision. Now such a change could evidently be of no possible advantage to the animal in which it might occur. On the contrary, it must tend to his uneasiness and confusion. Instead of being supported, therefore, and preserved, it must be aborted at once.

The incipient wing of a bird could not perform its function, and must, on the same principle, be promptly destroyed.

The tongue of the woodpecker, that ingenious contrivance which enables it to find and fasten its prey, could never have been developed by natural selection. Its first incipient elongation must have been checked as a useless encumbrance. And the same is true of very many of the important organs which animals now possess. It is difficult even to imagine how they could ever have been acquired by natural selection. The doctrine of development by this method is lacking in coherence and self-consistency.

(5) *Certain Reciprocal Organs are in the Way of Natural Selection.*

These are of two kinds: those found in the same organism, and those in different organisms. Of the first class, the poisonous fangs of serpents furnish a good example. This weapon comprises two distinct elements: the vesicle which contains the poison, and the tubular fang by which it is projected into an enemy. Now, which element was developed first? Whichever it was must have been useless without the other, and so must have perished.

Perhaps the best illustration of the second class is to be found in the genital organs of all bi-sexual animals. These organs cannot be developed by use, for their use presupposes their development. Furthermore, they could not be evolved for purposes of individual utility, for they exist in different animals and are both useless and injurious to the separate organisms which possess them. Their only utility is found in the persistent preservation of the species. But natural selection, which makes the individual every thing and the species nothing, cannot develop them or even endure them. Indeed, this whole matter of sex is an element of weakness to the individual, and those animals in whom its first tendencies were developed must, according to the hypothesis of natural selection, have invariably gone down in the struggle for existence. Natural selection fails to explain the universal fact of sex, or even to agree with it.

(6) *The Limit of Variability is Fatal to Natural Selection.*

Professor Haeckel's doctrine that the "variability of the organism is limited to the type of its phylum or tribe," is certainly suicidal.

In the first place, who established this "inalienable type"? And when, and how? Then if it were established, how could natural selection ever originate a new type? Surely the monern was not so handicapped, or it never could have varied into a sponge. Nor was the sponge, else all would have been sponges to this day.   If the higher orders cannot transcend their bounds, neither could the lower orders.   If a tree cannot branch at the top, neither could it branch at the bottom.   If animal types are now inalienable, as Professor Haeckel expressly states, then they must always have been inalienable.   Natural Selection is hopelessly destroyed by its own advocates.

(7) *Artificial Breeding Gives Little Comfort to Natural Selection.*

Varieties of plants and animals quite distinct from one another have been produced by mating individuals peculiarly developed.   Dove-cote pigeons, for example, have thus been varied into carriers, fantails, tumblers, and pouters.   The argument is, that if man can do so much in a short time, nature, in an indefinitely longer period, can produce all manner of new species imaginable.   Against this inference there are several weighty objections.

(*a*) Man produces his effects by arbitrary will.

But, according to mechanical evolution, there is no such thing as intelligent will-power in nature.

(*b*) Artificial Breeding is contrary to nature.

It operates for the good, not of the varieties bred, but of the man who breeds them.   What the man gains, the varied animal or plant loses.   The natural type is stronger and always prevails.   Developed varieties of pigeons, when freed from the hand of man, invariably return to the natural type of the dove-cote.   Weeds invariably choke out the finest plants and flowers of the garden.

(*c*) The mechanical evolutionist cannot pass from the operations of man to those of nature.   Natural phenomena, in which he admits nothing but mechanism, must not be compared with the conscious, voluntary, intelligent action of man.   And hence, (*d*) Even if man, by artificial breeding, should be able to produce hundreds of new species, that fact would give no proof whatever of nature's ability to produce a single one.

The entire hypothesis of the origin of species by Natural Selection is beset with troublesome difficulties.

4. REVERSIONS AND RUDIMENTARY ORGANS.

Individual animals sometimes show exceptional peculiarities of structure which belonged to some ancestor many generations back. This fact Mr. Darwin calls reversion, and attempts to explain by his famous " gemmule " theory. This theory supposes that free, minute atoms, called gemmules, remain in the blood, are transmitted in a dormant state to successive generations, and finally show themselves in the production of reversions. He states that this can be done after " characters have disappeared during scores or hundreds or even thousands of generations."

This explanation is not a good one. In the first place it depends upon atoms, whose origin, and whose existence even, are uncertain. Herbert Spencer well says that " the genesis of an atom is no easier to conceive than that of a planet." The Atomic Theory may do very well as a working hypothesis in physical science, but it cannot furnish an ultimate philosophical explanation of any thing. Then, again, these dormant gemmules, unlike all other atoms, are points of passive rest, and not of active force. But, worst of all, they are expected, in the outcome, to do a work which is inconceivably great. Mr. Darwin allows them to revert after thousands of generations. To be moderate, assume the lapse of one hundred generations only, and the gemmules of a given ancestor, still remaining in the organism, would be one out of 672,087,865,219,477,713,800,122,073,088—nearly seven hundred octillions. It is simply inconceivable that *one* should overcome such a multitude of its equals, and so revert to the ancestral type. It is far more probable that these so-called reversions are produced by the recurrence of similar external causes. But if so, they furnish no proof of evolution.

The argument from rudimentary organs is scarcely less doubtful. The evolutionist claims that a creature possessing such organs has descended from ancestors in whom these organs were perfect, but that by disuse they were slowly atrophied, and became rudimentary as we now see them. The theory of animal descent and mutation of species is supposed to be thereby established. Against this argument two forcible objections may be urged.

(1) *If True, It is Valueless.*

Let it be granted that certain animals have lost organs possessed by their ancestors, and that this loss has been caused by disuse. This admission is of no value to Evolution. The ability to lose an organ under natural processes by no means implies the ability to gain a new organ under natural processes. Because the fish of Mammoth Cave have lost their eyes in the darkness, is no reason that they could regain them in the light. The fact that the assassin has taken a man's life must not be urged to prove that he can likewise restore it. Even so the degradation or retrogression of animal organism throws no light whatever on the possibility of its evolution.

(2) *It is Possibly Not True.*

The supposition that an animal, having a useful organ, should systematically and persistently avoid using it, is immensely improbable. That the boa-constrictor, having a good pair of legs, should stubbornly refuse to use them until they are degraded into spurs ; that the three-toed horse should persistently stand on one toe until the others disappear ; and that the Greenland whale, having been a land animal, and having taken to the water, should obtusely refuse to use its hind legs for swimming and keep heroically flourishing its useless tail until, after thousands of generations, the legs drop off and the tail develops into proportions of utility and strength ; —these statements, and such as these, unsupported by a single fact in proof, are too improbable either to induce belief or to command respect. The products of a fruitful fancy must not be mistaken for the facts of science or the principles of philosophy.

5. ANATOMICAL RESEMBLANCES.

Comparative Anatomy establishes the fact that the various types of animal structure—man included—have many and striking resemblances; and that corresponding organs in different types are modified to meet the demands of the various functions to be performed. The evolutionist argues that family likeness proves a common parentage, and that, therefore, this " animal affiliation " shows that all animals must have come originally from the same parent stock. This argument is based on fact, is reasonable, and certainly has some weight. And yet it is not conclusive. The theist may grant that this similarity of structure points to a common origin ; but he may find that common origin in a conscious, intelligent Creator, rather than an unconscious, material organism. Products of the same mind, whether human or divine, may be supposed to be alike. The masterpieces of Raphael, Rubens, and Michael Angelo bear the impress of their authorship. Compositions of Mozart, Beethoven, and Wagner, and passages from Milton, Dante, Shakespeare, and Goethe, are readily distinguishable. Even so, if God created the existing species, either at once or successively, he need not have separated them by an impassable typical gulf. Probably he would not have so separated them. Certainly he would not, if it was any part of his creative design to enable his intelligent creatures to trace, in animate nature, the purposeful tokens of his handiwork. The prevalent fact of typical form gives evidence of an intelligent plan in nature, whether executed at once or successively. But this conclusion gives no aid to the theory of Mechanical Evolution.

6. GEOLOGICAL DEPOSITS.

The testimony of the rocks concerning Evolution is too long and complicated to be discussed, or even transcribed, in this place. It may be said in general that the oldest fossils, found in the Laurentian and Cambrian systems, are favorable to Evolution. And later formations have many facts of like import. But there are other facts to the contrary. In the Silurian rocks we find actinizoa side by side with cuttle-fish, which are nearly allied to the vertebrates. Spiders, first found in the carboniferous rocks, ought to appear much earlier. Fossils, in the form of man, have a cranial capacity quite up to that of the human race to-day. Virchow says, indeed, that the average is decidedly in favor of the fossil. Such facts as these, of which there are many, are directly opposed to the theory of Evolution by natural selection. But this subject must not be dismissed without a passing reference to Professor Huxley's famous horse argument. The professor claims to have shown, upon geological evidence, that the horse of our day has been evolved from the Hipparion of the Pliocene age, and that animal, in turn, from the Anchitherium of preceding ages. The evolution of species is supposed to be thereby firmly established. Against the force of this argument the following objections have been properly brought:

(1) "There are remains of the horse in the Upper Miocene period, which resemble in nearly every respect the horse which to-day runs wild in Asia and Africa."

(2) "There are remains of the hipparion found in the same deposit as the horse, viz., in the Upper Miocene."

(3) "Now this proves that the hipparion could not have been the ancestor of the horse. For, according to the hypothesis of evolution, there must have been many intermediate stages."

(4) "The remains of the anchitherium are found only in the Lower Miocene; so that there is a wider gap between it and the hipparion than between the latter and the horse."

Subsequent discoveries have cleared away most of these difficulties. But Professor Huxley's announced "demonstration" illustrates a strong and illogical tendency on the part of some naturalists to translate an inference or even an expectation into the language of certainty.

All the arguments in favor of Mechanical Evolution are found, upon candid examination, to be beset with obstacles great in number, and insuperable in character.

In answer to the question at the head of this section, and in accordance with the evidence submitted, the verdict must go against the Mechanical Evolutionist. He has not made out his case.

SECTION II.

IS EVOLUTION ANTI-THEISTIC?

There are two theories concerning God, and only two, between which the Mechanical Evolutionist must choose. First, he may hold that matter and force are eternal and that there is no God. This is atheism. Second, he may hold that there is a God, that he created matter and endowed it at the beginning with self-moving power to evolve the cosmos, and that, with this one creative act, he retired forever from the universe. This is deism. But it is not Theism. It relegates the Deity, as an "absentee God," to realms of obscurity and inaction. It projects him into the fathomless abyss of past eternity, forever beyond the possible knowledge of man.

This view, it is asserted, enhances the power, wisdom, and dignity of God. The mechanical evolutionist reminds us that a good watchmaker is not obliged to keep tinkering with his chronometer, but makes it so it will run itself. And so the Creator, in constructing this immense cosmical watch we call the universe, did, at the very beginning, wind up each individual atom contained therein, so completely and so divinely, that it has been keeping the most accurate time ever since. Now this theory of cosmogony views God as voluntarily cutting himself off from all possible communion or display of affection toward his human creatures, who alone, of all the works of his hands, he knew would need his presence and yearn after his love. Such a method may exhibit a certain dignity of power, but it comports not with wisdom or goodness. That monarch who wantonly neglects the highest interests of his subjects, and that father who willingly leaves his child in enforced and perpetual ignorance of his own existence and paternal regard, may be powerful indeed, but must be fatally lacking in those moral elements which are superior to any amount of mere physical power, even as mind is superior to matter. Deistical philosophy, whatever its source, can never commend the Deity to the intelligence or the affection of humanity. The theist cannot find his God in star-dust. His moral personality is gone. But again. Mechanical Evolution destroys the personality of man. If there is essentially nothing more in man than in primordial atoms, then man has no more personality than the atoms. A man of snow, or of clay, or of plaster, has no personality. If nature has patiently and ingeniously fashioned a man-of-clay, we may name him Alexander, Buddha, or Jesus Christ, but that does not make him a real man. He is only a lump of clay after all. Thus is man's personality blotted out. But so also is God's personality. If man be not a personal being, there is no evidence that God is. If there is nothing but forms of matter in the created universe, there is no evidence of a Personal Spirit beyond it.

Mechanical Evolution, the type herein discussed, while neither atheistic nor anti-deistic, is anti-theistic beyond a doubt. The theist may safely dismiss it as a hostile but harmless theory, with neither proof nor probability in its favor.

A word may be said, however, concerning other possible types of Evolution. Nearly all the objections heretofore mentioned lie, not so much against Evolution, as against this mechanical form of it. Nature is not a machine, for it is plastic, progressive, improvable, while a machine is neither of these. Matter may reveal higher and still higher forms of organism, but can never create them. Matter, motion, and force, without a directive idea, can do nothing toward explaining a rationally developed universe. But why exclude a creative and directive idea? Let that idea be God. There is not a single fact in nature against the existence of a personal God, or the occurrence of an act of creation. There are many facts in favor of both. Why not admit that God made the world and sustains it in being? That admission would not blot out Evolution, but would view it as a possible, or, it may be, probable, method of God's creative and providential work. The question would then be, not " Evolution *versus* Creation," but " Evolution, the method of Creation."

The cosmos may be reasonably viewed as evolving under the hand of Deity, with such new accretions from time to time as the evolving forms may be prepared to receive. This view does not compel us to get life out of death, mind out of matter, spirit and rationality out of instinct, something out of nothing, as does the theory heretofore considered. It leaves the Deity free to add these elements in his own good time. And it admits with equal freedom the affiliation of material organisms, the testimony of the rocks, and all other facts—of which there are many—that point toward some manner of development.

At the same time it admits another and vastly more important class of facts—those of man's rational, ethical, and religious nature. If God is over this world and in it and through it, creating, developing, upholding all, then these facts are easily explained. But if he has been inert and absent since the creation of atoms, these facts are utterly inexplicable. The divine origin of the Bible, the fall of man, the divinity of Christ, miracles, the new birth, and the efficacy of prayer, must all be rejected from the mechanical evolutionist's creed, as mistaken Hebrew myths. More than this. The very existence and universality of man's religious nature is a tantalizing puzzle to him. If there be no God, or if he be forever the Unknowable, why should these curious and numerous aggregations of dust familiarly known as human souls be so persistently and irrationally determined to find him, know him, commune with him, and enjoy him forever?

The truth is, that the mechanical theory of Evolution, while recognizing certain important facts in the material world, ignores the higher and profounder facts in the realm of mind and spirit. It is therefore neither sound philosophy nor true science. For true science never rejects a fact of any kind whatsoever.

But that modified kind of Theistic Evolution which would seem, from every standpoint, to be the better philosophy, can recognize and interpret all the facts, material, organic, rational, and spiritual. The Christian theist has no controversy with Evolution *per se*, but against those forms of mechanical and materialistic thought with which it is so often and so suspiciously associated, he declares eternal war.

REFERENCES :

Schmid's " Theories of Darwin."
Hall's " Problem of Human Life."
" Victoria Institute Pamphlets."
McCosh's " First and Fundamental Truths."

CHAPTER IX.

IMMORTALITY.

MAN universally believes that he is immortal. This conviction is both intellectual and emotional, both philosophic and religious. Theoretically it is not necessary to Theology. The science of God may be logically complete without including the immortality of man. In emotional and religious force, however, the doctrines of God must lose immeasurably if divorced from the belief that man is immortal. If death ends all for me, it matters little what may be the character of God, or, indeed, whether there be any God at all. If there be no life of holiness beyond, then why should I strive to learn the ways of holiness here? If on my purified vision the dawn of no immortal day shall ever rise, then why should I resolutely close my eyes to the allurements of the flesh? If I am born to be tantalized for a brief space by the animalism beneath me and the divinity above me, and then to perish forever, what care I to know any thing of God or of his ways? But, on the contrary, if I am to survive this earthly struggle, to fulfil an immortal destiny, to bear the image of the Divine, to see God and enjoy him forever, with what rational delight will I study his character and hasten to obey his holy will.

The doctrine of Immortality being thus practically involved in Theism, must not be entirely omitted from its discussion.

SECTION I.

PRESUMPTIONS AGAINST IMMORTALITY.

1. PHYSICAL DESTRUCTION.

Death destroys the body. The soul is not traceable thereafter. Hence it has been argued that all is destroyed with the body. This argument is not conclusive.

(1) *Disappearance is Not Destruction.*

A thing may exist and not be manifest. It may cease to be manifest without being destroyed. Latent heat is just as much *heat* when latent as when manifest. Even so death may interrupt the visible manifestations of the human spirit, but its destruction must not be thence inferred.

(2) *Bodily Mutilation Affects Not the Soul.*

Limbs may be amputated, physical functions cut off, and senses suspended, and still the operations of the soul may proceed with unabated regularity, and even with increased vigor. If the partial destruction of the body does not affect the soul, its total destruction may not.

(3) *The Soul may Not be Divisible.*

The body is. It can be returned to its original elements—carbon, nitrogen, hydrogen, iron, and the like. Hence its mortality ; it can die. But there is no evidence that the human spirit is composed of parts, or is in any wise divisible. Possibly Bishop Butler may go too far in arguing its absolute indiscerptibility ; and yet the unity of the human spirit is accredited both by universal consciousness and by profound metaphysical research. Until the soul can be analyzed as the body can, it will not do to infer the destruction of the one from the decomposition of the other.

2. PHYSICAL DEPENDENCE.

It is claimed that the soul is born with the body, developed with it, manifested through it, limited by it, dependent upon it, inseparable from it; and hence the soul must perish with the body. Against this argument there are two objections.

(1) *It is Contrary to Analogy.*

It proceeds upon the supposition that the present fleshly environment of the soul is its only possible habitat. But the analogies of nature are against this view. The caterpillar, chrysalis, and butterfly are marvellously unlike in development, mode of life, and relationship; and yet they are one and the same being. So the life of the disembodied human spirit may be totally unlike that in its earthly tabernacle, even as the butterfly transcends the worm.

(2) *The Soul is Not Essentially Dependent on the Body.*

For certain of its functions in sense-perception, it doubtless is. But for other and higher functions, such as memory, imagination, thought, and reason, the soul acts of itself without the body. These processes would not cease, even though the senses were paralyzed, and all communication with the material world suspended.

3. EMPIRICISM.

The empiricist argues that, since the immortality of the soul is utterly beyond our experience, and since no disembodied spirit has ever appeared or testified to its truth, we have a right to infer that the soul is not immortal. This position is not well taken.

(1) *It is Unreasonable.*

It demands physical proof of a spiritual fact. And because of the absence of such proof, it denies the existence of the fact.

(2) *It Goes Too Far.*

If our lack of experience concerning disembodied human spirits forms a presumption against their existence, it must go equally against that of other spirits. The same argument that would disprove immortality would likewise blot out God, angels, and devils. But in blotting out God it renders the first existence of human spirits impossible, and thus merges itself into materialism. Experience is not the only avenue of conviction. If we know the soul to be superior to the body, even while connected with it, why may not that superior existence continue when the body shall have been dissolved?

SECTION II.

ARGUMENTS FROM THE HUMAN SIDE.

All reasonable presumptions against immortality may be readily and fairly answered. But this is not enough. Positive arguments in its favor must be adduced. There are many such arguments. A goodly number of them may be drawn from the very character of the human constitution.

Before discussing them, a single caution must be observed. It is this. Physical science has nothing to say concerning the immortal life. It deals with the life of the flesh, and with that alone. It gives conclusive testimony concerning the embodied spirit. But of its disembodied state, if it have such a state, physical science has no testimony to give. Its operations are properly confined to material phenomena. If this evident truth be borne in mind, it will guard us against two possible errors:

First. It will prevent us from asking or expecting physical science to furnish any proof of the soul's immortality. Manifestly every such expectation is unreasonable.

Second. If physical science should forget herself, and assert that, inasmuch as she finds no evidence of the future life, therefore there can be no future life, then this reasonable caution will prevent an over-estimate of such a statement. It will assure us that all such assertions are mere assumptions, that in making them science is leaving her own appropriate sphere of knowledge, and assuming to speak where she knows nothing, and that any utterances she may be pleased to volunteer on this subject cannot, by the nature of the case, have any possible weight in determining the question of immortality. Let these truths be kept in view while arguments for the future life are being drawn from the constitution of man.

I. THE HUMAN ORGANISM AFFORDS A PRESUMPTIVE ARGUMENT.

Man is the highest of a progressive series of organic forms. The simpler the form, the more evanescent is its life. With few organs, an animal form has little correspondence to its environment, and hence little ability to adapt itself thereto. With a multiplication of organs, this ability increases, and the period of individual life is correspondingly lengthened. A man may outlive a thousand generations of the simpler organisms. This relation of organism to environment has been emphasized by the scientific philosopher. Herbert Spencer says: "Perfect correspondence would be perfect life. Were there no changes in the environment but such as the organism had adapted changes to meet, and were it never to fail in the efficiency with which it met them, there would be eternal existence and universal knowledge." Now here is a distinct intimation of immortality, from a purely scientific standpoint. For its realization, only two things are needful: a perfect environment and a perfectly adaptable organism. Apply this test to the human spirit. It is not a physical organism indeed ; but it has that " unity in complexity " which involves at once the highest possible unity and the greatest possible complexity. Nor is it perfect ; and yet it approaches a state of perfection which it seems plainly capable of attaining. If such perfection shall be attained in a perfect spirit-world with which the disembodied human spirit is in perfect harmony, and in which, by reason of its perfection, no harmful changes or " mechanical actions " can ever interrupt the processes of the finite spirit, then Mr. Spencer's scientific conditions of immortality will be fully met.

That this perfection may be so attained, is manifestly possible, if not probable. But one thing seems certain. The human organism itself, with its relative complexity, adaptability, and longevity, as compared with lower types on the one side, and with the human spirit on the other, furnishes a strong presumption, at least, in favor of the future life of the spirit.

2. THE PRESENT LIFE IS ONE OF PURPOSELESS IMMATURITY.

If this life be all, there is nothing in it to justify its existence, its growth, or its trend. The soul is scarcely ready for its fruitage when death cuts it off. If there be no harvest beyond, then all is fruitless and vain. Death is an untimely frost, that cuts down and destroys forever the whole garden of God. There is nothing left to the mind but the burden of disappointing toil, nor to the heart but the shock of broken hopes.

Neither can we solace ourselves with the thought of the perpetuity of the human race. The race is nothing more than the men and women composing it. The boasted " Grand-Etre " of humanity is a myth. If every

individual soul is to go out in darkness and death, the
mere continuance of the race can bring no relief.   On the
contrary, it adds to the general disaster.   Every additional
soul but increases the disappointing vanity of life.   And
so the very multiplication of souls becomes a huge and
horrifying iniquity.

Nor can we find comfort in the intellectual and spiritual
advancement of the race.   The grander and better human
life becomes, the stronger will be the argument for its
continuance, and the keener the disappointment in its
untimely cutting off.   If such a life, with its increased
powers and hopes, with its demonstrated capacity for indefinite progress in virtue and happiness, is to be throttled
at the very birthplace of its rational existence and laid
away forever in the grave, surely 'it must be a cruel
Demon who presides over the advancing destinies of the
race, only to increase the poignancy of the direful disaster
at the last.   If the toils and hopes of this life are ever to
ripen into a fruitful harvest for the soul, that harvest must
come in another life beyond.   It is not garnered here.

3. THE MORAL LAW ARGUES A FUTURE LIFE.

By moral law is meant that code of ethics which is
written, in ineffaceable characters, upon the tablet of
every man's heart.   It is that law which binds him to do
good and eschew evil ; to restrain his passions and malevolent desires, and cultivate his conscience and his judgment;
to sacrifice pleasure to duty, the present gratification to the
future good.

Now this universal law means a universal and life-long
struggle.   If this struggle is to be followed by enduring
peace, in a state of unalloyed bliss and confirmed virtue,
then the struggle itself is amply justified ; for surely such

a peace is worth conquering at any cost. But if the struggle is to end in utter extinction, it is worse than vain and useless. It imposes unmeaning and burdensome restraints, it carries too vast a sweep, it deceives us with lofty promises and empty threats. It vainly attempts the impossible and falsely hides its own failure. If death ends all, all is lost; and the moral law itself is the most ill-timed, deceptive, immoral enactment possible. If this prolonged struggle we call human life is to issue in eternal defeat, then it is immeasurably worse than failure. The unthinking life of the mere animal is better. And this is not a concession to animalism. The spiritual life is indeed superior to the animal life; but it maintains its superiority by virtue of its hold on the future, in which alone its vastness of sweep and fruition are to be found. If that is gone, all is gone. If there be no future life, then it were tyranny to establish the moral law, and moral madness to obey it.

4. DEATH DOES NOT EXHAUST THE POWERS OF THE SOUL.

It does exhaust the physical life. But there is a spirit in man which outgrows the body and keeps on expanding and strengthening, even after the physical powers begin to decay. And this expansion is felt to be but the beginning. When the body dies, the spirit is just ready to live. Its highest forces take hold on the future. The old man is just prepared for the life of the spirit. By a period of discipline he has matured his faculties, subdued his passions, enlarged his sympathies, refined his taste, broadened his knowledge, deepened his thought, purified his affections, and elevated his desires. By all these things is the human spirit brought to its true equipoise of virtuous attainment, and fitted for an unending

life of noble activity and of enduring peace. And shall
we suppose that all this preparation for life is but an
empty prelude to death, that all this gathered light is to
be put out in the grave, that this lofty endeavor after the
high and the holy is to be lost in final dissolution, that
the ineffable and unconquerable hope of an immortal life
is to be quenched forever in the tomb? Shall the animals even have time to round out their lives to satiety,
and shall man alone die unsatisfied? Shall the lower
powers be nicely adjusted to their ends, and the higher
powers never find adjustment? Shall intelligence and
spirituality, with their longing after a future life and their
conscious ability to improve and enjoy it forever, prove
at last to be a delusion and a cheat? Surely these powers of the soul in their present development do not indi-
cate any such pitiful future of oblivion and death. The
rather do they point to that broader and freer life wherein the spirit, having finally outrun the flesh, shall reach
its goal and wear its deathless crown.

5. BELIEF IN IMMORTALITY IS UNIVERSAL AMONG SPIRITUALLY MINDED MEN.

The best thinkers, though they may, like the gifted
Goethe, be without any realizing religious faith, still
agree with him as to a future life. Hear what he says:
" I should be the very last man to be willing to dispense
with faith in a future life. Nay, I would say, with Lo-
renzo di Medici, that all those are dead, even for the
present life, who do not believe in another. I have a
firm conviction that our soul is an existence of an indestructible nature. It is like the sun, which seems indeed
to set, but really never sets, shining on in unchangeable
splendor."

This is the common conviction of all men. To this statement there are two apparent exceptions. The Hindu belief in Nirvana forms the most noteworthy case. There is no doubt that millions of devout Hindu worshippers have included in their religious faith the belief and hope that they shall finally be absorbed in Deity. To them, however, this thought comes not as the stroke of annihilation, but rather as the gift of immortality. Other men cannot so regard it ; and even the possibility of their doing so is a mystery to Western thought. Its explanation, however, is to be found in their imperfect views of personality, both human and Divine, and not at all in their denial of immortality.

The other exception is found, in rare cases, among gifted men, who in all ages have denied or doubted the reality of the future life. This fact will be explained under the next topic. Meanwhile it may be asserted that the belief in immortality is quite as universal as any other belief among men. Moreover, it is among the strongest and most persistent of human convictions. But the objector may ask " What of that ? Are the universality and strength of a belief to be taken as an argument for its truth ? " Certainly they are ; and if not, then the most fundamental convictions of men must be rejected. When John Stuart Mill intimates, for instance, that, in some other world, two and two may not make four, the best and only answer is to be found in the universal and necessary conviction of mankind to the contrary. Even so man believes in his own immortality, by a necessity of his nature. He cannot divest himself of this conviction. The fact that he exists now, is all the proof he asks that he shall always exist. He cannot believe in his own non-existence any more than he can believe that somewhere two and two might make five instead of four. Now this universal and inexpugnable belief is a fact to be accounted for. It is best explained when taken as a sure token of the reality of the future life. Otherwise, our most profound and intimate convictions are utterly untrustworthy.

6. THE VERY REJECTION OF IMMORTALITY BY GIFTED MEN IS SOMETIMES AN ARGUMENT IN ITS FAVOR.

This statement may seem contradictory. Let it be explained. The *fact* of rejecting a belief can, in no wise, constitute an argument in favor of that belief. The exception cannot possibly prove the rule,—a silly proverb to the contrary notwithstanding. It is not the fact of rejection, but the *manner* thereof, that furnishes an argument for immortality. If great and good men, in a few cases, have given up this belief, their concession results from one of two causes: either an abnormal defect in the religious nature, or the adoption of some false system of philosophy. In the latter case, the immortal life is yielded with the greatest reluctance, and only at the relentless demand of empiricism, agnosticism, materialism, or some other one-sided philosophy. But in either case the man who denies immortality does so in plain violation of his better nature, and thereby gives an unintentional argument in favor of the very truth he denies.

Perhaps the correctness of this statement cannot be better enforced than by quoting from a gifted agnostic philosopher of modern times. After concluding from the force of his philosophy that there is no adequate evidence of God or of immortality, he closes his treatise in the following words:

" And now, in conclusion, I feel it desirable to state

that any antecedent bias with regard to Theism which I individually possess is unquestionably on the side of traditional beliefs. It is therefore with the utmost sorrow that I find myself compelled to accept the conclusions here worked out ; and nothing could have induced me to publish them save. the strength of my conviction that it is the duty of every member of society to give his fellows the benefit of his labors for whatever they may be worth. Just as I am confident that truth must in the end be most profitable for the race, so I am persuaded that every individual endeavor to attain it, provided only that such endeavor is unbiassed and sincere, ought, without hesitation, to be made the common property of all men, no matter in what direction the results of its promulgation may appear to tend. And so far as the ruination of individual happiness is concerned, no one can have a more lively perception than myself of the possibly disastrous tendency of my work. So far as I am individually concerned, the result of this analysis has been to show that, whether I regard the problem of Theism on the lower plane of strictly relative probability, or on the higher plane of purely formal considerations, it equally becomes my obvious duty to stifle all belief of the kind which I conceive to be the noblest, and to discipline my intellect with regard to this matter into an attitude of the purest scepticism. And forasmuch as I am far from being able to agree with those who affirm that the twilight doctrine of the 'new faith' is a desirable substitute for the waning splendor of 'the old,' I am not ashamed to confess that with this virtual negation of God the universe to me has lost its soul of loveliness; and although from henceforth the precept to 'work while it is day' will doubtless but gain an intensified force from the terribly intensified meaning of the words that 'the night cometh when no man can work,' yet when at times I think, as think at times I must, of the appalling contrast between the hallowed glory of that creed which once was mine and the lonely mystery of existence as now I find it,—at such times I shall ever feel it impossible to avoid the sharpest pang of which my nature is susceptible. For whether it be due to my intelligence not being sufficiently advanced to meet the requirements of the age, or whether it be due to the memory of those sacred associations which to me at least were the sweetest that life has given, I cannot but feel that for me, and for others who think as I do, there is a dreadful truth in those words of Hamilton—Philosophy having become a meditation not merely of death, but of annihilation, the precept *know thyself* has become transformed into the terrific oracle to Œdipus—' Mayest thou ne'er know the truth of what thou art.' "

These are the words of an honest doubter—the piteous wail of a soul ruined by false philosophy. But the very greatness of the ruin they disclose only serves to emphasize the folly of rejecting that fundamental belief which binds all men to the future life.

7. IMMORTALITY IS THE LAST ARTICLE IN THE NECESSARY RELIGIOUS FAITH OF MANKIND.

The faith-faculty insists upon the existence of human spirits and a Divine Spirit. But this creed is incomplete and disappointing without a third article—the immortal fellowship of spirits. It is thus that faith, the highest possible function of the mind and heart, gathers the best that is in us about the future life as the only living centre of its inspiration. From that immortal clime the clearest voices of duty and the sweetest voices of love come thronging into our hearts. Heeding their kindly words of admonition, comfort, and hope, and lifting the eye of faith above the horizon of sordid sense to the regions of purity beyond, we are made conscious of the highest and the holiest that is within us, and are filled with an unutterable longing to become meet for the exalted inheritance to which we are called.

Henry Drummond, speaking on this subject, and arguing the necessary correspondence of the soul with its future environment, says: " The quality of the Eternal Life alone makes the heaven; mere everlastingness might be no boon. Even the brief span of the temporal life is too long for those who spend its years in sorrow. Many besides Schopenhauer have secretly regarded consciousness as the hideous mistake and malady of Nature. Therefore we must not only have quantity of years, to speak in the language of the present, but quality of correspondence. When we leave science behind, this correspondence also receives a higher name. It becomes communion. Other names there are for it—religious and theological. It may be included in a general expression, Faith; or we may call it by a personal or specific term, Love. For the knowing of a Whole so great involves the coöperation of many parts."

Eternal communion with God—this is the culmination and resting-place of all truly spiritual philosophy. It may not be uttered in the measured phrase of exact science; but it transcends science, and speaks to the heart in the clearest possible language of truth and duty and love. It leads to the noblest life, the loftiest thought and feeling, the most heroic endeavor, the strongest faith, and the purest hope. It contradicts not a single fact of material science, but it interprets, harmonizes, and justifies the otherwise inexplicable facts of human life and the human spirit. It unites the sublimest thought of the mind with the purest sentiment of the heart, and lays upon both the enduring blessing of Heaven. Immortality is the final leverage in the grand up-lift of the human spirit.

SECTION III.

ARGUMENTS FROM THE DIVINE SIDE.

The preceding arguments find their warrant in the constitution of man. Bnt they are not the only possible proofs of immortality. Another and entirely distinct system of arguments may be drawn from the nature of God. Doubtless the best argument for immortality from the God-ward side is to be found in the Word and work of Jesus Christ. Natural Theism cannot use this argument, however, since its validity plainly depends upon the fact of a Revelation. And yet, without opening any Book of Revelation, it may be seen that the Divine Being possesses attributes which demand an immortal life for man. A brief compend of this argument for immortality from the Divine side, as usually presented by theistic writers, is all that need be given here.

I. THE WISDOM OF GOD REQUIRES IT.

If we believe in God at all, we must believe him to be a Being of infinite wisdom. And if so, all he does must be perfectly wise. Now, the creation of man in his present environment and with his present constitution, is evidently an act of God, no matter how it may have been done. It must therefore be perfectly wise. But its wisdom can never be vindicated by the experience of man as a mere denizen of the earth. If there be no future for him, he would far better never have been. It is no irreverence to say that while the wisdom of his creation can be clearly seen in the light of immortality, it cannot be seen at all without that light. This world is a scene of perpetual moral disorder and confusion. If there be any wise purpose in it, or any moral harmony to result from it, the future alone can disclose that fact. If this momentary life of the flesh is the prelude to an eternal life of the spirit, then the present confusion appears as only the marshalling of those moral forces within the soul which are to carry it, in harmony and victory, into its native domain of enduring peace. But if there be no life of the spirit, if the forces are perpetually mustering without plan or purpose, and never engaging for the crown of immortal victory, then the present life is but the merest by-play—a childish farce, a comedy of errors with a tragic end. Surely the creation of such a being, and his endowment with such a life, could reflect no credit upon the wisdom of the Creator.

2. THE GOODNESS OF GOD IS A PLEDGE OF IMMORTALITY.

The infinite goodness of God calls for the goodness and happiness of his moral intelligences. Man, one of these intelligences, is evidently fitting in this life for a state of goodness and happiness beyond. His spirit is manifestly capable of such a beatific state of being. In his best and supremest moments he longs for it more than for all things else, and gives himself up to the all-absorbing desire. This desire is high and holy. Its gratification would honor the Creator and bless the creature. It is therefore the dictate of infinite love. But God's love

must be infinite, like himself; and must continue its outflow to the human soul, so long as the human soul is
capable of receiving it.   He will not then create that soul
only to destroy it at the very moment when it is best
fitted to receive his own love.   The rather will He manifest the Divine strength of that love more and more in
the perpetual enlargements of an immortal life.

3. THE VERACITY OF GOD CALLS FOR IMMORTALITY.

Man has been universally endowed with what Max
Müller calls the faith-faculty.   By the nature of this
faculty he is constrained to believe in the truthfulness of
God.   He feels sure that God will not and cannot
deceive him.   But man likewise finds within him a universal hope of immortality, and a continual longing for it.
He also recognizes in his own being powers and possibilities that promise a future life.   By this promise he is
lifted to the highest hope and urged to the strongest
endeavor.   If, therefore, there be no future life, then the
very constitution of man must be a perpetual delusion,
and the God who made him thus must be an arch-
deceiver from the beginning.   But this cannot be.   A
wise and truthful parent will not raise in the bosom of his
child an ardent and all-absorbing hope which he knows
can never be realized.   Neither will he permit such a
hope to be awakened by another if he have power to prevent it.   But the Infinite Father of us all has allowed this
fervid hope of immortality to glow incessantly in the
hearts of his human children; nay, more, He has kindled
it there with his own creative hand.   And will he permit
it to go out in unutterable despair?   Has he formed us
but to deceive us? to toy with our affections, make grim
sport of our hopes, and then turn us into nothingness

forever? Surely not; his wisdom and truthfulness forbid it. Both are pledged to fulfil every promise of his hand.

4. THE FELLOWSHIP OF GOD IMPLIES IMMORTALITY.

Men have always believed in the fellowship of God. The communion of the Infinite Spirit with the purest spirits of earth has, in all ages, been held as a possibility and a sacred fact. That the Divine is in some way communicable to the human, is a cardinal doctrine of Christian Theism. Sufficient proofs of its truth have already been given. God evidently can hold communion with man; or rather, to speak more exactly, man has been made capable of communing with God. And if so, God will surely bring him into fellowship with himself. His goodness and love demand it. It is the very nature of love to communicate itself. All true love gives itself to its object. If God loves man he will not shut himself up in perpetual isolation; he will find means to manifest his love. There will be a communion of spirits. But the very existence of such love argues its continuance. Love cannot die; true affection can never cease. And surely the infinite and loving God will not bestow his love in order to recall it. He will not awaken human love in order to disappoint it. That same Divine affection which has made fellowship with man both possible and necessary, will also make it eternal. The immortal fellowship of all good spirits is as sure as the immortality of God himself; its pledge is written in his infinite being.

5. THE VERY EXISTENCE OF GOD IS AN ARGUMENT FOR IMMORTALITY.

Theoretically and logically, as has been before stated, there may be no necessary connection between the being

and character of God, and the immortal life of man.   A
tolerable system of Theism might possibly be constructed
without reference to a future state.   There would doubtless be many obscure places in it, but the possibility of its
construction need not be denied.   One thing, however, is
very certain.   No such system could have any practical
power over the lives and consciences of men.   It would
be essentially cold and valueless.   Every realizing, inspiring, vivifying view of God's being includes immortality.
It is quite true that men have sometimes lost their hold
on immortality, but it is because they have first lost their
hold on God.

He who lives with God now, confidently hopes to live
with him forever; but he who expects to pass the period
of his earth-life and then lie down and perish like a beast,
has never been touched by the inspiration of the Almighty.
He is spiritually dead already ; there is no light in him.
He is without hope because he is without God in the
world.

Now these arguments for the future life are neither
exact nor demonstrative ; and yet they are rational and
convincing, unless one bars his mind against them and
prefers the thrall of death to the thrift of life.

For such a one, life has no joy, no peace, no hope.   It
is but an empty chaos of blackness ; the soul-sickening
shadow of the tomb is over it all.   The light has faded
from the sky, and the soul that has once tasted the delu-
sive sweets of life must be filled at last with the bitter-
ness of death.   Every avenue before it leads at last to a
dark and lonely pathway.   Of its entrance upon that
solitary journey, there is a lifetime of agonizing dread,
but not a single moment of friendly warning.   The whole
earth is one vast charnel-house of departed spirits.   The

voices of vanished hopes break into one dirge-like wail of despair, and the doomed spirit is hurried away into the dread silence of eternal dissolution. There is an inexpressible sadness in the orphanage of such a soul. It has lost its God, its Heaven, itself. The spell of the destroyer has come upon it and covered all with the ashen hue of death.

There is but one voice that can avail to break the spell and set the spirit free. That voice is the pledge of immortality. It is the final utterance of a true spiritual philosophy. It restores the faded light, revives the vanished hopes, relights the quenchless fires of life, proclaims eternal victory over death, and crowns the purified spirit with an immortal diadem of fellowship with God.

CONCLUSION.

IN concluding this system of theistic studies, three reflections present themselves :

1. The personality of man, the being, eternity, and sovereignty of God, the moral character and responsibility of human acts, the immortality of the soul, and the enduring rewards and retributions of the future life are basal truths of human belief. They are firmly and ineradicably implanted in the heart. No circumstance, environment, or system of thought has ever been able to remove them or destroy their force. Either they are received in their simplicity and purity, or else they are distorted into monstrous beliefs, which, by their very enormity, demonstrate their necessity. Man can neither rid himself of them nor render himself indifferent to them. He is born to them, bred in them, fed on them, buried with them. What he is, they make him ; what he has, they give him ; what he hopes, they pledge to him. They voice his deepest thoughts, control his purest sentiments, inspire his noblest deeds. To renounce them is to reject one's spiritual birthright in the impossible attempt to feed the hungry soul on the sodden pottage of materialism. To cherish them and live by them is to make the most of life and character and destiny. It is to choose, in the supreme election of life, that spiritual philosophy which alone is both rational and satisfying.

2. In their last analysis all these truths depend upon the faith-faculty. Religious faith, so called, is that in man which construes and justifies the basal truths of Christian Theism. All its arguments must finally be brought to this test. Faith in testimony justifies all historical proofs. Faith in the uniformity of nature is the ultimate ground on which all inductive and deductive arguments must rest. Faith in the necessary intuitive truths of the mind gives all their force to the intuitional and causal proofs therein employed. And this is no disparagement to the proofs themselves. They are rational, and their convincing force is irresistible. And yet it must never be denied or doubted that without faith it is impossible, not only to please God, but even to know his being, recognize his hand, or read his words wherever written, in nature, providence, or grace.

3. This resort to faith is not a mere weakness or religious makeshift. It is the ultimate resort in all things, the crucial test of human knowledge, the very citadel of truth itself. Without faith it is indeed impossible to know God. Be it so. The theist makes no apology; for, if this analysis is just, it is equally impossible to know man or earth or ocean or star or sky. All objects of knowledge are on precisely the same footing in this regard. There is no department of truth, physical, philosophical, social, or historical, which, at the last thrust, rests not on this same basis of universal faith. More than this. There is not a single truth established in any field of human thought which can be proved without an ultimate resort to some principle of simple belief. Let this statement be tested by the fundamental truths of science, of mathematics, of philosophy, or of common life, and it will be found universally and intensely true. Even the most rigorous demonstrations of logic depend at last upon

propositions which, though universally believed, can never be proved. And yet this truth is by no means irrational. On the contrary, faith is the very groundwork of all reason. He who will believe only what he can prove must believe nothing. But he who believes nothing can prove nothing, and therefore knows nothing. There is no rational stopping-place between faith and blank agnosticism.

The science of God is based on faith. But this is neither surprising nor alarming. For all science is equally based on faith, and all true science recognizes faith as its only firm foundation. Upon this foundation let it continue to build. Let the structure rise into a beautiful and sacred temple of truth. Let the truth-seeker, of every name and purpose, come hither to worship. Let the deepest thought of the mind and the holiest sentiment of the heart be offered upon its pure shrine together. Then shall the myriad forms of error disappear. Then shall the triumph of truth be complete, and the whole earth be filled with the knowledge and glory of God.

INDEX.

THE SCRIPTURES,

HEBREW AND CHRISTIAN.

ARRANGED AND EDITED AS AN INTRODUCTION TO THE STUDY OF THE BIBLE.

Rev. EDWARD T. BARTLETT, D.D.,

Dean of the Divinity School of the P. E. Church in Philadelphia, and Mary Wolfe, Prof. of Ecclesiastical History.

Rev. JOHN P. PETERS, Ph.D.,

Professor of Old Testament Literature and Language in the Divinity School of the P. E. Church in Philadelphia, and Professor of Hebrew in the University of Pennsylvania.

} EDITORS.

The work is to be completed in three volumes, containing each about 500 pages. Vols. I. and II. now ready.

Vol. I. includes Hebrew story from the Creation to the time of Nehemiah, as in the Hebrew canon.

Vol. II. is devoted to Hebrew poetry and prophecy.

Vol. III. will contain the selections from the Christian Scriptures.

The volumes are handsomely printed in 12mo form, and with an open, readable page, not arranged in verses, but paragraphed according to the sense of the narrative.

Each volume is complete in itself, and will be sold separately at $1.50.

The editors say in their announcement: "Our object is to remove stones of stumbling from the path of young readers by presenting Scriptures to them in a form as intelligible and as instructive as may be practicable. This plan involves some re-arrangements and omissions, before which we have not hesitated, inasmuch as our proposed work will not claim to be the Bible, but an introduction to it. That we may avoid imposing our own interpretation upon Holy Writ, it will be our endeavor to make Scripture serve as the commentary on Scripture. In the treatment of the Prophets of the Old Testament and the Epistles of the New Testament, it will not be practicable entirely to avoid comment, but no attempt will be made to pronounce upon doctrinal questions."

The first volume is divided into four parts:

PART I.—HEBREW STORY, FROM THE BEGINNING TO THE TIME OF SAUL.

" II.—THE KINGDOM OF ALL ISRAEL.

" III.—SAMARIA, OR THE NORTHERN KINGDOM.

" IV.—JUDAH, FROM REHOBOAM TO THE EXILE.

The second volume comprises :

PART I.—HEBREW HISTORY FROM THE EXILE TO NEHEMIAH.
" II.—HEBREW LEGISLATION.
" III.—HEBREW TALES.
" IV.—HEBREW PROPHECY.
" V.—HEBREW POETRY.
" VI.—HEBREW WISDOM.

The third volume will comprise the selections from the New Testament, arranged as follows:

I.—THE GOSPEL ACCORDING TO ST. MARK, PRESENTING THE EVAN-
    GELICAL STORY IN ITS SIMPLEST FORM ; SUPPLEMENTED BY
    SELECTIONS FROM ST. MATTHEW AND ST. LUKE.
II.—THE ACTS OF THE APOSTLES, WITH SOME INDICATION OF THE
    PROBABLE PLACE OF THE EPISTLES IN THE NARRATIVE.
III.—THE EPISTLES OF ST. JAMES AND THE FIRST EPISTLE OF ST. PETER.
IV.—THE EPISTLES OF ST. PAUL.
V.—THE EPISTLE TO THE HEBREWS.
VI.—THE REVELATION OF ST. JOHN (A PORTION).
VII.—THE FIRST EPISTLE OF ST. JOHN.
VIII.—THE GOSPEL OF ST. JOHN.

Full details of the plan of the undertaking, and of the methods adopted by the editors in the selection and arrangement of the material, will be found in the separate prospectus.

" I congratulate you on the issue of a work which, I am sure, will find a wide welcome, and the excellent features of which make it of permanent value."—Rt. Rev. HENRY C. POTTER, Bishop of New York.

"Should prove a valuable adjunct of Biblical instruction."—Rt. Rev. W. E. STEVENS, Bishop of Pennsylvania.

"Admirably conceived and admirably executed. . . . It is the Bible story in Bible words. The work of scholarly and devout men. . . . Will prove a help to Bible study."—Rev. HOWARD CROSBY, D.D.

" We know of no volume which will better promote an intelligent understanding of the structure and substance of the Bible than this work, prepared, as it is, by competent and reverent Christian scholars."—*Sunday-School Times.*

G. P. PUTNAM'S SONS

NEW YORK :   LONDON :
27 AND 29 WEST 23D STREET   27 KING WILLIAM ST., STRAND

Knickerbocker Nuggets.

NUGGET—"A diminutive mass of precious metal."

"Little gems of bookmaking."—*Commercial Gazette*, Cincinnati.

"For many a long day nothing has been thought out or worked out so sure to prove entirely pleasing to cultured book-lovers." — *The Bookmaker.*

I—Gesta Romanorum. Tales of the old monks. Edited by C. SWAN $1 00

"This little gem is a collection of stories composed by the monks of old, who were in the custom of relating them to each other after meals for their mutual amusement and information."—*Williams' Literary Monthly.*

"Nuggets indeed, and charming ones, are these rescued from the mine of old Latin, which would certainly have been lost to many busy readers who can only take what comes to them without delving for hidden treasures." .

II—Headlong Hall and Nightmare Abbey. By THOMAS LOVE PEACOCK $1 00

"It must have been the court librarian of King Oberon who originally ordered the series of quaintly artistic little volumes that Messrs. Putnam are publishing under the name of Knickerbocker Nuggets. There is an elfin dignity in the aspect of these books in their bindings of dark and light blue with golden arabesques."—*Portland Press.*

III—Gulliver's Travels. By JONATHAN SWIFT. A reprint of the early complete edition. Very fully illustrated. Two vols. . . . $2 50

"Messrs. Putnam have done a substantial service to all readers of English classics by reprinting in two dainty and artistically bound volumes those biting satires of Jonathan Swift, 'Gulliver's Travels.'"

IV—Tales from Irving. With illustrations. Two vols. Selected from "The Sketch Book," "Traveller," "Wolfert's Roost," "Bracebridge Hall" $2 00

"The tales, pathetic and thrilling as they are in themselves, are rendered winsome and realistic by the lifelike portraitures which profusely illustrate the volumes. . . . We confess our high appreciation of the superb manner in which the publishers have got up and sent forth the present volumes—which are real treasures, to be prized for their unique character."—*Christian Union.*

"Such books as these will find their popularity confined to no one country, but they must be received with enthusiasm wherever art and literature are recognized."—*Albany Argus.*

V—Book of British Ballads. Edited by S. C. HALL. A fac-simile of the original edition. With illustrations by CRESWICK, GILBERT, and others $1 50

"This is a diminutive fac-simile of the original very valuable edition. . . . The collection is not only the most complete and reliable that has been published, but the volume is beautifully illustrated by skilful artists."—*Pittsburg Chronicle.*

"Probably the best general collection of our ballad literature, in moderate compass, that has yet been made."—*Chicago Dial.*

VI—The Travels of Baron Münchausen. Reprinted from the early, complete edition. Very fully illustrated $1 25

"The venerable Baron Münchausen in his long life has never appeared as well-dressed, so far as we know, as now in this goodly company."

"The Baron's stories are as fascinating as the Arabian Nights."—*Church Union.*

"The book-lover who has not yet seen the Knickerbocker Nuggets issued by the Putnams, should at once make their acquaintance, as we have done, through Baron Münchausen."—*Fremont Journal.*

G. P. PUTNAM'S SONS, NEW YORK AND LONDON

VII—Letters, Sentences, and Maxims. By Lord CHESTERFIELD. With a critical essay by C. A. SAINTE-BEUVE $1 00

"Full of wise things, quaint things, witty and shrewd things, and the maker of this book has put the pick of them all together."—*London World.*
"Each of the little volumes in this series is a literary gem."—*Christian at Work.*

VIII—The Vicar of Wakefield. By GOLDSMITH. With 32 illustrations by WILLIAM MULREADY $1 00

"Goldsmith's charming tale seems more charming than ever in the dainty dress of the 'Knickerbocker Nuggets' series. These little books are a delight to the eye, and their convenient form and size make them most attractive to all book-lovers."—*The Writer*, Boston.
"A gem of an edition, well made, printed in clear, readable type, illustrated with spirit, and just such a booklet as, when one has it in his pocket, makes all the difference between solitude and loneliness."—*Independent.*

IX—Lays of Ancient Rome. By THOMAS BABINGTON MACAULAY. Illustrated by GEORGE SCHARF $1 00

"The poems included in this collection are too well known to require that attention should be drawn to them, but the beautiful setting which they receive in the dainty cover and fine workmanship of this series makes it a pleasure even to handle the volume."—*Yale Literary Magazine.*

X—The Rose and the Ring. By WILLIAM M. THACKERAY. With the author's illustrations $1 25

"'The Rose and the Ring,' by Thackeray, is reproduced with quaint illustrations, evidently taken from the author's own handiwork."—*Rochester Post-Express.*

XI—Irish Melodies and Songs. By THOMAS MOORE. Illustrated by MACLISE $1 50

"The latest issue is a collection of Thomas Moore's 'Irish Melodies and Songs,' fully aud excellently illustrated, with each page of the text printed within an outline border of appropriate green tint, embellished with emblems and figures fitting the text."—*Boston Times.*

XII—Undine and Sintram. By DE LA MOTTE FOUQUÉ. Illustrated $1 00

"'Undine and Sintram' are the latest issue, bound in one volume. They are of the size classics should be—pocket volumes,—and nothing more desirable is to be found among the new editions of old treasures."—*San José Mercury.*

XIII—The Essays of Elia. By CHARLES LAMB. Two vols. $2 00

"The genial essayist himself could have dreamed of no more beautiful setting than the Putnams have given the *Essays of Elia* by printing them among their Knickerbocker Nuggets."—*Chicago Advance.*

XIV—Tales from the Italian Poets. By LEIGH HUNT. Two vols. $2 00

"The perfection of artistic bookmaking."—*San Francisco Chronicle.*
"These include selections from Dante, Tasso, Ariosto, and Pulci, with critical notices and biographical sketches of the immortal writers."—*Newark Advertiser.*
"This work is most delightful literature, which finds a fitting place in this collection, bound in volumes of striking beauty."—*Troy Times.*

G. P. PUTNAM'S SONS, NEW YORK AND LONDON.

The Story of the Nations.

Messrs. G. P. PUTNAM'S SONS take pleasure in announcing that they have in course of publication a series of historical studies, intended to present in a graphic manner the stories of the different nations that have attained prominence in history.

In the story form the current of each national life will be distinctly indicated, and its picturesque and noteworthy periods and episodes will be presented for the reader in their philosophical relation to each other as well as to universal history.

It is the plan of the writers of the different volumes to enter into the real life of the peoples, and to bring them before the reader as they actually lived, labored, and struggled—as they studied and wrote, and as they amused themselves. In carrying out this plan, the myths, with which the history of all lands begins, will not be overlooked, though these will be carefully distinguished from the actual history, so far as the labors of the accepted historical authorities have resulted in definite conclusions.

The subjects of the different volumes will be planned to cover connecting and, as far as possible, consecutive epochs or periods, so that the set when completed will present in a comprehensive narrative the chief events in the great STORY OF THE NATIONS; but it will, of course not always prove practicable to issue the several volumes in their chronological order.

The " Stories " are printed in good readable type, and in handsome 12mo form. They are adequately illustrated and furnished with maps and indexes. They are sold separately at a price of $1.50 each.

The following is a partial list of the subjects thus far determined upon :

THE STORY OF *ANCIENT EGYPT. Prof. GEORGE RAWLINSON.
" " " *CHALDEA. Z. A. RAGOZIN.
" " " *GREECE. Prof. JAMES A. HARRISON,
                                    Washington and Lee University.
" " " *ROME. ARTHUR GILMAN.
" " " *THE JEWS. Prof. JAMES K. HOSMER,
                                  Washington University of St. Louis.
" " " *CARTHAGE. Prof. ALFRED J. CHURCH,
                                  University College, London.
" " " BYZANTIUM.
" " " *THE GOTHS. HENRY BRADLEY.
" " " *THE NORMANS. SARAH O. JEWETT.
" " " *PERSIA. S. G. W. BENJAMIN.
" " " *SPAIN. Rev. E. E. and SUSAN HALE.
" " " *GERMANY. S. BARING-GOULD.
" " " THE ITALIAN REPUBLICS.
" " " *HOLLAND. Prof. C. E. THOROLD ROGERS.
" " " *NORWAY. HJALMAR H. BOYESEN.
" " " *THE MOORS IN SPAIN. STANLEY LANE-POOLE.
" " " *HUNGARY. Prof. A. VÁMBÉRY.
" " " THE ITALIAN KINGDOM. W. L. ALDEN.
" " " *MEDIÆVAL FRANCE. Prof. GUSTAVE MASSON.
" " " *ALEXANDER'S EMPIRE. Prof. J. P. MAHAFFY.
" " " THE HANSE TOWNS. HELEN ZIMMERN.
" " " *ASSYRIA. Z. A. RAGOZIN.
" " " *THE SARACENS. ARTHUR GILMAN.
" " " *TURKEY. STANLEY LANE-POOLE.
" " " PORTUGAL. H. MORSE STEPHENS.
" " " *MEXICO. SUSAN HALE.
" " " *IRELAND. HON. EMILY LAWLESS.
" " " PHŒNICIA.
" " " SWITZERLAND.
" " " RUSSIA.
" " " WALES.
" " " SCOTLAND.
" " " *MEDIA, BABYLON, AND PERSIA.
                                      Z. A. RAGOZIN.

* (The volumes starred are now ready, November, 1888.)

G. P. PUTNAM'S SONS
NEW YORK   LONDON
27 AND 29 WEST TWENTY-THIRD STREET   27 KING WILLIAM STREET, STRAND

www.ingramcontent.com/pod-product-compliance
Lightning Source LLC
Chambersburg PA
CBHW021216270326

41929CB00010B/1160